Principles of
Safety
in Physical Education and Sport

Third Edition

Edited by

Neil J. Dougherty

Rutgers University
New Brunswick, New Jersey

A project of the

National Association for
Sport and Physical Education

an association of the American Alliance for
Health, Physical Education, Recreation and Dance

1900 Association Drive • Reston, VA 20191 • (703) 476-3410 • www.aahperd.org/naspe

Principles of Safety in Physical Education and Sport

Preface

The ever present threat of litigation in connection with student injuries, the inescapable fact that the guidelines and recommendations of the National Association for Sport and Physical Education (NASPE) are frequently considered in assessing potential liability, and most importantly, the desire to promote the safest programs possible precipitated the development of the first edition of Principles of Safety in Physical Education and Sport in 1987.

The same quality of authorship and validity of content that led to the wide use of the first two editions have been followed in this edition. The text is designed to provide the professional with a straightforward and complete resource of those factors that must be considered in the provision of safe units of instruction in the commonly taught physical activity forms in physical education programs. Using a format that relies heavily on checklists, the authors have provided the essential information in a manner that facilitates incorporation of key safety concepts in the development of unit and lesson plans as well as for quick pre-class safety checks.

It is the intention of the National Association for Sport and Physical Education that this book will assist the teacher in the implementation of a safe and well-balanced program of activities in physical education. It should help the teacher provide students with information about safe participation in various sports and activities from which they can benefit throughout their lifetime.

Principles of Safety in Physical Education and Sport can serve as a companion resource to another text published by NASPE, Physical Activity and Sport for the Secondary School Student. The latest edition of this comprehensive and authoritative textbook provides teachers and students with information on skill and technique acquisition, safety, scoring, rules and etiquette, strategies, equipment, and related terminology for a variety of sports and activities included in contemporary physical education programs.

Judith C. Young, Executive Director
National Association for Sport and
Physical Education

Principles of Safety in Physical Education and Sport

Acknowledgements

I would like to extend my sincere thanks to the individual authors who collaborated on this project. Chosen because of their professional knowledge and prominence, they committed an enormous amount of time and energy to produce a book in which they all can, justifiably, take great pride.

I am also very grateful to Adam Bixby. He stepped in as an emergency replacement for an exceptional secretary and immediately found himself retyping chapters as they were edited and re-edited, organizing correspondence, keeping track of the progress of the individual chapters, solving computer compatibility problems, and generally keeping a very complex project well under control. Even more important, he did it all without ever losing his composure or his sense of humor. Thanks Adam—you made my job much easier and more enjoyable.

Finally, I would be remiss if I failed to acknowledge the efforts of Pia McCarthy, Kathy Stark, and the rest of the NASPE staff. Always open-minded and supportive, they were, nevertheless, unyielding in their commitment to professional excellence. One cannot work with such people and fail to recognize why NASPE is such a successful and highly respected professional association.

Neil J. Dougherty, Editor
Rutgers University
New Brunswick, New Jersey

Principles of Safety in Physical Education and Sport

Table of Contents

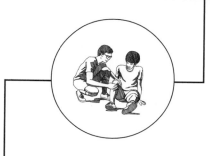

CHAPTER I

The Injury Problem

Murray Mitchell
University of South Carolina
Columbia, South Carolina

David A. Feigley
Rutgers University
New Brunswick, New Jersey

Disease is a high profile killer. There are telethons and foundations that raise awareness and funds to support the important and specialized work of trying to find cures for a whole host of diseases that, in a variety of terrible forms, are a major cause of death in the United States. A much lower profile cause of pain, suffering, loss of time at work and/or school, financial mayhem, and liability is injury. Injuries are insidious in that few realize either the nature or magnitude of their impact on our lives.

Scope of the Problem

Injuries touch most citizens in a variety of ways across their lifespan, from the nearly inconsequential to the traumatic. Injury, as a category, is the single greatest killer of children, accounting for 51 percent of deaths in the 1-14 age group. It has been estimated that at least one adolescent (10-19 years) dies of an injury every hour of every day, and about 15,000 adolescents die each year of injury (Runyan & Gerken, 1989); approximately 6.4 percent of all deaths to residents of the United States are attributable to injuries (Annest et al, 1998).

Although not all injuries lead to death, on any given day more than 170,000 injuries occur that are serious enough to require medical care (National Center for Health Statistics,

1987), and these injuries are costly. The cost to society for sports-related injuries to persons 65 years of age and older grew from about $364 million in 1990 to about $516 million in 1996 (Rutherford & Schroder, 1998). Estimates for the cost to society for baby boomer (ages 35-54) sports-related injuries was about $18.7 billion in 1998 (Rutherford, 2000), and sports-related injuries to youths (age 0-14) cost society a little more than $49 billion in 1997 (National Youth Sports Safety Foundation, 2000).

Clearly, injuries, especially sports-related injuries, are not limited to the young anymore. Sports-related injuries have increased substantially in the baby boomer generation (ages 35 to 54) and in the retired segment of the population (65 and older). Presented in Table 1 are the top sources of sports-related injuries across age groups for 1999. A growing source of injuries across ages appears to be the unpowered scooter, accounting for 27.6 thousand incidences of injuries from January through October of 2000 (Rutherford & Ingle, 2001).

Table 1. Top 5 Sports-Related Injury Activities (in Thousands) Across Age Groups for 1999							
Ages 0-14		**15 - 24**		**25-64**		**65+**	
1. Bicycles	378.3	Basketball	273.3	Bicycles	136.2	Ex. & Equip.	13.7
2. Playground	231.6	Football	160.8	Basketball	127.5	Bicycles	13.5
3. Basketball	195.8	Base/Softball	89.6	Base/Softball	109.7	Swimming	4.6
4. Football	173.3	Bicycles	86.3	Ex. & Equip	105.7	Rqt. Sports	3.9
5. Base/Softball	138.7	Soccer	65.8	Swimming	45.4	ATVs	1.9

Source: *Consumer Product Safety Review,* Fall 2000, pp. 3-4.

Statistics are difficult to gather on the full impact of injuries because agencies that collect data on the topic have a variety of definitions for the term. This variance is partially a result of the fact that different agencies have different purposes for such data collection (e.g., knowing what injuries require treatment vs. determining the cause of such injuries) and because agencies differ in their organizational responsibility to the participating individuals (e.g., national survey systems vs. a local coaching staff). Hence, comparisons of injury or fatality rates for the general population versus the rates for athletes are difficult to make because of the lack of information and because of different criteria used in collecting the data.

Nonetheless, according to experts in epidemiology and public health, nearly two-thirds of all illnesses and injuries could be prevented. Nowhere is this fact more relevant than with sports-related injuries. Although many assume that most sports injuries are the result of "accidents," these accidents are frequently the result of factors that lead predictably to injuries. Often these accidents and injuries can be traced directly to social, environmental, and behavioral factors, that, if regulated, would result in dramatic reductions in deaths and injuries. The fact that injuries are often considered "accidental" or as part of the inherent risk of sports is one of the major reasons why these social, environmental, and behavioral factors remain uncontrolled and, thus, why accidents and injuries continue to occur. If such accidents and injuries were perceived as predictable results of the lack of public health and accident control policies, actions would likely be taken to reduce "accidents" in terms of both frequency and severity.

Perceptions of injuries and their causes are shaped by operational definitions. Definitions serve two functions: First, they provide a specific *focus* as to what is to be studied; second, they provide peripheral *boundaries* concerning what to include and what to exclude from the topic to be analyzed. Paradoxically, definitions can be both enlightening and obstructing at the same time. Whereas it is necessary to limit the field of possibilities when attempting to study a phenomenon, overly restrictive definitions can limit potential insights. Attributing the cause of injuries to "accidents," for example, contributes to perceptions of helplessness and unpredictability in the search for injury prevention strategies. And, as noted earlier, when different groups (with different motives) collect data on injuries while using different definitions, trends and patterns of injuries may be hidden from policy makers. With caveats stated, an attempt will be made to address the definition of injuries.

Defining an Injury

Haddon (1980) defined injury as "damage or trauma to the body caused by exchanges with environmental energy that are beyond the body's resilience" (p. 1). Two practical considerations are often part of injury definitions. First, an injury is deemed to have occurred if the victim loses time from an activity such as work, school, or play. For example, the National Athletic Injury/Illness Reporting System (NAIRS) defines a reportable injury as "any injury/illness [that] causes the cessation of an athlete's customary participation throughout the *participation day following day of onset.*" Thus, time lost from practice is often used as the threshold to determine whether damage sustained by an athlete is considered severe enough to be classified as an injury. The second practical consideration is the referral to a medical professional such as a trainer, nurse, physician, or emergency staffer. Bumps, bruises, and chronic stiffness that do not necessitate a visit for medical treatment are rarely counted in injury statistics. Only if their severity prompts a formal visit to a medical professional do they typically become classified as an injury. A number of efforts have been made to classify the severity of injuries with a score or rating that would allow comparisons across different types of injuries (cf., Baker, et al., 1974; Committee on Medical Aspects of Automotive Safety, 1971).

Within the context of sports, distinctions are often made between injuries *directly or indirectly* attributable to participation in a sport. Damage sustained from mechanical energy tends to be more commonly associated with injuries resulting from accidents termed "directly attributable" to sport than to other forms of energies. For example, an accident caused by being hit by a ball or bat is likely to be seen as directly attributable to sport whereas heat stroke caused by a lack of water while training in hot, humid conditions is more likely to be classified as an *indirect sports injury.*

Another common distinction made with regard to sport injuries is the classification as either acute or chronic. The American Academy of Orthopedic Surgeons (1991) character- ized acute injuries as a sudden onset or "sudden crisis, followed by a fairly predictable, though often lengthy, resolution to healing" (p. 104). Chronic injuries were characterized as "insidious onset, implying a gradual development of structural damage," which may result in a condition that "lasts months or even years and is characterized by persistence of the symptoms" (p. 104).

Following is a discussion on the prevention of injuries. Once again, distinctions must be made between the related but different concerns of safety and risk.

Defining Safety

Although the term "safety" is generally understood, its scientific meaning is often quite vague. According to Lowrance (1976), an activity is safe if its risks are deemed acceptable; acceptability is a matter of personal and societal value judgments. Thus, what is judged "safe" varies from time to time and from situation to situation. Furthermore, Lowrence argues that what is typically measured scientifically is not safety but degree of risk. An activity is judged safe if the risks associated with that activity are judged acceptable. Stated differently, risk is the calculation of the probability of harm—a scientific measurement. Safety involves the judgment of the acceptability of those risks—a value judgment. Thus, risks are something we measure, whereas safety is something we must judge.

Defining Risk

Thygerson (1986) defines "risk" as "possible loss or the chance of a loss" (p. 39). Theoreti- cally, measuring risks is quite straightforward. Taking into consideration the population data, the exposure data, and the injury data, the calculations for determining risk are quite simple. From a practical standpoint, measuring such risks is rarely carried out because gathering the appropriate data is often quite a substantial task. There are three general methods of measur- ing risk: (1) relative risk methods; (2) probability of occurrence methods; and (3) relative exposure rate methods.

1. Relative risk methods. An activity or hazard is rated according to a standard that can be ranked along a dimension of more or less. For example, a boxing glove with nine ounces of padding is considered to be more risky than a glove with twelve ounces of padding. Sometimes a rating scale is adopted to reflect the approximate degree of risk. For example, in women's artistic gymnastics, athletes select skills rated from level "a" (easy) to level "d" (extremely risky).

2. Probability of occurrence. The likelihood of future injuries can be accurately esti- mated if records have been kept over reasonable periods of time for sizable populations that will continue the activity under similar conditions. Just as the National Safety Council can predict the number of fatalities for a given holiday period, the American Football Coaches Association Committee on Football Injuries can predict the number of football-related fatalities for the upcoming season. Both groups have compiled a long history of fatality statistics that permit such prediction. If the future circumstances were changed from the situation upon which the original data were based, the estimates would differ more radically from the actual observed fatalities. For example, if the weather changed (e.g., it rained) or if a rule change were implemented (e.g., spearing were eliminated in football), the actual number of deaths or injuries would change.

3. **Relative exposure.** Risks may be portrayed in terms of exposure rates in order to compare different risks. Table 2 reports the number of cervical cord injuries directly attributable to participation in high school and collegiate football across a 20-year period from 1980 to 1999. Although it is clear that such injuries declined in the 1990s compared to the 1980s, the mean number of cervical injuries annually was 6.95 for secondary schools compared to only 1.05 in collegiate programs. That is, there were approximately seven times as many cervical injuries in secondary school programs than in collegiate programs during both

Table 2. Cervical Cord Football Injuries from Sandlot, Pro and Semipro, High School and College 1980 - 1999				
5-Year Block	Sandlot	Pro and Semipro	High School	College
1980-84	3	1	40	7
1985-89	0	1	41	6
1990-94	0	3	27	3
1995-99	1	1	31	6
Annual Mean	0.20	0.30	6.95	1.05

Source: Mueller & Cantu (2000), *Annual Survey of Catastrophic Football Injuries,* National Center for Catastrophic Sport Injury Research, Chapel Hill, North Carolina, 2000.

Table 3. Incidence of Cervical Cord Football Injuries per 100,000 Participants:* High School and College 1980 - 1999		
Year	Secondary School	College
1980-84	0.62	1.87
1985-89	0.61	1.60
1990-94	0.36	0.80
1995-99	0.40	1.60
20-Year Rate (mean)	0.50	1.47

*Rates based on 75,000 college players, 1.3 million secondary school players from 1980-88 and 1.5 million secondary school players from 1989-99.

Source: Mueller & Cantu (2000), *Annual Survey of Catastrophic Football Injuries,* National Center for Catastrophic Sport Injury Research, Chapel Hill, North Carolina, 2000.

decades. However, this comparison is misleading. When cervical injuries per 100,000 are compared between collegiate and secondary school athletes, the rate of collegiate injuries is almost triple the rate of the younger athletes (See Table 3). Thus, the actual risk appears to be significantly lower for secondary school athletes.

Exposure rates can take into consideration not only the number of participants but also the number of practices, number of hours per practice, and the number of actual sporting attempts, depending on the degree of sophistication of the measurement of exposure. An advantage of this technique of expressing risk is that different sports or different dimensions can be compared on a rate basis (See Table 1). For example, Reif (1981) estimated that, whereas the risk of death in collegiate football was 1 in 33,000 exposures, the risk of injury or long-term disability was as high as 1 in 18 exposures. In this estimate, exposures were based on a per year basis in which 25 days of participation per year were assumed.

Overuse Syndrome Injuries

Overuse injuries are the result of purposeful, repetitive training. They are clearly injuries although they are not accidental. In fact, they are clearly predictable and often endured specifically in the quest for higher levels of performance. Monitoring overuse injuries was once restricted to adult activities, such as those of the construction worker, clerical worker, or the weekend tennis player, who tended to be afflicted with bursitis and tendinitis. Now they are seen with increasing regularity in highly trained children.

According to Micheli (1986), children are particularly susceptible to these types of injuries for two reasons. First, the growing cartilage of the joint surfaces may be more susceptible to stress, especially shear stresses, both in terms of single-impact trauma (e.g., growth plate fractures) and repetitive microtrauma (e.g., Osgood-Schlatter disease, patellofemoral stress syndrome). Second, the process of growth itself renders children more susceptible to certain injuries. As growth occurs in the bones, the muscle-tendon unit spanning the bones and joints becomes progressively tighter with growth, particularly during growth spurts. This reduced flexibility heightens the child's chances of both single-impact injuries and repetitive microtrauma because of increased tension across the joints and growing surfaces.

Understanding the Injury Problem

Effective understanding and control of the injury problem in physical education and sport requires a multistep approach. A model for analyzing injuries in sport is presented in Figure 1.

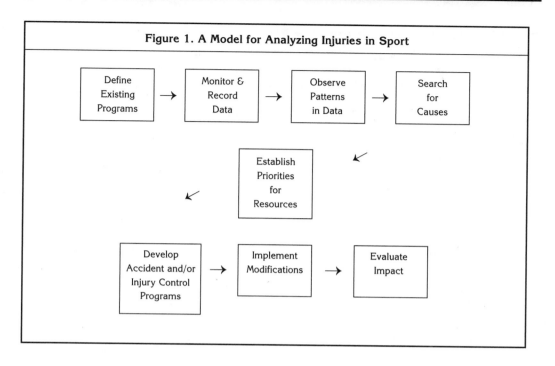

Figure 1. A Model for Analyzing Injuries in Sport

Define Existing Programs

First, the specific programs to be analyzed must be designated. At first glance, this step may seem obvious; on closer inspection, a variety of complicating factors become evident. If, for example, you wish to analyze football in terms of injury occurrence, you must decide what constitutes "football." Does your study include only organized programs? Will you include instructional classes, intramurals, or "sandlot" games? Are you looking only at injuries during games, or will you also include practices?

The problems associated with collecting data from organized programs are likely to differ from those encountered while collecting data from parks, playgrounds, and "sandlot" football. In addition, you must decide if you are interested in injuries both directly and indirectly attributable to the activity or sport. For example, an injury resulting from tackling is likely to be directly the result of playing football, whereas a stroke occurring to an athlete on the sidelines may be unrelated to the individual's participation in sport. Other injuries may be caused by a combination of factors—some direct and some indirect. Heat exhaustion may be both attributable to weather conditions and to the wearing of heavy uniforms and the intense training regimens during high heat/humidity conditions.

Monitoring and Data Collection

Once the conditions defining the sport have been specified, an analysis of injury patterns requires an accurate monitoring of the frequency, type, and severity of injuries as well as the circumstances under which they occur. Here again, the problem of definition arises. What constitutes an accident or an injury? Depending on the purpose of the monitoring institution, the definitions of injuries may differ dramatically. A coach concerned about the welfare of young athletes may define an injury as a bruise that creates discomfort. An organization concerned about medical treatment may define injury as any physical problem that requires medical treatment. A league concerned about the severity of accidental injury may define an injury as any physical problem that requires the athlete to miss a day or more of training or competition. The data collected under each of these examples may be quite different and reflect decidedly different patterns.

The collection of accident and/or injury statistics appears deceptively simple. Even assuming that clear and adequate definitions of accident and injury have been established, the substantial problems of collecting, storing, and retrieving data remain. Not only must data forms be developed and provided, but the responsibility for reporting the data must be assigned to specific individuals who have the authority to obtain the appropriate descriptive data. Data collection requires many costs in terms of time, effort, and material supplies—not to mention time away from other tasks often thought to be more pressing.

Subtle and not-so-subtle distortions of injury data are quite common. Coaches and administrators often feel pressure to portray their programs in as positive a light as possible. Documenting injuries often appears to be self-defeating to people held responsible for safety. An administrator who introduces an effective injury reporting system should be prepared to explain to superiors why a dramatic increase in injuries is now being recorded. Even the athletes themselves often minimize the reporting of injuries in order to avoid playing restrictions. Failure to complain and direct avoidance of reporting injuries is a major factor distorting accurate injury surveillance data.

Pattern Analysis

An examination of the data often reflects patterns that are not obvious to the casual participant because these patterns occur over long periods of time or across large populations of athletes. For example, Sands (1984) found that women collegiate gymnasts were significantly more likely to be injured in November and January than in any other months of the season and that the most common types of injuries occurred from the knee down. Further, heavier, taller gymnasts were more prone to injury than lighter, shorter gymnasts. Some of these findings are obvious. Few coaches would be surprised to find that heavier gymnasts are more prone to injury. Other findings are not so obvious or easily interpreted. The answer to why injuries occur more often in one month over another requires further information and analysis.

Klafs and Arnheim (1981) concluded that injuries in high school sports were more likely to occur during the first three to four weeks of practice because athletes frequently lacked flexibility, were overweight, or had little cardiovascular conditioning when they first reported to practice. These patterns have changed over time as more trainers advocate what Arnheim and Prentice (2000) describe as "periodization" (p. 76). This concept is used to describe different training and conditioning needs of serious athletes year-round rather than just during preseason and in-season competition. Consequently, the search for patterns of injury incidence requires substantive searching for underlying explanations.

The Little League's analysis of injury patterns in organized youth baseball revealed a number of obvious and nonobvious factors contributing to injury. Klafs and Arnheim (1981) suggested that "the result has been the elimination of steel spikes and the on-deck-circle, screening dugouts, mandating the use of face and head protectors for the batters, and installing breakaway bases, all of which have resulted in a decrease in injuries" (p. 9). More recent studies of bike helmet usage have indicated the merits of wearing helmets on bikes (e.g., reduce risk of head injury up to 85%) but not on playground equipment, and studies of the effectiveness of public education programs suggest substantive improvements in helmet use and ownership from 1991 to 1998 (Rodgers, 1999).

Determine Causes

Once the descriptive data have indicated certain patterns, the cause of the patterns must be determined. Why do injuries typically occur during the third and fourth week of training? One possible explanation might be that this is the period during which athletes are shifting their training emphasis from conditioning to sport-specific game skills. An equally plausible explanation might be that during the fall sports season, the third and fourth weeks are a period during which the athletes are more tired and distractible; they have switched from a summer schedule to a winter schedule in which they are attending academic classes as well as training on the athletic field. In fact, both of these reasons, in combination with others, might be causing the increased rates of injuries. Multiple causation of a class of injuries is more often the case than not. Attributing the "cause" of injuries to a single antecedent event is often incomplete, if not directly misleading.

Some safety experts believe that the human element is the fundamental cause of virtually all accidents. Such a belief focuses on controlling human behavior as the main basis for reducing accidents and injuries. Safety education programs, reward and punishment contingencies for safe and unsafe behaviors, respectively, and the identification of accident-prone individuals are all safety approaches that rely on the assumption that human frailties create accidents and injuries. Clearly, there are circumstances in which human error leads to increased accident and injury rates. Individuals who lack knowledge of accepted safety practices may be more prone to injury. For example, athletes who have not been taught the fundamentals of falling safely appear to be at a higher risk than athletes who possess such skills. Nonetheless, the assumption that teaching falling automatically leads to reduced risk is unwarranted. Athletes who feel in control of the risk because they believe

their skill at falling protects them may actually attempt more risky maneuvers and thereby increase their exposure to risk. The fact that as many accomplished swimmers as
nonswimmers drown each year suggests that increased skill does not guarantee a
reduced accident rate.

Furthermore, unsafe behavior may occur even though the individuals possess an
awareness of what constitutes safe behavior. When safe behavior is inconvenient, uncomfortable, "unheroic," or reduces one's effectiveness at the sport, unsafe behavior becomes
predictable. Often the value of behaving safely is less prominent than the value of the unsafe
behavior. For example, the absence of injury is more difficult for a soccer player to observe
than the fact that he or she can run faster without shin guards. In such cases, coaches and
administrators must arrange the circumstances so that the athlete realizes that safety is
important. For example, a rule that bars any soccer player from playing unless proper
equipment is worn will demonstrate the need to wear shin guards.

Whereas careless human behavior may often be the culprit in creating accidents and
injuries, perceptive analyzers of safety should also be alert to opposing points of view.
Robertson (1983) pointed out that although many "experts" insist that the injury problem
is essentially a human behavioral problem, some of these opinions may be deliberately
self-serving. That is, such opinions are offered by those who manufacture or provide the
hazardous equipment and/or activity and, thus, who may wish to avoid regulation and
being held responsible. Such biased perspectives may also come from those in the "human
services" sectors such as educators, behavioral scientists, police, and others who benefit
from labor-intensive behavior-change programs.

As Robertson (1983) stated:

> The widespread acceptance of the premise of correctable human error
> cannot be entirely attributed to brainwashing by those with obvious self-
> interests, however. The assumption that human beings are for the most
> part rational actors in complete control of their actions is embedded in our
> mores and laws. To question the assumption is to question both a cultural
> theme and a basis for self-esteem. It is true that in many contexts this
> cultural myth is harmless. Where split-second decisions mean the dif-
> ference between life and death or health and disability, however, as is
> frequently the case in handling highly concentrated energy, reliance
> on the myth of the rational, fully informed, constantly alert, lightning
> quick human being is, paradoxically, an irrational act. (pp. 65-66)

Establish Priorities

Clearly, some types of injuries warrant more concern than others. Fatalities need to be dealt
with at a higher priority than minor cuts and abrasions. Acquired immune deficiency syndrome (AIDS) and human immunodeficiency virus (HIV), on the other hand, are conditions
that have recently required renewed attention to cuts and abrasions relative to the safety of

participants in athletic events. Some injury prevention is also more feasible and/or requires less investment of resources. Providing access to water during training in order to reduce heatstroke requires less of a resource investment than building a foam pit for safe landings in high-risk gymnastic skills. Although the arguments over the value of a human life have both philosophic and practical overtones, the issue is one that goes beyond the scope of this chapter. (The interested reader is referred to Thygerson, 1986, Chapter 6). Any reader who feels that practical value considerations are not a current issue is invited to sit in on a jury trial in civil litigation following an accidental death.

Develop Effective Prevention Programs

Haddon (1980) outlined ten strategies for controlling injuries once the causes of those injuries have been determined. Those who use this list to analyze injury control options should realize that effective analysis requires that all options be initially considered. Whereas some options are already in use or can be easily applied, others appear difficult, if not impossible, to implement and are often casually dismissed during the initial stages of injury-control analysis. The practical aspects of implementation should be set aside until all possibilities have been outlined.

1. Eliminate the hazard. Sports injuries can certainly be reduced by eliminating the sports or activities that cause injuries. Although few would advocate the wholesale elimination of sport, there are a variety of examples where steps have been taken to eliminate specific sports. In 1977, the American Academy of Pediatrics advocated that trampolines be banned from instructional programs and eliminated as a competitive sport. Periodic cries for the elimination of boxing (usually prompted by a death) are relatively commonplace. The swinging rings in gymnastics have been eliminated both in physical education classes and in competition. In a different venue, commercial motels and hotels throughout the United States have virtually eliminated diving boards from their recreational swimming pools.

A less dramatic interpretation of this strategy might include the elimination of select parts of activities. For example, eliminating the full contact aspect of tackle football to play touch or flag football would be another way to "eliminate" hazards while preserving the spirit of the game.

2. Reduce the amount of the hazard. Often, sports have been modified to reduce the amount or degree of risk incurred by the participants. This strategy involves a quantitative intervention. That is, the basic nature of the activity is not changed; participation is simply scaled down. For example, young platform divers train and compete on 5-, 6-, and 7-meter platforms rather than the 10-meter tower required by international rules. Limiting the degree of vertical drop on novice ski trails to intentionally curtail the speeds that beginner skiers can attain reduces the amount of hazard. Similarly, specifying shortened playing periods and age categories and weight classes for young, less experienced players provides a quantitative degree of hazard reduction.

3. Prevent or reduce the likelihood of the release of already existing hazards. In this category of interventions, attention is focused on changing the conditions under which the activity will continue to be performed. In gymnastics, for example, performers are concerned about slipping off of some pieces of apparatus. To be competitive, performers must include skills in their routines that involve the risk of unexpectedly leaving the apparatus. The use of magnesium carbonate ("chalk" or "mag") by gymnasts to reduce the likelihood of slipping is an example of one approach to reducing the likelihood of such an occasion.

4. Modify the rate or spatial distribution of the release of the hazard from its source. In some activities, hazards exist as part of the nature of the activity and will never be totally removed. One can, however, take steps to reduce the amount of force that such hazards can exert on the body. In skiing, for example, participants will fall and risk twisting or even breaking ankles, knees, or other body parts. One of the major problems encountered when falling is that the skis may force the lower extremities to bend in unplanned ways. The use of rapid release bindings on skis that are adjusted to the skill level of the performer is an example of this principle. A similar example is seen in the use of seat belts in motor vehicles.

5. Separate, in time or space, the hazard and the participant. Providing bicycle and jogging paths that are isolated from streets and highways separates the hazards (faster vehicles) from the participants (cyclists and joggers). The separation of spectators, benches for nonplaying athletes, and an equipment storage area from the playing field also reduces the likelihood of injuries caused by colliding with other players or objects after running out of bounds. Likewise, isolating playing fields from such potential hazards as streams, roads, and construction sites reduces the potential for accidents and injuries.

6. Interposition material protective barriers. The use of football and lacrosse helmets, gymnastics mats, chest protectors in baseball and fencing, protective eyeglasses in racquetball and squash, and mouth guards in contact sports are prime examples of the use of such a strategy.

7. Modify the basic relevant qualities of the hazard. Children often fall on playgrounds. The hazard in such situations is the actual surface of the playground-hard surfaces and soft skin and bones are bad matches. The surfaces of playgrounds and playing fields can be covered with materials that are softer than asphalt, concrete, or crushed stone. Making the surface softer would be an example of an appropriate modification in this category.

8. Make what is to be protected more resistant to damage. Conditioning athletes to be stronger and more flexible decreases their susceptibility to certain types of injuries. Providing unlimited access to water and gradually increasing workout intensity during periods of high temperatures allows the athletes to become acclimated and more resistant to heat disorders.

9. Counter damage already done. Emergency first aid training to stop bleeding and CPR training to restore heart function and breathing are fundamental to effective sports medicine programs. Recognizing potential spinal injuries and knowing that immobilization of such injured athletes is essential to prevent further injury is a prime example of preventing further damage resulting from a sports injury. Well-situated, well-trained and well-equipped professionals ready to respond quickly can make substantial differences in the fatality rate and the severity of damage occurring from traumatic injuries.

10. Stabilize, repair, and rehabilitate the damage. Rehabilitative physical therapy programs, reconstructive surgery, and the use of knee and ankle braces to facilitate recovery from sprains and strains illustrate this approach.

Implement Safety Modifications

Knowing the cause of a type of injury may suggest a variety of prevention techniques, not all of which are equally effective. Knowing, for example, that being hit in the chest with a baseball or softball is the major cause of death among baseball/softball players suggests that chest protectors may be warranted. Getting players to actually wear such protective devices is yet another matter. Implementing programs often requires much lead time and substantial resources. Resistance to change also impedes the effectiveness of prevention programs. Although the use of face masks for goalkeepers and helmets for all players is now accepted in ice hockey, it was resisted by players and coaches alike during the early stages of implementation. Paradoxically, the implementation of effective injury reduction programs is most difficult in areas in which the individual participant carries the most responsibility for his or her own safety.

Assess the Influence of Prevention Programs

Again, the monitoring of ongoing programs is required in order to assess the effectiveness of prevention programs. Often, the frequency of injury experienced by an individual instructor, participant, or program is so small that patterns are difficult to detect without a record-keeping system that extends over a period of years and across many similar programs. Contact information for several data collection organizations are included in Appendix A. Individuals may contribute their statistics to the larger database, compare their statistics to data from the larger database, or gain insights into potential problem areas identified through the existing data to modify prevention programs.

Researchers at the University of North Carolina have compiled statistics of football fatalities annually since 1931. The pattern of injuries in high school football programs, plotted in five-year blocks between 1961 and 1990, are described in Table 2. There has been a steady decrease in the number of fatalities directly related to football since the peak observed between 1961 and 1965. A similar decline has occurred in indirect fatalities during this same period. Whereas a variety of factors have contributed to this steady decline, a significant rule change was implemented in 1976. Initial contact with the head while blocking and tackling (spearing) was ruled illegal. This rule change was introduced because of an awareness not only of fatalities in football, but because statistics revealed that the vast majority of fatalities since 1960 were due to injuries to the head and neck. This information led to the development of a prevention program involving protecting this area of the body via improved equipment and rule changes to eliminate the use of the head as a tackling technique. Continued monitoring of injury frequencies indicated that such programs have achieved the desired effect of reducing injuries and fatalities. Penalties for spearing and rigid enforcement of those penalties, plus an increased awareness on the part of coaches and athletes regarding the nature and severity of injuries produced by spearing, have all contributed heavily to the reduction of fatalities resulting from head and neck injuries. Data continue to indicate that deaths in football, although significantly reduced in number, are still primarily caused by head and neck injuries. Efforts continue to develop even more effective prevention of such injuries.

A Practitioner's Analysis

The professional in sport and physical education can gain an understanding of the factors that should be controlled by using a simple, yet effective, approach to analyzing the safety requirements of the program. Although the number of specific concerns to which attention must be focused can be overwhelming, virtually all can be subsumed under the following classification plan. When analyzing a specific program, ask the following three questions:

1. Are the athletes prepared for the activity? Has there been a medical screening? Have they been properly conditioned for the demands of the sport? Have they been taught the appropriate prerequisite skills? Have they been taught to appreciate the risks inherent in their particular sport? Have the basic safety regulations been taught to them in terms they can understand? Has the instructor/coach clarified exactly what is expected of the athlete during the learning and/or performance stages?

2. Is the instructor prepared to teach the skill and supervise the activity? Does the instructor have the prerequisite knowledge of the biomechanical and teaching progressions of the skill? Is the instructor capable of individualizing the learning sequence and teaching progressions to accommodate the needs of the athlete, both real and imagined? Is the instructor aware of the common errors made by beginners and the likely hazards to be confronted by both the student and the instructor during the learning of the skills? Is the instructor familiar with the level of mental and physical preparation of the athlete, and can the instructor modify the learning progressions to match the learner's preparation with the difficulty of the task?

3. Is the environment adequately prepared for the performance of the skill? Is the protective equipment available and properly positioned? Are the apparatus and/or protective equipment properly adjusted for the athlete? Has the activity been properly designed for the space, lighting, facilities, and number of athletes available? Have the athletes been properly matched for size, skill, and maturity? Have activity areas been clearly defined and separated from traffic lanes, resting stations, and teaching stations?

Clearly, the number and type of questions that one can ask under each heading has not been exhausted. Appropriate questions depend on the specifics of the activity taught and the degree of risk associated with that activity. This strategy does, however, provide direction in terms of systematically examining the three primary areas in which coaches, teachers, and administrators are responsible for providing adequate care and supervision for their students and/or athletes.

References

American Academy of Orthopedic Surgeons. (1991). *Athletic training and sports medicine* (2nd ed.). Park Ridge, IL: Author.

Annest, J. L., Fingerhut, L. A., Conn, J. M., Pickett, D., McLoughlin, E., & Gallagher, S. (1998). *How states are collecting and using cause of injury data*. San Francisco: The APHA Challenge Grant Program and the Trauma Foundation.

Arnheim, D. D., & Prentice, W. E. (2000). *Principles of athletic training* (10th ed.). Boston: McGraw-Hill.

Baker, S. P., O'Neil, B., Haddon, W., et al. (1974). The injury severity score: A method for describing patients with multiple injuries and evaluating emergency care. *Journal of Trauma, 14,* 187.

Committee on Medical Aspects of Automotive Safety. (1971). Rating the severity of tissue damage. *Journal of the American Medical Association, 215,* 277-280.

Consumer Product Safety Review. (2000). NEISS Data Highlights-1999. *Consumer Product Safety Review, 5*(2), 3-7.

Haddon, W. (1980). Advances in the epidemiology of injuries as a basis for public policy. *Public Health Reports, 95,* 411-421.

Klafs, C. E., & Arnheim, D. D. (1981). *Modern principles of athletic training* (5th ed.). St. Louis: CV Mosby.

Lowrance, W. W. (1976). *Of acceptable risk.* Los Altos, CA: William Kaufmann.

Micheli, L. J. (1986). Pediatric and adolescent sports injuries: Recent trends. In K. B. Pandolf (Ed.), *Exercise and sport sciences reviews.* New York: Macmillan.

Mueller, F.O., & Cantu, R.C. (2000). Annual survey of catastrophic football injuries, 1977-1999. Chapel Hill, NC: National Center for Catastrophic Injury at University of North Carolina. *www.unc.edu/depts/nccsi/CataFootballInjuries.htm.*

National Center for Health Statistics. (1987). *Advance report of final mortality statistics, 1985.* Washington, DC: U.S. Government Printing Office.

National Center for Health Statistics. (1988). *Vital statistics of the United States, 1986.* Vol. 2, Mortality, part A. Department of Health and Human Services Publication No. (PHS) 88-1122. Washington, DC: U.S. Government Printing Office.

National Federation. (1991, May). Injury prevention pays dividends; no direct death reported in football. *National Federation News, 8,* 14-17.

National Youth Sports Safety Foundation. (2000). *The cost of injuries fact sheet.* Boston, MA: Author.

Reif, A. E. (1981). Risks and gains. In P. F. Vinger & E. F. Hoerner (Eds.), *Sports injuries: The unthwarted epidemic* (pp. 56-64). Littleton, MA: PSG Publishing.

Robertson, L. S. (1983). *Injuries: Causes, control strategies, and public policy.* Lexington, MA: Lexington Books.

Rodgers, G. B. (1999). Bike helmets. *Consumer Product Safety Review, 4*(1), 1-5.

Runyan, C. W., & Gerken, E. A. (1989). Epidemiology and prevention of adolescent injury: A review and research agenda. *Journal of the American Medical Association, 262,* 2273-2278.

Rutherford, G. W. (2000). Baby boomer sports injuries. *Consumer Product Safety Review, 4*(4), 3-4.

Rutherford, G. W., & Ingle, R. (2001). Unpowered scooter-related injuries-United States, 1998-2000. *Journal of the American Medical Association, 285,* 36-37.

Rutherford, G. W., & Schroeder, T. J. (1998). *Sports-related injuries to persons 65 years of age and older.* Washington, DC: U.S. Consumer Product Safety Commission.

Sands, B. (1984). Injury data NCAA female gymnasts 1983-84: Data reveals potential patterns. *Technique: The official publication of the United States Gymnastics Association, 4,* 7.

Thygerson, A. L. (1986). *Safety* (2nd ed.). Englewood Cliffs, NJ: Prentice Hall.

Appendix A

The following is a partial registry of agencies that provide information on product safety and injury patterns in general and specifically related to sports. Although not exhaustive, this list provides a starting point for many valuable information links.

American Academy of Pediatrics
www.aap.org

American Society for Testing and Materials
1916 Race Street
Philadelphia, PA 19103
(215) 299-5585
www.astm.org

American Trauma Society
www.amtrauma.org

Canadian Pediatric Society Injury Prevention Pages
www.cps.ca/english/carekids/safety&prevention/index.htm

Center for Injury Research and Control, University of Pittsburgh
www.injurycontrol.com/icrin

Centers for Disease Control and Prevention
www.cdc.gov
(at the same site, connect to Morbidity and Mortality Weekly Report)

Harborview Injury Prevention and Research Center
http://depts.washington.edu/hiprc/

Harvard Injury Control Research Center
www.hsph.harvard.edu/hicrc

Injury Prevention Web
www.injuryprevention.org

The Johns Hopkins Center for Injury Research and Policy
www.jhsph.edu/Research/Centers/CIRP

National Center for Catastrophic Sport Injury Research
www.unc.edu/depts/ncsi

National Pediatric Trauma Registry
New England Medical Center
750 Washington St. #75 K-R
Boston, MA 02111-1901
(617) 636-5031 (voice)
(617) 636-5513 (fax)
www.nptr.org

National Youth Sport Safety Foundation
333 Longwood Avenue, Suite 202
Boston, MA 02115
(617) 277-1171 (voice)
(617) 277-2278 (fax)
NYSSF@aol.com (E-mail)
www.nyssf.org

United States Consumer Product Safety Commission
www.cpsc.gov

Web-Based Injury Statistics Query and Reporting System (WISQARS)
An interactive system that provides customized injury-related mortality data useful
for research and for making informed public health decisions
www.cdc.gov/ncipc/osp/wisqars_intro.htm

CHAPTER 2

Legal Responsibility for Safety in Physical Education and Sport

Neil J. Dougherty
Rutgers University
New Brunswick, New Jersey

The number of lawsuits brought against physical educators and coaches has reached an unprecedented high and, from all indications, will continue to rise in the foreseeable future. Consider the following reasons why this may be the case:

- The overwhelming majority of all school-related injuries occur in conjunction with physical education and sport.

- A tort is a legal wrong for which one may seek recompense through legal action.

- Under the civil laws of the United States, it is possible for practically any person to sue any other person at any time for any reason. Although the outcome of the suit is by no means guaranteed, the right to initiate it is virtually unquestioned.

- The overwhelming majority of all negligence suits are settled prior to the completion of the trial process.

- Both the number of lawsuits and the size of the settlements or awards have increased dramatically in the last several years. This has, of course, been reflected in the cost and availability of liability insurance as well as the nature and continuation of many programs.

The field of physical education and sport unquestionably carries with it a higher risk of injury than most other areas of the curriculum. The relative ease with which one can institute a lawsuit and the high likelihood of some form of settlement, regardless of the relative strength of the case, have led to an increasing level of professional concern over issues related to risk management and liability.

Although there are many negative aspects to the liability problem, such as spiraling insurance costs and the loss of some programs and activities, the increased concern over liability has also resulted in safer programs and has been used by knowledgeable teachers and administrators as a highly persuasive argument for program and facility improvements. Further, although no amount of planning or preparation can guarantee freedom from injuries and subsequent lawsuits, a thorough understanding of the legal process and the elements of risk management can greatly increase one's chances of success when such a situation arises. This chapter will, therefore, examine the fundamentals of the legal process as they relate to physical education and sport. Those factors that most commonly give rise to lawsuits will be discussed in sport-specific safety principles in the remainder of the text.

The Legal Process

Tort claims in physical education and sport are primarily the result of personal injuries caused by the alleged negligence of the teacher or the coach. In order for the plaintiff or injured party to prevail in such a suit, several elements must be proved by the greater weight of evidence.

Duty. The defendant must be shown to have had a responsibility to provide for the safety and welfare of the plaintiff. If the injured party was a student in the defendant's class, or a player on his/her team, then the duty is virtually assured.

Breach of duty. It must be shown that the defendant failed to provide the standard of care that could reasonably be expected of a reasonable, prudent, and up-to-date professional under the same or similar circumstances. A duty can be breached either by omission or by commission. That is, the defendant either failed to do something that he/she should have done or did something he/she should not have done. Additionally, it must be shown that the breach entailed a *foreseeable* risk. That is, the defendant should have been able to predict the likelihood of an accident or injury arising out of the specific circumstances in question.

Harm. In order to institute a tort claim, the plaintiff must have suffered an actual loss to his/her person, property, or interest.

Proximate cause. The mere presence of an act of negligence is not sufficient grounds to allow the plaintiff to prevail. It must be shown, further, that the injury for which recompense is sought was actually caused or aggravated by the specific act of negligence in question.

A key point in this entire process is the establishment of the standard of care required of the defendant. In this regard, the prudent person principle is most commonly employed. We are obligated to perform as would a reasonably prudent individual under the same or similar circumstances. Although this statement is essentially correct, remember that it is also very superficial. The yardstick by which professional conduct will be measured in court is the current established standards and practices of the profession as applied and explained by a prudent professional (an expert). It is essential, therefore, that we take every reasonable precaution to guarantee that our teaching and coaching behavior always meets or exceeds the currently accepted practices and procedures of the profession.

Legal and Quasi-Legal Defenses

There are several legal arguments and professional procedures that can help to form the basis of a defense in the event of a lawsuit. Whereas these are useful tools in the litigation process, they are even more valuable as indices of administrative and supervisory responsibilities with regard to risk management.

Contributory/comparative negligence. In states that adhere to the principle of contributory negligence, the plaintiff is barred from recovery if it is proved that his/her own negligence helped to cause or aggravate the injury. In the majority of states, however, the doctrine of comparative negligence is applied. In such a situation, the jury will be asked to apportion a relative percentage of responsibility to the plaintiff and to the defendant(s). The size of the award that the plaintiff could receive would then be diminished by his/her percentage of responsibility. If, for instance, May Addams was seeking $250,000 damages for an injury sustained in a soccer class, and if the jury found her to have been comparatively negligent in the amount of 45%, then the maximum award she could receive would be 55% of $250,000, or $137,500. Obviously, the amount of responsibility that a student can assume for his/her own welfare is a function of age, intelligence, skill, and background in the activity. In general, the more thorough the instruction, the more explicit the warnings, and the more consistent the feedback, the more the students will be expected to assume some reasonable share of the responsibility for their own safety.

Assumption of risk. It is often argued that an individual who takes part in certain types of vigorous physical activities must assume the risk of accident or injury that is normally associated with that activity. Assumption of risk, however, is a technical term that many feel has no validity as a separate defense. Reduced to simplest terms, no one can be expected to assume a risk of which he/she is unaware. If the teacher fails to warn the student of the dangers involved in the activity and/or fails to guarantee the level of instruction, skill, and feedback necessary for the student to reasonably protect him/herself from those dangers, then the teacher may very possibly have been negligent in the fulfillment of his/her duties and the student cannot be held to have assumed any risk or responsibility. If, on the other hand, the student was properly instructed, warned, and provided with reasonable feedback regarding his/her performance, and despite this, acted in a manner that increased the likelihood of his/her own injury, then there may be grounds for a valid claim of contributory or comparative negligence. In either case, however, the assumption of risk terminology is merely excess verbal baggage that has no real place as a separate defense in today's law.

Informed consent. Although written documents such as waivers and permission slips cannot provide absolute legal protection from our own acts of negligence, they can, when properly understood and executed, be very useful tools in the reduction of liability.

For our purposes as physical education teachers and coaches, the most commonly used informed consent documents can be grouped into two major categories: release forms, often called waivers, and participation agreements, which include permission slips.

Release. A release or waiver is a contract, signed by the participant and/or his/her parents, that purports to absolve the teacher or coach from liability in the event that an accident or injury arises from some specifically named activity. Waivers have limited legal value in school programs for several reasons: (a) The courts are reluctant to allow one to be contractually protected from the consequences of one's own negligent actions; (b) since no person can legally waive the rights of another, parental waivers executed on behalf of a minor child cannot be held valid; and (c) the requirement of a release prior to participation in a public program is frequently held to be a violation of public policy and therefore invalid.

Participation agreement. A participation agreement is of particular value in circumstances where a release or waiver may not apply. It is, in essence, a signed statement indicating that the participant and/or his/her parents understand the dangers that are inherent in the activity, know the rules and relevant safety procedures and the importance of following them, fully appreciate the possible consequences (i.e., specific types of injuries or even death) of the dangers involved and, knowing all this, request to participate in the activity. Van der Smissen (1985) has indicated that, in order to be effective, participation agreements should meet the following criteria:

1. They must be explicitly worded.
2. If there are rules that must be followed, it is preferable that the rules be listed in the agreement or listed on the reverse side of the paper.
3. The possible dangers inherent in the activities must be spelled out in detail, along with the consequences of possible accidents to the participants.
4. The participants must sign a statement expressly assuming the risks of the participation.

Although a participation agreement will not prevent a lawsuit or absolve the teacher or coach of the responsibility for his/her negligence, it clearly establishes the awareness level of the participant and his/her willingness to assume reasonable responsibility for his/her own welfare and compliance with appropriate rules and procedures. It can, therefore, be a very valuable tool in the establishment of a contributory or comparative negligence defense.

Risk Management

The best possible means of avoiding costly liability claims and judgments is by recognizing those circumstances in which injuries are most likely to occur and by taking appropriate steps to eliminate or minimize the chances of their occurrence through a carefully applied process of risk management.

Most activity-related lawsuits allege that the teacher or coach was negligent in the fulfillment of his/her professional responsibilities with regard to one or more of the following areas: supervision, selection and conduct of the activity, or environmental conditions. This is not surprising since it is possible, through careful analysis of these areas, to identify virtually all controllable injury-causing factors within an activity. For this reason, the areas of supervision, selection and conduct of the activity, and environmental conditions provide an excellent organizational focus for a general program of risk management and prevention as well as for identifying specific safety principles within individual activities.

Supervision

The structure of the educational environment and the nature of the students dictate the absolute necessity for effective supervision. A skilled supervisor (teacher, coach, group leader, etc.) can, in the normal course of his/her duties, prevent many needless accidents. Effective supervision is, therefore, recognized as an essential element in the delivery of safe and successful programs of physical activity and is called into question virtually every time a negligence suit is instituted. In developing educational programs, therefore, it is necessary to provide a sufficient number of supervisory personnel to manage the group in question and to ensure that the supervisory personnel employed possess the necessary knowledge and skills to fulfill their responsibilities.

The individual teacher or coach is responsible for the provision of both general and specific supervision. The broad overall supervision of a class or team is referred to as general supervision. In providing effective general supervision, one is expected to maintain visual contact with the entire group, to be immediately accessible to them, and to apply a high level of professional skill in the detection and remediation of deviations from safe and prescribed procedures. Specific supervision, on the other hand, refers to situations of direct interaction between the teacher and one or more students. Direct supervision might be required in order to correct some noted deviation from safe practices or procedures, to provide individual feedback, or to lend direct assistance when a student is about to attempt a new or particularly dangerous skill. The intensity and specificity of the supervision is inversely proportional to the ability of the student to understand and appreciate the dangers of the activity, to assess his/her performance and skill level, and to adhere to required safety procedures. Generally speaking, therefore, as the age and ability of the students decrease, the need for specific supervision can be expected to increase, and the advisability of allowing extended periods of time with only general supervision can be expected to decrease.

Decisions regarding the relative proportion of general to specific supervision are, of course, dependent on the particular group and situation in question. It should be remembered, however, that the need to provide specific supervision to one or more individuals does not remove the need to provide general supervision for the remainder of the group. The teacher cannot, therefore, become so engrossed in providing individual feedback to students in the northeast corner of the gym that he/she fails to detect and correct the hazardous situation that may be occurring in the southeast corner.

The following general guidelines should prove helpful as you seek to provide effective supervision for all activities:

1. Take whatever steps are necessary to guarantee your own competence in the activity being taught. You must be the expert!

2. Establish general safety rules for the gymnasium, locker rooms, etc. Rules should be explained to the students, posted, reinforced, and consistently enforced.

3. Develop the habit of writing detailed lesson or practice plans. The act of planning will help to identify and correct many potential hazards. Moreover, the plans themselves can serve as valuable legal evidence of your preparation and knowledge with regard to the subject matter as well as the preparation of your students.

4. Never leave your class or team unsupervised. A quick phone call in the office or a brief stop in the equipment room to retrieve some forgotten item presents a period of supervisory absence and, thus, is a potential source of negligence. In such a case, if it is determined that the presence of the teacher would have resulted in the correction or the prevention of the injury-causing behavior, then the injury sustained by the student can be proximately related to the negligence of the absent teacher.

5. Take care to arrange your classes so that the entire group is in your field of vision. Move about the area in a manner that maximizes student contact and minimizes the length of time during which your back may be turned to any portion of the group.

6. Be sure to secure the facilities and equipment when they are not in use. If facilities are left open and equipment is left out, it is reasonable to expect people to use them. Unplanned and unsupervised activities of this nature frequently lead to injuries and lawsuits.

7. In the event of an emergency, you will be expected to render necessary first aid until appropriate emergency personnel (trainer, nurse, doctor) arrive. Be sure that you are adequately prepared to do so.

8. Establish a list of emergency procedures to be followed in all accident cases. This will prevent student confusion, unnecessary delays in treatment, and supervisory breakdowns. Who goes for help? Who supervises the class? How is he/she contacted? What do the unaffected students do?

9. The actions of one or more students should never be allowed to endanger other students or interfere with their learning. Maintain effective control of the activity at all times. Situations involving horseplay or aggression are rarely resolved satisfactorily by themselves.

Selection and Conduct of the Activity

As professionals, we are expected to select activities that are appropriate for the age and ability levels of our students. Having selected an appropriate activity, we are further expected to provide instruction that is factually accurate and presented in a manner that maximizes the likelihood of student success. This instruction should be supplemented by warnings with regard to any potentially hazardous conditions involved in the activity, the provision of appropriate safety devices and protective measures, and the provision of feedback through which the student can gauge and modify his/her performance.

The courts have been relatively consistent in their recognition of the fact that very few activities are inherently unsafe. The issue in question, therefore, should an injury occur, is whether the injured student was physically capable of successful participation and was properly prepared and instructed. Whereas certain risks may be deemed necessary in the interests of good programming and total student development, such risks must be well-thought out and justified, and the potential for student injury must be minimized.

The following guidelines should be considered when selecting and developing any activity:

1. Always select activities that are within the reasonable ability limits of the students.

2. Readiness is an individual matter. Pretesting and screening, careful record keeping, and the development of individualized progressions are, therefore, essential to safety and success.

3. The development and maintenance of comprehensive lesson plans and curriculum guides is essential both to instructional success and a sound legal defense in the event of a lawsuit. They provide evidence regarding the nature and organization of the instruction as well as previous student experiences and background.

4. Always have planned rainy day activities to correspond to planned outdoor activities. It is both difficult and embarrassing to try to justify an injury occurring in an ad-libbed activity that had to be pulled together because an outdoor lesson was rained out.

5. All activities should be justifiable within the context of the educational objectives of the school. Too frequently, activities selected solely on the basis of expressed student enjoyment are not particularly enjoyed by all and result in needless injuries. Such injuries are very difficult to justify.

6. Procedures should be developed for the acceptance of medical excuses and for return to activity after serious injury or illness. Never allow an injured or ill student to participate without a medical clearance.

7. Do not attempt to coerce students to perform when they are, by their own admission, fearful or unequal to the task. Such action is almost impossible to justify when it results in an injury.

8. Provide all necessary protective measures and devices, and require their use.

9. If adequate protective measures cannot be provided, then the activity itself should be modified.

10. Be sure that all instruction is consistent with the most professionally accepted information and procedures and includes warnings regarding the dangers involved and the manner in which they can be avoided or minimized.

11. Provide ongoing review feedback and corrective instruction with regard to the performance of motor skills. Remember that practice without effective feedback and appropriate remediation tends to result in well-established bad habits.

12. Take whatever steps may be necessary in order to avoid mismatch situations in activities where there is a strong likelihood of physical contact. It should be remembered, however, that a mismatch is a function of size, strength, skill, and experience. The gender of the participant is not a controlling factor.

13. Above all, remember that the focus of the educational process is the student, not the activity. Our responsibility, therefore, is to tailor the activity according to the skills of our students in order to provide the safest and most productive learning experience for all.

Environmental Conditions

In addition to providing a safe activity under competent professional supervision, one must also take appropriate measures to provide safe facilities and equipment. Before allowing students to use an instructional area or a piece of equipment, it should be carefully inspected for safety and proper function. Such things as debris or potholes on the playing fields or loose racquet heads can lead to participation injuries. When this occurs, the teacher/coach will, almost invariably, be called on to explain the procedures he/she followed in order to prevent injuries due to unsafe environmental conditions.

Although obvious hazards such as water on a court surface or a cracked bat usually result in immediate remediation, many teachers unknowingly create environmental hazards by the manner in which they use an otherwise safe facility. Instructing students to run across the gym, tag the far wall, and return, for instance, is simply inviting an injury due to a collision with the wall. This is not the fault of the facility. It is a function of the manner in which the facility is used. Similar situations can be seen where one fails to provide a sufficient buffer area around a playing field or court. Participants must be expected to run out of bounds and beyond finish lines. A sufficient buffer zone is, therefore, essential to safe play. Other teacher-imposed and easily corrected environmental hazards include the following: relays where the turning directions and running lanes have not been clearly specified; the use of improper substitute equipment such as candy wrappers for bases; or the use of equipment that requires a level of skill beyond that of the participants. An example of the latter circumstance would be the use of fixed-post bases with unskilled participants where sliding is allowed. Although these bases offer distinct advantages with skilled sliders who recognize their unyielding characteristics, they are unsafe for those who lack such skill and knowledge. If, therefore, they were to be used with an unskilled group, sliding should be disallowed in the interest of safety.

The following general guidelines should prove helpful in reducing the number of injuries due to hazards in the environment.

1. Start every day with an inspection of the facilities your classes will using. Note any hazards such as broken glass, slippery or uneven surfaces, loose fittings, etc., and take steps to eliminate them.

2. Make appropriate planning modifications to keep students away from hazardous areas until repairs can be completed. If a problem is located in a general use area, consider some form of marking as a warning to others.

3. All equipment in use should be inspected daily.

4. Teach students to inspect equipment and require them to do so each time it is issued. This double check system virtually eliminates the possibility of teacher negligence associated with equipment failure.

5. Under no circumstances should students be allowed to use equipment that is in a state of disrepair.

6. Be sure all facilities and equipment meet or exceed recommended size and safety specifications, e.g., thickness of mats, free area around courts, and landing pits.

7. Do not hold running activities on an uneven or slippery surface.

8. Provide and require the use of appropriate safety equipment. Post signs and reminders to keep the importance of this issue clearly in the minds of the students.

We are living in an age of litigation. Disputes and losses, whether real or imagined, are commonly brought before the courts for adjudication. It is not surprising, therefore, that in a profession such as physical education and sport, where the possibility of participant injury is present, there should be a great concern for matters of legal liability. To the degree that this concern manifests itself in careful attention to standards of safety and professionalism and thoughtful program planning, it is healthy and should be cultivated. Care must be taken, however, to prevent overreaction. It is one thing to eliminate unnecessary risks; it is quite another to eliminate programs or activities entirely because some risk happens to be involved.

Risk is an unavoidable component of sport. It cannot be eliminated, but it must be controlled. The task of the teacher is to eliminate all unnecessary risks and to reduce as much as possible those that remain. If, after doing this, the educational value of the activity can be shown to substantially outweigh the risks, then the activity has a valid place in the curriculum and should be retained. If, however, the potential risks cannot be justified in this manner, or if all reasonable steps have not been taken to guarantee the safety of the participants, then program modifications must be implemented in order to prevent needless injuries and costly lawsuits.

Reference

van der Smissen, Betty. (1985, March). Releases, waivers, and agreements to participate. *National Safety Network Newsletter, 1*(4), 2.

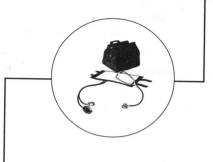

CHAPTER 3

First Aid and Safety Concerns

Phil Hossler
East Brunswick High School
East Brunswick, NJ

"It is wiser to prepare than to repair"

Physical education classes present a unique set of situations and potential for both good and bad. No other classroom is as large and has as many bodies in motion as does the physical education classroom. For that reason, more attention must be given to safety and anticipatory responses in a physical education/athletic classroom than in any other in the building. Within the confines of this chapter, "teacher" may be replaced with "coach" because coaches should be, first and foremost, teachers.

The teacher/student relationship in physical education is unique because the students have entrusted their physical well-being to the teacher. The board of education and the community assume that the teacher is versed in the skill and has taken steps to eliminate hazardous practices and conditions that might endanger the health of the student/athlete. Injuries in physical activity classes may occur from lack of proper supervision, improper progression, and physical contact between students or environmental conditions.

The following checklist may be helpful in establishing cooperation between the instructor and the student, which will promote safety in the classroom:

- Establish general safety rules for the gymnasium, locker room, equipment handling, and traffic patterns to remote locations. Post and share them with each class and be certain they are faithfully enforced.

- Establish a coding system in your roll book that will enable you to document your impressions about a student's unsafe or disruptive behaviors that might endanger them or another student.

- Establish a coding system for hazardous field/court or equipment conditions so that you can record them when detected during class or practice.

- Your students have the right to expect proper maintenance of equipment, organization, and promptness when it comes to classes beginning and ending on time, as well your presence when in transit. Inconsistency in these areas demonstrates possible laxity of supervision and the potential for injury.

- Talk to the class in the beginning and explain what they can expect from you and what you expect from them. Make them a part of the solution so that they won't become a part of a problem.

- In the event of an injury, you will be expected to render necessary first aid until appropriate emergency personnel arrive. Be sure that you are adequately equipped and trained to do so.

Preparing Your Emergency Action Plan

The key component of an effective emergency action plan is getting professional care to the student as quickly as possible. Recognize that despite your very best efforts, injuries can and will occur.

Establish a districtwide creation and implementation of an Emergency Action Plan (EAP) for the physical education staff. The EAP must be designed to care for both the injured and noninjured class members. Each emergency action plan must be individually developed, taking into consideration the program, the population, the facility, and the personnel involved.

While preparing your EAP, ask yourself these questions:

- Do your teachers routinely receive a list of students who have any noteworthy medical conditions such as diabetes, epilepsy, and exercise-induced asthma?

- Has your staff been instructed in the immediate care that might be necessary with any of these identified medical conditions that they might encounter during class?

- Does your district provide opportunities to obtain CPR training for the staff?

- How far is the nurse's office from the farthest field that is used for class?

- What method do you currently use to communicate with the nurse/athletic trainer when an injury occurs?

- Do you have a system in place by which teachers can report and document hazardous conditions on your fields or courts?

Components of an Effective EAP

Who does what? Outline the specific responsibilities of each responder. Use simple language. Leave nothing to chance. It will, almost certainly, be the unplanned elements that cause additional problems. Avoid assignments to specific individuals; instead, use titles such as "instructor" or "first on the scene" to avoid the problem of a specific person not being there that day.

What communication is available? How quickly and effectively can further assistance be obtained? Time delays are critical to the health of the injured student as well as to the supervision necessary for the remainder of the class.

What is the sequence of actions? Although no two emergency situations will be identical, it is important to visualize the injury and the reaction to it. What will be the first action taken and by whom? What happens next? Who is responsible for each step in the EAP?

What emergency equipment is available? It should be routine for every physical education teacher to go to outdoor classes equipped with a fanny pack containing sterile gauze pads, protective gloves, and a means of communicating with the main office or nurse's office such as a walkie-talkie or wireless phone.

Figure One. Emergency Action Plan

EAP for the Injured Student

1. Assess the nature and severity of the injury
2. Assume the existence of the worst-case injury and act accordingly until you are certain it is not
3. Activate EAP communication system to summon assistance if necessary
4. Control bleeding and treat for shock as needed
5. Assist emergency personnel as needed and practical
6. Complete your report as soon as possible
7. In the event of a serious injury, get accounts from eyewitnesses

EAP for the Noninjured Students

1. Remove all students from the injury site
2. Stop all activity; separate students from all equipment that might make continued supervision difficult
3. Remember you are responsible for the well-being of every student, not just of the injured one

---

First Aid Considerations

The application of emergency care during a physical education class is truly the epitome of the definition of first aid: "the immediate and temporary care given until further help can be obtained." The physical education teacher's first aid may be as much knowing what not to do as it is what to do.

The teacher must see to several areas and decide which one needs to be addressed first. These areas include the following:

- Assess the nature and severity of the injury. Injuries are generally of two types: life-threatening/altering and non-life threatening/altering. Become proficient at recognizing the type and take appropriate steps

- Determine the need for additional trained medical personnel
- Provide supervision for the noninjured students
- Provide the appropriate first aid
- Activate the communications system

Ideally, each staff member should have constant access to the supplies necessary to care for bleeding, such as sterile gauze pads and protective gloves, as well as a form of communication and transportation. The issuance of staff fanny packs should be routine. School districts should create their EAP with the most difficult scenario in mind; this will make every other situation easier to address.

Universal Precautions

Education in the use of universal precautions to guard against blood-borne pathogens should be routine in each school district for all employees. Check with the health supervisor in your district for the presence of this program.

General guidelines of implementing universal precautions:

- Avoid contact with bodily fluids
- Place barriers (e.g., gloves) between the injured and yourself
- Wash your hands before and after giving care whenever possible
- Dispose of soiled materials properly

General Injury Conditions

Opportunities to acquire a general knowledge of first aid should be a routine part of each district's in-service agenda. Physical education teachers need to have a basic knowledge of the conditions enumerated below. This section should not be viewed as a substitute for additional courses in first aid and cardiopulmonary resuscitation. Immediate first aid is threefold: control bleeding, prevent infection, and prevent shock.

Additionally, in the near future, the presence of equipment such as automated external defibrillators (AED) will be more commonplace in schools, athletic arenas, factories, and office buildings. Districts are encouraged to research cost, availability, and individual state regulations about AEDs to determine individual district advisability.

Shock

Traumatic shock results from a depressed condition of the body due to failure of the circulatory system. When blood flow is slowed, the heart and brain receive less than normal amounts of oxygen. Shock can occur with any injury regardless of apparent severity or blood loss. Shock can be fatal even when the wound itself is not life threatening. It is easier to prevent shock than to treat it. Any injured student can go into shock; so anticipate it and treat it early.

The injured student may present with rapid breathing; pale, cool, clammy skin; disorientation; and nausea or vomiting. The student should be placed face up on the ground with the feet elevated 8-12" in order to facilitate blood flow to the heart and brain. If there is breathing difficulty or leg, neck, or back pain or head injury, the student should be placed flat on the ground with no leg elevation. Maintain normal body temperature; additional blankets or coats may or may not be necessary.

Severe Bleeding

Bleeding that cannot be controlled quickly can be life threatening. These injuries are often deep and/or extensive. The wound should be covered with sterile gauze (or the cleanest white cloth you can find) or your gloved hand.

Direct pressure to the wound site (with adjustments made for deformity or protruding bones) and elevation will control most bleeding. If the dressing becomes saturated with blood, do not remove it; instead, place additional dressings on top and continue with direct pressure. Shock is a real possibility in the presence of blood. Take steps to prevent it.

Head Injuries

Scalp wounds bleed freely and often appear worse than they are. Nevertheless, the presence of blood often alarms and agitates students. Be prepared to deal with the remainder of the class as well as the possibility of shock in the injured student.

A concussion is one type of injury to brain tissue. There are three degrees of concussions; the grading of concussions is an ongoing discussion as to which signs and symptoms determine levels of severity.

A mild (first-degree) concussion is the least serious traumatic brain injury and is a large category into which many minor "bell-rung" episodes can fit. Consciousness is not lost, but the athlete may experience some changes in consciousness, mental alertness, and memory. The student may experience ringing in the ears, headache, dizziness, and an inability to recall recent events. The presence of a headache should be taken as a sign for the student to immediately stop further activity until he or she is symptom-free. This injury requires medical clearance prior to returning, and even mild concussions may require 7-14 days of no activity/contact. Moderate or severe concussions that involve longer memory loss, unconsciousness, and possible nerve and neck trauma can be long-term, potentially devastating injuries. They should be evaluated by a physician and may require weeks of restricted activity.

Summary

Today's litigious society demands forethought and planning by those conducting athletic, exercise, and education programs for children. Electronic communication has become commonplace; its absence is noticeable. The absence of an established emergency action plan and in-service training for the staff in how to implement this plan is unfair to both staff and students.

During any physical activity there is the possibility of injury. It is the responsibility of those persons charged with governing and implementing the activity to prevent and properly handle injuries through the following:

- Proper conditioning and progression
- Observation of rules of the game and safety rules
- Proper use and maintenance of equipment
- Elimination of hazardous practices, situations, and playing surfaces
- Creation and implementation of an effective emergency action plan
- Establishing a means of communication between the instructor and additional medical personnel

There are few situations as scary as when you are supervising an activity and someone gets hurt. Your immediate reaction is "I hope it is only minor" (and most of the time you are correct). However, there are those occasional times when the potential for a serious injury can be great. It is at these moments that your reactions and actions can keep a simple situation from becoming serious. Physical education teachers have the responsibility of knowing what to do when an injury occurs. This does not imply that everyone involved in the activity must know how to evaluate all athletic injuries, but it does mean that everyone involved should know basic first aid, CPR, and how to activate the district emergency action plan.

Consider the following situation and decide which reaction your school is closer to:

> It is a warm, sunny day in late May. You are conducting a class in softball about 500 yards from the school building. One of the students hits the ball, and, as he starts to run, he releases the bat over his shoulder. You have warned the class about this, but it happens anyway. The bat flies about five feet, striking the next batter across the bridge of her nose. The struck girl falls to the ground, bleeding profusely from her nose and upper lip. When you reach her, she is conscious but in a great deal of pain. What do you do?

Alarmed Reaction

1. Try to sop the bleeding with the palm of your hand. It is not working very well so you ask a student for his T-shirt.
2. Send a student into the school to retrieve the nurse.
3. Hope the injured student doesn't need CPR because you missed that class the last two times it was offered.
4. The student returns and tells you, "I couldn't find the nurse!"
5. What are you doing with the rest of the class? Are they helping the situation or making it worse?
6. Now you must decide between walking the girl up, having someone else walk the girl up, or taking her and the entire class up to the building.

7. Have you thought about and treated her for shock yet?

8. Keep checking your watch (now covered with blood) and wonder if another teacher will ever become visible.

Armed Reaction

1. Pull out two sterile gauze pads from your waist pack (which every teacher was given by the department). Hand them to the girl while you put on protective gloves.

2. Have the entire class sit where they are as you assess the injury.

3. Using the department walkie-talkie in your waist pack, call the nurse's office and apprise her of the situation. You tell her that although the girl is in pain, she is responsive and conscious and you have placed her into shock position.

4. Her answer is that she will be enroute as soon as she gets the athletic department's electric cart.

5. Once the nurse arrives, assist her as needed and allow another student to accompany and assist the injured girl.

6. Assemble the class together, taking this opportunity to reinforce the need for constant vigilance when it comes to sport safety.

7. When you return to the building at the conclusion of class, stop at the nurse's office to check on your student and fill out the necessary forms.

All activity injuries, regardless of severity, are best handled by preventing their occurrence. Prevention requires forethought and planning. The emergency action plan must take into consideration the respective first aid training of those persons working within it, the geography of the area, the communications system available, and the demands of supervising the noninjured students.

CHAPTER 4

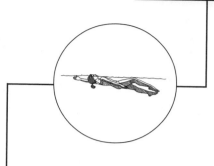

Aquatics

Ralph L. Johnson
North Greenville College
Tigerville, South Carolina

Construction of new swimming pools and rehabilitation of existing pools continued unabated in the last two decades of the 20th century. This trend is likely to continue, driven by curriculum expansion in progressive schools, Title IX's influence on women's aquatic sports, and the demands being placed on school boards by taxpayers to build and provide access to school swimming pools and other recreational facilities. Unfortunately, the increase in aquatic facility construction and the demand for pool time by citizens ranging in age from infants to senior citizens will also increase risk potential.

Major Risks in School Aquatic Facilities

Drowning

Drowning has always been a concern in school facilities. Whereas there appears to be a modest decline in the number of drownings across the U.S., an increase has been noted among certain racial groups, specifically, Hispanics and African-Americans. In aquatic classes, the primary cause of drowning is oversized classes or classes with mixed abilities and a lack of continuous direct supervision by the teacher. Second is the failure of schools to provide a lifeguard in their aquatic classes. The leading cause of drowning in school recreation programs is breath-holding activities and long distance underwater swimming. The primary cause of drowning in competitive swimming is hypoxic (low-oxygen) training sometimes referred to as 2-stroke, 3-stroke, 4-stroke breathing, etc. Low oxygen levels lead to cerebral anoxia, resulting in unconsciousness and, subsequently, a passive drowning.

Although teachers and coaches need to supervise their activities more closely, school districts that won't provide lifeguards must not continue to place the entire burden of supervision on their teachers and coaches.

Shallow Water Diving

Spinal cord injuries (SCI) most often occur from striking the pool bottom in water 3 1/2- 5 feet in depth. Although this type of injury has declined in America's schools in the past 20 years, the result of an impact with the bottom is usually permanent quadriplegia. According to the YMCA of the USA's Medical Advisory Committee, it is unsafe to conduct diving instruction and for recreational divers to make a head first entry into less than nine feet of water. The American Red Cross also supports the nine-foot standard for safe instructional and recreational diving. Diving skills should always be taught in sequential progressions in nine or more feet of water, and recreational diving from poolside must be restricted to nine-foot depths or greater.

Starting Block Spinal Cord Injuries

Since the mid-1970s, high school and college competitive swimmers have suffered permanent quadriplegia from diving off starting blocks located in the shallow end of pools with $3^1/_2$ feet of water depth. In addition, the belief by some coaches and swimmers that the Pike Dive (sometimes called the scoop, shoot start, or dive in the hole start) is a faster start has been proven wrong. The Pike Dive theory was disproved in a research study by Counsilman (1985), who not only showed that it was slower than other racing starts but also demonstrated that 10% of his sample group went deeper than $4^1/_2$ feet with the Pike entry. Gehlsen and Wingfield (1994) conducted starting block research for the NCAA and determined that at least 1.4 meters, or $4^1/_2$ feet, of depth is required for any racing dive. Subsequent spinal cord injuries occurring in high school competitive swimming have shown Gehlsen and Wingfield's results to be correct. This fact has been further demonstrated by the YMCA of the USA, whose competitive swimming program has not had a single spinal cord injury from starting blocks in over a decade since recommending that all blocks be moved to the deep end of YMCA pools where the water is 5 feet or more in depth.

Class Trips, Field Experiences, and School Social Events

Drowning and quadriplegia accidents continue to occur across America while students travel on senior trips to water parks, during studies of pond or river ecology, and when school social events such as after-prom parties occur in hotel pools and spas. The risk of death or serious injury increases greatly when well-meaning teachers chaperone these types of activities without first investigating the site with an aquatic professional. A risk analysis of the site and providing a lifeguard for nonguarded facilities along with the use of throw bags, reaching poles, and PFD's at locations in the natural environment, along with carefully planned and practiced emergency procedures, are responsible risk-reduction techniques that should be employed by all schools.

Additional Aquatic Facility and Program Risk Concerns

Two facility issues—water quality and pool design—have been responsible for a number of injuries and deaths in school swimming pools.

Water Quality - This includes cloudy water that precludes a teacher or a lifeguard from seeing a student on the pool bottom. Classes should not be conducted in any pool where the drain is not clearly visible in the deep end. Water-quality standards that will prevent cloudy water include chlorine levels of 1.5 – 2.0 ppm, a pH level of 7.2 – 7.5, a Langelier Saturation Index calculation of 0 (zero), and clean filters, with all of these responsibilities coordinated by an aquatic director currently certified in pool operation.

Pool Design - Several pool design issues have been responsible for serious injuries and deaths in school-owned facilities. They include the hopper and spoon-shaped bottom design in both new and older facilities. These designs have frequently caused paralyzing diving injuries when students have struck their heads on the bottom or transition slope in the deep end. An inadequate diving envelope for springboard diving is also a significant risk, especially in older pools with high-performance aluminum diving boards. Other major design issues of concern include low levels of lighting (below 50-foot candles at the water surface), pool dressing room entrances at the deep end, and slippery decks.

Classes with Mixed Swimming Abilities - Schools sometimes combine nonswimmers together with swimmers because they are also similarly grouped together for social studies, math, etc. Although this concept may work in other physical education classes, it doesn't work in the aquatic environment. Nonswimmers must remain in shallow water for most of a grading period while swimmers need to be challenged with deep-water skills and activities. A teacher cannot be in both areas simultaneously. The only responsible and safe solution for this issue is two teachers assigned to the pool at this time, each one with a separate lifeguard.

End-of-Class Security Procedure - Drownings have occurred in some school classes because lifeguards were not provided, because teachers were assigned to swimming classes with 40 – 50 students, or because some teachers were required to instruct students with mixed swimming abilities in the same class. In light of these conditions, a final check or closing security procedure should be implemented at the end of every class. Such a procedure requires a teacher to circle the entire pool, checking the bottom while being directly observed by another teacher, teacher's aide, lifeguard, or even a student. Following the inspection, the teacher and observer should sign out on the pool log as indicated below:

Pool Closed & Locked By   Date   Time (Circle one)

    / /   am or pm

_____

(Teacher's Signature)

Pool Closure Witnessed By   Date   Time (Circle one)

    / /   am or pm

_____

(Witness Signature)

This procedure will effectively insure that no one was left behind and that the pool was secured properly in the presence of a witness.

Supervision

Swimming and aquatic activities have long been recognized by the aquatic profession and the court system in the United States as hazardous, requiring close, direct supervision and careful instruction and administration. All aquatic activities, including instruction, competition, recreation, fitness, therapy, etc., require supervision by a teacher or coach and a certified lifeguard. Safe aquatic supervision includes eight basic components: 1) Knowledge of the Standard of Care, 2) Supervisory Competency, 3) Planning, 4) Participant Abilities, 5) Safe Environment, 6) Warnings and Instructions, 7) Emergency Management, and 8) Lifeguard Support.

These eight components of aquatic supervision represent the minimum standards for proper aquatic facility and program supervision.

1. Knowledge of the Standard of Care - The standard of care for aquatic facilities in the United States is usually defined by a governmental body and by the aquatic profession. Most states, as well as some counties and large cities, have enacted laws that regulate aquatic facilities. These laws are enacted because aquatic facilities inherently include two issues of concern related to aquatic activities: safety (drowning and traumatic injury potential) and health (waterborne disease potential). Teachers, coaches, and aquatic directors have a professional responsibility to obtain, interpret, and apply these statutes to their facility and programs.

In recognition of the fact that laws and regulations represent the minimum standard of care, teachers, coaches, aquatic directors, and aquatic safety professionals have developed and promulgated standards that represent the opinions of the aquatic profession. These professional opinions are often published in the form of professional standards, in textbooks, journals, and position papers. Professional aquatic facility and program standards are developed and published by the following organizations:

1. Aquatic Council of AAALF/AAHPERD
2. YMCA of the USA
3. NCAA
4. USA Swimming
5. USA Diving
6. U.S. Coast Guard
7. American Red Cross
8. American Camping Association
9. National Recreation and Parks Association
10. National Intramural and Recreational Sports Association

Aquatic Council of AAALF/AAHPERD Standards can be obtained from the Aquatic Council web site http://www.aahperd.org/aaalf/.

Depending on the position held by an aquatic professional and his or her employer, it is a teacher's professional obligation to acquire these standards and apply them appropriately. Willfully ignoring aquatic standards is unprofessional and could have serious legal consequences in the event of an injury and a subsequent lawsuit.

2. Supervisory Competency - Instruction of aquatic classes and the administration of school aquatic facilities are usually conducted by a person with a bachelor's degree in physical education. However, due to the health and safety issues involved with water, additional knowledge and experience is desirable. Standards in aquatic supervision are often defined by state and county regulations. Many states and counties require a pool operator's license or certification to meet the legislated standard of care. In addition, curriculum and certification requirements for teaching and lifeguarding have been defined by the Aquatic Council of AAALF/AAHPERD, the YMCA of the USA, and the American Red Cross. To demonstrate evidence of supervisory competency in lifeguarding, facility operation, and swimming instruction, aquatics administrators often must earn a certificate from an agency certifying in these areas. The Aquatic Council of AAALF/AAHPERD offers Teacher of, Master Teacher of, and Master Clinician Certifications in Swimming, Pool Chemistry, and Aquatic Facility Management, among others. The YMCA of the USA aquatic curriculum includes Lifeguard Training, Aquatic Facility Management, and Instructor Certification in Y Swim Lessons (Preschool and Children and Youth and Adult), and the American Red Cross offers certification in Lifeguarding and Water Safety Instructor (W.S.I.). Each of these certifications is considered to be helpful in establishing supervisory competency for teachers and aquatic facility managers. Similar certification courses are offered and sometimes required by USA Swimming, USA Diving, and the American Swimming Coaches Association. School teachers, coaches, and facility managers should earn these certifications, along with obtaining a membership in AAHPERD and attending the many annual aquatic seminars and workshops sponsored by AAHPERD at state and national levels.

3. Planning - Planning has always been a distinguishing characteristic of teachers, coaches, and facility managers. Safety planning should be inherent in lesson plans, team workouts, and in-service training when professionals develop their plans. Planning should be accomplished in accordance with state regulations as well as standard professional practices in aquatics. All lessons, competitive workouts, and in-service training plans should be committed to writing, dated, and retained for at least five years. Comprehensive planning should be used to identify methods of instruction that are related to individual ability and sequential progressions.

4. Participant Abilities - Swimming strokes and diving are complex motor skills that require several considerations related to participant abilities. Teachers should always employ individual skill assessments (pre-tests) before assigning students to a class. Another important consideration is participant readiness. Because swimming and diving instruction is conducted in water, teachers must be ready to deal with real and imagined fears and also be prepared to use developmentally appropriate skills and instructional techniques. In addition, teachers and coaches should never use coercion or forced participation to achieve skill development and should realize there is a fine line between encouragement and coercion. They must also be very careful not to certify or pass a student whose skills and knowledge are below competency. Likewise, teachers must avoid succumbing to the desire to extend the standards required to pass a skill, keeping in mind that most students are not Olympic hopefuls or candidates for a Navy S.E.A.L team.

5. Safe Environment - The provision of a safe environment for students is a vital characteristic of aquatic education that includes several important components. A safe environment is a product of both preventive and remedial maintenance. Ongoing inspections of the facility—its roof and ceiling and fixed equipment such as diving mounts, ladders, and lifeguard chairs—should be conducted regularly, some as frequently as once a month (lifeguard chairs) and others every five years (ceiling and roof). Inspections of first aid kits, blood-borne pathogens precautionary kits, rescue equipment, and class equipment should be made weekly.

Another vital component of a safe environment is the use of instructional and warning signs. These signs should be created by following sign standards developed by the American National Standards Institute (ANSI-Z 535.1, .2, and .3). Along with proper signage, a safe pool environment includes the selection of reliable class equipment. Equipment that has achieved a reliable reputation and has become a standard in the field is often safer than equipment purchased from the lowest bidder. Since most school swimming pools are indoor facilities, a safe environment includes the need for clean air and chemically safe water. Attention by teachers, coaches, and/or aquatic facility managers to air turnover, heat, humidity, and removal of carbon dioxide, chlorine, and chloramines gases will prevent students and staff members from encountering aerosol diseases such as R.I.S. (Respiratory Insufficiency Syndrome), Lifeguard Lung, and Legionnaires Disease.

Clear water and disease-free water requires an understanding of the relationship among the operational components of water chemistry, disinfection, and filtration systems. If aquatic instructors or facility managers do not have this knowledge, pool water can become cloudy enough to obscure the bottom and permit the growth of intestinal parasites, as well as waterborne diseases.

6. Warnings - Warnings and safety instructions are important components of good supervision. Warnings fall into three categories: verbal, written, and signage. Verbal warnings include initial warnings by teachers and coaches about facility, equipment, and program risks. Verbal reminders (repetition of previous warnings) are vital components of good supervision because learning is enhanced through repetition. Verbal warnings should also be expressed during the orientation of students on the first day of class. Professional aquatic teachers will conduct a pool tour pointing out equipment risks (diving boards and starting blocks), unsafe activities (diving into water less than nine feet deep), and pool rules (no running, etc.), prior to the first class or team practice.

Written warnings can also be conveyed through course syllabi, topical safety handouts, and instruction sheets. Behavioral rules and instructions posted on the rear of dressing room doors and lifeguard chairs and on large signs in several places around the pool are another way to communicate warnings. Informed consent letters sent home to parents of participants contemplating field trips with aquatic opportunities and a form seeking approval for student participation in potentially hazardous activities are both examples of warnings that also require parental or guardian consent to participate in aquatic activities.

Proper signage, constructed in conjunction with ANSI sign standards and pool markings, are also common methods used to convey warnings in aquatic facilities. They include accurate depth markers, lane lines (on the pool bottom), break point lines, contour lines, and international picture signs.

7. First Aid and Accident Management - The primary goal of planned supervision is to prevent as many accidents as possible; however, not all accidents can be prevented. Therefore, supervision must include a component dealing with first aid and accident management. American courts have consistently demonstrated through their opinions that teachers, coaches, and aquatic facility managers owe four duties to accident victims:

1. They must activate the impact zone around the accident scene, requesting an ambulance from EMS and/or aid from police, firefighters, or HAZMAT teams.

2. The victim must be protected from further injury or physical harm.

3. First aid and CPR, along with proper equipment (i.e., backboards, cervical collars, mechanical suction devices, oxygen administration equipment and AEDs) must be provided to sustain or restore life functions.

4. The victim must be comforted and reassured that everything necessary is being done for his or her well-being.

In order to accomplish these four duties, aquatic staff must develop a well-constructed accident management plan that includes a staff response by personnel currently certified in first aid and CPR who are equipped with lifesaving equipment and barrier protection. Minimum accident management equipment includes the following items:

Basic First Aid and Resuscitation Equipment List

1. Resuscitation masks for each lifeguard and teacher or coach.

2. A bag valve mask resuscitator.

3. Manual suction devices to maintain a clear airway.

4. Oxygen administration equipment.

5. An AED (Automated External Defibrillator).

6. Blood-borne pathogens precautionary kit with face shield, protective gown, latex gloves, and foot coverings.

7. Hazardous waste kit with clean-up supplies.

Note: The YMCA of the USA and American Red Cross lifeguard programs are now in a transition phase during which lifeguard candidates are voluntarily being trained in blood-borne pathogens prevention, O_2 administration, and the use of an AED. This training will become mandatory for lifeguard certification by January 2003. Blood-borne pathogen kits, hazardous waste kits, and clean-up materials, as well as oxygen units and an AED, will need to be in place at all school pools across the United States by January 2003. Employing lifeguards trained in the use of this equipment and not having an AED or oxygen administration unit on hand will present insurmountable liability for any school in America that fails to purchase these standard equipment items.

In addition to the aforementioned basic equipment, a well-maintained, comprehensive first aid kit will continue to be necessary. Aquatic facility personnel will also need to develop, write, and rehearse accident management procedures if these procedures are not already in place. Below is a minimum list of procedures fundamental to all school aquatic facilities.

Fundamental Accident Management Procedures Checklist

1. Near drowning or drowning
2. Spinal cord injury
3. Fractured bone
4. Facility evacuation for fire, explosion, or chemical spill
5. Stroke or cardiac arrest
6. Uncontrolled bleeding
7. Respiratory emergency (exercise-induced asthma, seizure, allergy reaction)
8. Weather or natural disaster
9. Bomb threat
10. Missing person
11. Assault or civil disturbance
12. Power failure

Once these procedures have been developed and written, regular in-service training must be implemented to test the aquatic staff and their preparation to be sure that each procedure will function properly. Developing and testing the drowning, spinal cord, and chemical spill procedures should also involve input from and cooperation with local police, fire, EMS, and hazardous materials team personnel to ensure coordination necessary for successful completion of each procedure. There should also be follow-up counseling available for witnesses and aquatic staff members who may experience Post Traumatic Shock Syndrome.

8. Lifeguard Supervision - Lifeguards are a recognized standard of care; no school swimming program should function without a lifeguard on duty for each class and aquatic activity. This has been a standard ever since the American Red Cross published its Swimming and Aquatic Safety text in 1981. It has been proven repeatedly in the courts that the teacher cannot adequately provide instruction while working simultaneously in the capacity of a lifeguard. Many school districts have employed an adult or teacher's aid who resides in the community to provide lifeguard services for their classes; other schools have employed their own students as lifeguards. Lifeguards, however, must not be assigned instructional or maintenance tasks while on duty. Their responsibility must be entirely devoted to the observation and supervision of students in the pool area.

Instruction and Conduct of Aquatic Activities

Instruction

The key elements of safe, quality instruction include lesson plans, participant readiness, identifying high-risk activities, teacher qualifications, and the conduct of the activity. The following list contains important concerns for the safety-conscious teacher:

1. Lesson plans - Daily lesson plans should be developed in accordance with school district requirements, aquatic texts, and safety and instructional standards developed by the Aquatic Council of AAALF/AAHPERD, the YMCA of the USA and the American Red Cross.

2. Participant readiness - Students should be screened with a swim test to determine if their skill level justifies being assigned to a particular class. A procedure should be developed regarding student health and medical evaluation that will determine when students can go back in the water after a period of illness. Psychological readiness is also a very important consideration. Some students come to class with learned or perceived fears about drowning. Coercion, embarrassment, or force should never be used with these students as a means of gaining participation, especially in high-risk aquatic activities.

3. Aquatic activities that have high risk potential:

   a. Diving - teaching or permitting diving from poolside or starting blocks located in shallow water (less than 9 ft. deep.)

   b. Springboard diving

   c. Skin and scuba diving

   d. Beginner classes for nonswimmers

   e. Water polo

   f. Special-population aquatic classes and activities

4. Teacher qualifications:

   a. Teachers must be certified in swimming and other specialty activities that they will be teaching.

   b. Continued certification in swimming, lifeguard training, first aid, and CPR must be maintained.

   c. Teachers must update when national agencies such as the YMCA and American Red Cross change their courses and standards.

   d. Updating in aquatics also includes attending the variety of workshops and courses offered by the following:

      - Aquatic Council of AAALF/AAHPERD

      - Colleges and universities

      - National Recreation and Park Association

      - State and county health departments

Conduct of Aquatic Activities

The actual conduct of the aquatic activity is the final step in assuring a safer aquatic experience for all students. Conduct of an activity involves the following:

1. The Lesson Plan:

    a. Psychomotor objectives must be realistic for the swimmer's skill level, justifiable, and consistent with the Aquatic Council of AAALF/AAHPERD, the YMCA or the American Red Cross standards.

    b. Relate all class activities directly to objectives written in the lesson plan.

    c. Provide clear verbal descriptions of skills, a demonstration video or film of the skills, and a great deal of closely supervised practice.

    d. Include written safety considerations in each lesson plan identifying equipment, lifeguards' roles in the accident management procedures, and resuscitation equipment.

    e. Do not deviate from the plan without careful thought and professional judgment.

2. Course Syllabus - A handout should be provided that identifies course requirements and performance standards. Participants should also be requested to identify any medical condition such as exercise-induced asthma, hypoglycemia, diabetes, seizures, or allergies that might affect their safety while participating in swimming and diving.

3. Checking Safety, Instructional, and Fixed Equipment - Items used for rescue or instruction should be checked daily, and fixed equipment (e.g., ladders, diving mounts, and boards) should be assessed monthly. Equipment in need of repair should be taken out of service and repaired or replaced promtly. A safety assessment form should be used, dated, signed filed, and retained for at least 5 years.

4. Emergency/Accident Management Procedures - During the first day of class, several students should be identified to assist the teacher and lifeguard in an organized response to a class emergency. These students can assist by calling 911, clearing the pool, keeping other students away from an accident victim, and securing assistance from other school officials.

5. Lifeguard Rescue and Emergency Equipment - Never begin class without a lifeguard on deck equipped with a rescue tube and rescue pack (resuscitation mask and latex gloves). Before roll is taken, have the lifeguard check the telephone, first aid kit, O_2 devices, and AED to make sure that all emergency equipment is ready for use.

6. Professional Attitude - The teacher must be a good role model. Pushing students into the pool and clowning on the diving board are examples of unacceptable behavior.

7. Teacher/Student Ratio - Acceptable ratios have been identified by aquatic agencies and the Aquatic Council of AAALF/AAHPERD:

    a. Beginner/nonswimmer: 1 teacher for 15 students

    b. Intermediate/advanced courses: 1 teacher for 20 students

Teachers should not be expected to instruct a class with diverse swimming abilities unless teacher aides (properly certified) or other teachers are assigned to co-teach the class. A lifeguard should be assigned to any class, intramural, or competitive aquatic sport (swimming, diving, water polo, or synchronized swimming) practice or event.

8. Class Orientation - The teacher should develop a standardized first-day written orientation. This written document should contain a standardized script that is presented to students in every class on the first day. It should have a place where it can be dated and signed by each student when it is presented. A roll and absentee sheet should be attached to this document before it is filed. Teachers must make sure that any student who was absent during the orientation is presented with the material before they are allowed to participate in the class. This first-day orientation should include but not be limited to the following items:

Orientation to Aquatic Instruction

1. Pool tour
2. Staff introductions
3. Role of the student, teacher, teacher aides, and lifeguard
4. Pool and locker room rules
5. Class and school rules and regulations
6. Classroom and locker room procedures
7. Emergency situation procedures - what is expected of students in the class
8. Special-situation procedures
   a. Evacuation procedures for both warm and cold weather
   b. Fire drills in warm and cold weather
   c. Pre-arranged meeting places outside the pool
   d. Weather emergencies
9. Reporting of accidents to the lifeguard or teacher
10. Procedures for entering and leaving the pool area; students must be reminded frequently of class protocol such as the following:
    a. Staying out of the water until being told to enter by the teacher
    b. Abstaining from chewing gum and smokeless tobacco during class
    c. Abstaining from drugs and alcohol before class
    d. Obeying the rules of the pool
    e. Identifying other expected behavior

      f. Taking medications and bringing medical appliances such as asthma inhalers to the pool for classes and team practices.

11. Warnings - Clearly identify high-risk activities such as diving into shallow water and tell students what the consequences are (e.g., quadriplegia) and identify and warn about the proper use of equipment, such as starting blocks and springboards.

12. Aquatic equipment - Be sure to use equipment as it was intended to be used by the manufacturer.

Class Trips, Field Experiences, and School Social Events

When a school uses a facility other than its own to conduct aquatic activities, the principles of safety and risk management procedures discussed in this chapter are the same.

The primary responsibility for the students' supervision and safety is with the school and the teacher who chaperones or supervises that activity at the facility—just as if it were the school's pool. The standards of supervision and care do not change, and while they are shared with the host facility they cannot be passed on to that facility totally. Teachers and schools are the primary caregivers for their students and must ensure that students are provided with proper supervision at all times.

The aquatic director should assist in the planning process for biology field trips, school club trips to water parks, and class trips to campgrounds or other facilities with a pool, lake, or water slides. An inspection of the site should be conducted prior to the class activity. If the facility or site does not have lifeguard supervision, the school should supply an adequate number of lifeguards, along with a teacher who possesses current aquatic, first aid, and CPR certifications. Emergency medical information should be brought along by the aquatic teacher, along with a first aid kit, AED, an oxygen unit, a manual suction device, and a cellular phone. In addition, an emergency procedure should be developed that includes teachers, lifeguards, and students, if necessary.

Pool Environmental Concerns

Because swimming activities are conducted in and around water, additional health and safety precautions must be taken related to the facility and its equipment. Check your pool for dangerous conditions with the pool design and operation hazard checklist below to determine risk potential.

Pool Design and Operation Hazard Checklist

Design Item	Acceptable Standard
1. Pool entrance:	Entrance at shallow end
	Locks are operational
2. Pool deck:	Slip resistant
	Slope - good drainage

Depth markers 4-6 inches high, black on
    contrasting background (white)
Depth markers on vertical wall
Depth markers on deck and vertical pool wall
Depth markers display in feet, inches and meters
No obstructions or tripping hazards

3. Pool walls:
    (underwater)

Smooth finish
No obstruction or protrusions

4. Pool bottom:

Smooth surface
Marked for depth perception - lane lines
    or contour line
Breakpoint line across the bottom and vertically
    up each pool wall
Minimum of 2 drain grates, fastened in place
    and requiring tools to remove them
Safety ledge visible from above and below water
Hopper/spoon-shaped bottom marked for
    depth perception

5. Ladders:

Attached securely
Slip resistant steps

6. Lifeguard chair:

No less than 5 ft. high and no more than 6 ft. high
Positioned at pool edge
Safe seat and steps, positioned for 90º observation
on a pool corner or 180º along the side of a pool

7. Starting blocks:

Located at deep end (more than 5 feet)
Clean, slip resistant surface anchored securely
Clean, slip resistant step

8. Diving boards:

Anchored securely to the diving mount
Clean, slip resistant surface
Mount-anchored
Slip resistant steps
Double guardrails extending to the edge of the pool
No more than 12" space between double guardrails

9. Diving area:

11'6" depth - 1 meter
12'8" depth - 3 meter
Depth extends forward 20 feet from board tip
Depth extends 8 feet on either side of board
Depth extends under board back to wall

10. Lighting:	Deck (50-foot candles per square foot of deck area) Water surface (50-foot candles) Underwater (100 lamp lumens)

11. Signs and warnings:

Pool rules large enough to see from a distance
Pool rules located at entrance
Diving rules located on or near diving mounts
Exit signs
Men's and women's locker room signs
"Danger - Shallow Water - No Diving" placed above
  a Universal No Diving Sign, with the consequences
  ("You can be paralyzed or fatally injured") written
  beneath the Universal No Diving Sign. Place this
  sign on the pool coping every 25 ft. where water
  depth is less than 5 ft.
International picture signs on indoor pool walls
  or outdoor pool fences to provide warnings and
  information to individuals who do not speak or
  read English.

12. Safety equipment:

Ground fault interrupters - all outlets
Telephone with direct outside line
Telephone emergency script message and
  emergency numbers posted next to phone
Emergency lighting system and generator
Self-contained breathing apparatus for chlorine
  gas emergencies
First aid kit
Oxygen administration unit
Reaching poles and ring buoys
Rescue tubes
Non-absorbent backboards with head immobilizer
  and six sizes of cervical collars (Adult sizes S, M, L;
  Children's sizes S,M,L)
Biohazard precautionary kit and clean-up supplies
Resuscitation masks
Automatic External Defibrillator
Manual suction device
Bag valve mask resuscitator

13. Water quality:

Free chlorine - 1.5-2.0 ppm
pH - 7.2-7.5
Water temperature - 82-85°
Total alkalinity - 100 ppm
Calcium hardness - 200-300 ppm
Total dissolved solids - less than 300 ppm
Langelier index - 0
Chloramines less than .3 ppm
Bacteria - 0 coliforms
Clear enough to see bottom drains plainly

References

American National Standards Institute, Inc. (1991). *Criteria for safety symbols*, ANSI Z535.3. New York, NY: Author.

American National Standards Institute, Inc. (1991). *Environmental and facility safety signs*, ANSI Z535.2. New York, NY: Author.

American National Standards Institute, Inc. (1991). *Safety color code*, ANSI Z535.1. New York, NY: Author.

American Red Cross. (1988). *Basic water safety*. Washington, DC: Author.

American Red Cross. (1990). *Lifeguarding*. Washington, DC: Author.

American Red Cross. (1992). *Swimming and diving*. St. Louis, MO: Mosby Lifeline.

American Red Cross. (1996). *Safety training for "swim coaches."* Washington, DC: Author.

Care and prevention of competitive diving injuries: A training program for United States diving coaches (1st ed.). (2000). Indianapolis, IN: USA Diving.

Council for National Cooperation in Aquatics. (1987). *Swimming pools: A guide to their planning, design and operation* (4th ed.). Champaign, IL: Human Kinetics.

Gabrielsen, M. Alexander, et al. (1991). *Diving Injuries* (2nd ed.). Ft. Lauderdale, FL: Nova University.

Johnson, Ralph L. (1994). *YMCA pool operations manual* (2nd ed.). Champaign, IL: Human Kinetics Publishers.

Johnson, Ralph L. (1996). *The swimming pool manger's manual*. Harrisburg, PA: Pennsylvania Department of Conservation and Natural Resources.

Sawyer, Thomas H. (Ed.). (1999). *Facilities planning for physical activity and sport (guidelines for development)*. American Association for Healthy Lifestyles and Fitness. Dubuque, IA: Kendall/ Hunt Publishers.

YMCA of the USA. (1999). *Y swim lessons: Teaching swimming fundamentals*. Champaign, IL: Human Kinetics Publishers.

YMCA of the USA. (1999). *Y swim lessons: The youth and adult aquatic program manual*. Champaign, IL: Human Kinetics.

YMCA of the USA. (2001). *On the guard II, the national YMCA lifeguard manual* (4th ed.). Champaign, IL: Human Kinetics Publishers.

CHAPTER 5

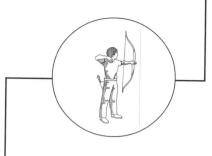

Archery

Kathleen M. Haywood
University of Missouri-St. Louis
St. Louis, Missouri

Introduction

People have enjoyed the challenge of "hitting their mark" with an arrow for more than 20,000 years. In earlier times the bow was used in defense, as a weapon, and for hunting. Once firearms were invented, the bow was rarely used in war, yet even today individuals enjoy the challenges of bowhunting and target shooting. So, even in sport and educational settings, we must remember that a shot arrow is potentially harmful and lethal.

You can teach archery just as safely as any other physical activity. To do so requires continuous vigilance and attention to detail. On the one hand, you want to provide a safe environment in which the risk of injury to your students and others in the community is minimized and your risk of liability is negligible. On the other hand, you want your students both to learn a lifetime skill and to learn to participate safely for a lifetime, long after they leave your supervision.

Perhaps more with archery than many other sports, running a safe class has as much to do with your activities before classes begin as it does with your activities during classes. Before classes begin, you must secure the archery range, prepare equipment for safe use, post safety rules, plan a lesson on safety, and prepare a unit with logical skill progression. During classes you must monitor not only your students for proper technique and equipment usage, but also the environment for unexpected intruders.

The major dangers associated with archery, then, are a failure to establish and follow safety rules, improper use of equipment, and improper use of technique. There are inherent risks in archery participation. These include equipment failure, even when that equipment is well-maintained and inspected, and fellow participants who overlook safety rules. If you make your students partners in taking responsibility for a safe environment, you will minimize the risk to all involved.

Let's look more closely at your role in conducting safe archery classes. We will begin with how to best supervise archery classes, including what you need to know and organize. Then we will review conduct of archery units and classes. Finally we will discuss facility and equipment concerns.

Supervision

There are several aspects of an archery course that you, as instructor, must supervise. These require that you know about the equipment and techniques of archery. Be sure that you have received instruction yourself in equipment maintenance and execution of the archery shot. Read extensively about these topics, too. Naturally, anyone who supervises shooting in your absence must be a knowledgeable adult. A responsible but nonexpert adult can monitor some of the necessary activities of the archery class but cannot be expected to detect improper techniques. Therefore, exercise the greatest discretion in turning over supervision of an archery class to another, even for a brief time.

Here are some additional considerations in first organizing, then supervising, your students:

1. Prepare a set of safety rules adapted for your shooting environment. Post them where students can read them daily and discuss them on the first day of your unit. A basic set of rules is suggested in Figure 1. Adapt this list for your needs, students, and setting.

2. Hold a safety discussion at the beginning of your unit. Review your rules as well as the inherent risks in archery. Consider having students sign a statement of informed consent (see Haywood & Lewis, 1989, p. 20, for an example). Such a signed statement demonstrates that you, the instructor, took a reasonable step to make students aware of the risks of archery.

3. Consider testing students on their knowledge of archery safety after your discussion but before they shoot for the first time.

4. Keep your class small, or, in the early lessons of your unit, have students shoot in groups, one after the other, so you can monitor a small number of shooters at a time.

5. Consider using a partner system wherein one student monitors another for aspects of technique that are important to safety. You must provide the student monitor with sufficient, specific details so that he or she knows what to watch.

6. Stand where you can monitor the students shooting as well as the area behind and next to the targets; that is, stand behind the shooting line. Obviously, you would never want to stand in front of the line when students are working with arrows, even if just mimicking with arrows.

7. In helping students with their technique, avoid placing your hand in the path of the string in case a student tires and releases the bowstring unexpectedly.

8. Establish specific signals to begin shooting (1 whistle blast or a verbal "begin shooting"), to retrieve arrows (2 whistle blasts or a verbal "retrieve"), and to stop shooting immediately (4 or more whistle blasts or a verbal "hold your arrows"). Practice the emergency "stop shooting" signal periodically, even when there is no danger or emergency. Practice both the whistle and verbal signals so that you can use either.

9. Be prepared to provide first aid and have an established plan of action for emergencies.

10. Monitor the physical and mental health of your students and allow individuals to shoot only if they are fit to do so.

11. Review proper attire with students on the first day of class and monitor students for compliance daily. Explain that loose clothing, hair, and jewelry, especially that worn around the face, can catch in the bowstring, as can bulky clothing, and that flat-soled shoes provide the most stable base for shooting. Shoes also protect the feet from wayward shot arrows that embed in the grass.

12. Supervise the retrieval of arrows as closely as the shooting itself. Stress that students should move forward only on the established signal and that they should walk, not run, to the target. Eye injuries can occur if an archer trips and falls into the arrows sticking from a target. Students should be taught to check behind them when removing arrows from the target and to help others at their target locate lost arrows. Arrows embedded in the grass should be pulled carefully forward and out of the grass.

Figure 1. Basic Safety Rules

1. Inspect your bow, bowstring, and arrows every day before shooting.
2. Dress appropriately and wear an arm guard and finger tab.
3. Straddle the shooting line; when not shooting, stay behind the waiting line.
4. Nock an arrow only when signaled to begin shooting. Once you nock an arrow, keep your bow pointed toward the target.
5. Step forward of the shooting line only when signaled to retrieve arrows.
6. Leave any equipment that falls forward of the shooting line, including an arrow, until the signal to retrieve unless you can pull it back to the shooting line with your bow.
7. Always obey an emergency signal to stop shooting.
8. Walk, rather than run, to the target to retrieve arrows, picking up those that have fallen short on the way.
9. Be sure the area behind you is clear when pulling arrows from the target and hold the arrow tips in your palm when walking or place your arrows in a quiver.
10. Stay at the target until all the archers in your group looking for arrows behind the target have located their arrows and are ready to walk back to the shooting line.

Selection and Conduct of Activity

Earlier, we said that some of the dangers in archery can be associated with using improper technique. You are responsible for teaching your students the proper way to execute the archery shot. Doing so increases their enjoyment of the sport, too. You also must monitor beginners for the typical technique flaws that can compromise their safety and that of their classmates. Your attention must be given to the following:

- What you tell students
- What you demonstrate to students
- What you have students practice, and
- The sequence into which you organize activities

We will focus first on what you say and demonstrate. We won't review the entire archery shot here but will attend to several aspects of technique that are related to safety:

1. Insist that your students straddle a marked shooting line so that no shooter is slightly ahead of or behind another adjacent shooter. If you have students shooting in groups (flights), make sure those not shooting stay behind the waiting line.

2. Teach students to hold their bow in front of them and pointed toward the target at all times, but especially once they nock an arrow.

3. Make sure students do not get into the habit of gripping the bow too high on the handle. In this position they are vulnerable to hand cuts from the feathers on the arrow as it clears the bow.

4. Teach students to nock their arrows on the string next to the nock locator. This prevents the arrow from leaving the bow at an unusual upward or downward angle. Later, in the section on equipment, we will discuss attaching a nock locator.

5. Teach students a string hand hook with the fingers curled (to hook onto the string) but the back of the hand flat. Beginners tend to cup the hand, twisting the bowstring and hence pulling the arrow off the side of the arrow rest (see Figure 2). This can cause the arrow to shoot much farther to the side than it is aimed if the bowstring is released as the arrow is falling.

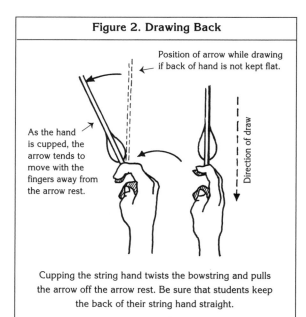

Figure 2. Drawing Back

Position of arrow while drawing if back of hand is not kept flat.

As the hand is cupped, the arrow tends to move with the fingers away from the arrow rest.

Direction of draw

Cupping the string hand twists the bowstring and pulls the arrow off the arrow rest. Be sure that students keep the back of their string hand straight.

6. Teach students to rotate their bow arm down and away from the path of the string. When the arm is hyperextended, the bowstring will slap the forearm. Even with an arm guard, it is possible for the string to slap the arm above the guard or get caught between the arm and the arm guard.

7. Teach students an anchor point-a place on the face, jaw, or neck to which they draw back their string hand on each and every shot. Beginners sometimes over-draw the bowstring (pull too far back) and pull the arrow off the back of the arrow rest. The arrow point can then jam into the bow or even the bow hand and cause injury if the bowstring is released (see Figure 3).

8. Teach archers to start the shot over if an arrow does fall off the arrow rest, rather than use their bow hand index finger to hold the arrow on the rest.

The second aspect of conducting archery classes is how you sequence your instructional and practice activities. It is best to arrange activities so that the most important aspects of the activity are taught early in the unit and learning activities are arranged from easier to more difficult. This is both sound instructional practice and conducive to safe conduct of your archery course. Although archery has but a single "skill," you can still arrange learning activities in sequence. Make sure, too, that students have sufficient practice in a learning activity before you move on to something more difficult, especially something requiring proficiency in the first activity. Here are several principles to consider:

1. Use mimicking. You can have students mimic parts of the shot (the draw and anchor, for example) and then the entire shot sequence. You can have them mimic first without equipment, then with equipment. [Note: Bows can be damaged if the bowstring is drawn and released without an arrow, so students cannot mimic the release with equipment.]

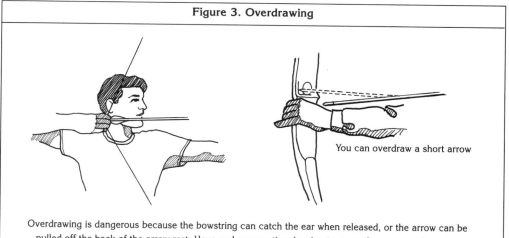

Figure 3. Overdrawing

You can overdraw a short arrow

Overdrawing is dangerous because the bowstring can catch the ear when released, or the arrow can be pulled off the back of the arrow rest. Have archers practice drawing to an anchor point and provide arrows that are slightly longer than desired once shooting form has been refined.

2. Teach students a shot sequence such as the following: 1. Stance, 2. Bow in front, 3. Nock arrow, etc. Practice this sequence with students, first by mimicking without, then with, equipment. Consider testing students, either individually or as a group, on execution of the sequence before shooting the first arrow.

3. Begin with short shooting distances. Increase the distance as your students improve and become more comfortable with shooting. If some students are ready to be challenged with longer shooting distances before others, stagger your targets (rather than your shooting line), or you can provide some with a smaller target.

4. Provide rest periods. Archery requires arm and shoulder strength. Especially in the early days of a unit, intersperse practice with activities or discussions that allow students to recover if the upper body muscles are fatigued. This is doubly important if you are not having students shoot in staggered groups (flights). Rest will help assure that students release when their shot is set up properly and their arrow is aimed at the target, rather than prematurely, due to fatigue.

Environmental Concerns

Archery classes must be taught in a safe and secured location and with equipment that not only maximizes the enjoyment of the activity for students but also minimizes their risk of injury. Following are factors to consider regarding the facilities and equipment needed for archery classes.

Facilities

To teach archery safely, you will need an indoor or outdoor space where access can be controlled and where errant shots will not cause damage. You must have target butts that will stop arrows shot by bows of the weight you use in your class. Here are some specific considerations:

1. If your range is outdoors, have a minimum area of 40 yards behind and 20 yards to the side of your targets that is visible so that you can monitor the area for unexpected intrusions. Access should be blocked and signs should be posted ("archery in progress" or "archery range-do not enter"). An alternative is to use a hillside behind the targets to stop errant arrows from traveling far and to prevent access (although signs should still be posted). Request that the grass be cut frequently so that arrows embedded in the grass can be seen.

2. If your range is indoors, make sure that any doors giving access to the area downrange are locked from the outside and that signs are posted for those with keys. You should be able to see the area behind and next to the targets so that you can monitor these areas. Use a backdrop to catch arrows that miss the target. This should be a curtain made for the purpose, bound cardboard, or bales of hay. Arrows hitting a hard surface can bounce off the surface and reverse their direction because the tip is heavier than the arrow shaft and nock. For this reason, too, remove obstacles or equipment from the area. You can pad hard surfaces that cannot be

removed. If your target stands tend to slide on an indoor floor, place rubber mats under the legs of the stand.

3. Make sure that other members of the staff know the days and hours the range will be in use. They can help keep the area secure.

4. On any range, have a clearly marked shooting line that archers straddle when shooting. If students will be shooting in groups, mark a waiting line at least 5 yards back for students who are not shooting. A shooting distance of 15 yards is quite sufficient for novice secondary school students. Targets should be approximately 10 yards apart.

5. Provide targets that will stop arrows shot by the bows you use in class. If the targets are mounted on stands, be sure they are secured and will not fall on participants as they pull their arrows from the target.

Equipment

As stated earlier, equipment can fail even if well-maintained, but a good maintenance program and frequent inspections minimize risk. Maintenance and inspection should be a habit, both for you, the instructor, and for your students. Equipment should be inspected daily, and in the case of arrows, on every "end" or turn of shooting. Below, we will consider specific pieces of equipment, then discuss fitting equipment to students to provide for safety.

Arrows

1. Damaged arrows should not be used. Splits or cracks in the shaft, bent aluminum shafts, or loose tips or nocks all mean an arrow should be taken out of service. Tips and nocks can be replaced later, but a split shaft should be destroyed. Bent aluminum shafts can be straightened later, to assure they will shoot true to the direction aimed.

2. Arrows are often hit by other arrows, so they should be inspected after retrieval on every end.

3. Arrows with some sections of feather missing can be used, but arrows with dangling fletching should be set aside because the dangling feather can cut an archer's bow hand as the arrow leaves the bow.

4. If an arrow hits a hard surface, the tip should be closely inspected. Blunted tips can later be sharpened, but when tips are pushed back into and split the shaft, the arrow should be destroyed.

5. Arrows should be stored flat, preferably in a way to prevent damage to feathers, or stored in a rack. Leaning wood or fiberglass arrows can cause them to warp over time.

6. The broadheads mounted on arrows for hunting are particularly dangerous. They should never be allowed in a class setting. Broadheads have two, three, or four razor-sharp blades mounted on a tip. They must be handled with care,

especially when being carried. Archers can be fatally injured by falling on an arrow mounted with a broadhead. An archery course, though, is a good opportunity to teach students interested in hunting about the safe handling of broadheads. Consider inviting a bowhunter to class to talk about these safe handling procedures.

Bows

1. Instruct students in the proper stringing technique of recurved limb bows that must be strung, or braced, for shooting. These bows are designed to bend in one direction. During stringing, the limbs should be bent in this plane to avoid damage to the bow and possible breakage. Consider leaving bows strung for the duration of your archery unit. You can teach students to string a bow properly, but avoiding daily stringing and unstringing minimizes associated accidents and saves time.

2. Inspect bows for splits, cracks, or other damage. Limber up each bow with quarter or half draws after a period of time in storage. Have students inspect bows daily.

3. Direct students to make sure the bowstring is properly seated in the notch made for the string during and after stringing. Consider purchasing a rubber tip protector for the bottom limb or using tape to assure the bowstring will not slip from the notch. Have students check for proper routing of the cables on compound bows.

4. Inspect, and teach students to inspect, the bowstring for wear and tear, including frayed or broken fibers in the string. Wax the bowstring periodically and teach students how to wax a bowstring. When replacing a worn bowstring, be sure to replace it with one of proper length.

5. Place a nock locator on the bowstring approximately one-quarter inch above the point where a straight line from the arrow rest intersects the bowstring at 90 degrees. Commercial locators are available, as are installation pliers, but nock locators also can be made by wrapping waxed dental floss around the string enough times to make a nocking point that prevents an arrow from sliding up the string.

6. Store bows by hanging them rather than leaning them against a wall. Over time, leaning a bow against a wall will cause the limbs to twist, and this could eventually lead to breakage.

7. Be cautious about letting students use their own equipment. You must be sure your target butts will stop arrows if personal bows are higher in draw weight than your class bows. You also do not know if personal bows have been properly maintained. If you do allow students to use personal equipment, consider having them sign a waiver (see Haywood & Lewis, 1989, p. 20 for an example).

Other Accessories

1. Periodically treat leather goods such as finger tabs and arm guards with a leather cleaner and preservative so that the items don't crack and catch the bowstring when used.

2. Be sure target sights are in proper working order.

3. Store equipment in a dry location to help maintain it and be sure to lock equipment away when not in use.

4. Target mats should be stored in a dry location where air can circulate between mats. Mats can spontaneously combust if stored improperly and in a hot location. If mats are stacked, 2 x 4s can be placed between them to allow for air circulation.

Fitting Equipment

Equipment can be in good working order but not well-matched to the size and strength of the archer. Safe, as well as successful, shooting depends on the proper fitting of equipment to archer. Here are the steps to take in fitting equipment to your students:

1. Make sure the arrows assigned to a shooter are long enough for his or her arm length and warn students not to trade arrows with each another once they are assigned a set of arrows. You can assure that arrows are long enough by using the longest length of arrow as a measuring stick and having each student in turn draw back to an anchor point while you note the location on the measuring arrow that corresponds to the arrow rest. It is prudent to give beginners an arrow that is at least two inches longer than this distance. It is better to err on the side of giving archers arrows that are too long than too short. As archers perfect shooting form, they can use arrows more precisely matched to their draw lengths.

2. Determine each archer's dominant eye and have each shoot with a right-handed bow if the right eye is dominant (left arm holds the bow, right arm draws the bow-string) but with a left-handed bow if the left eye is dominant. Alternatively, you can allow archers to shoot according to their dominant hand if they close the eye on the side of their nondominant hand when aiming. The reason for this is that it is preferable to aim with the eye on the side of the draw arm. This eye is more closely aligned with the arrow shaft. If archers vary the eye that aims the arrow at the target (which can happen if the opposite eye is dominant), they will have a greater variance in left/right accuracy.

3. Assign archers a bow length suited for their draw length and a draw weight suited for their strength. Information on selecting the proper length is available (Bolnick et al., 1993; Haywood & Lewis, 1997). It is preferable to have light draw weights available for beginners and to shoot short distances if necessary. Lighter weights decrease the likelihood that novice archers simply "let go" of the bowstring for not being able to hold it any longer and despite where the arrow is aimed. Better that beginning archers develop good form and gradually increase muscle strength and endurance than to worry about shooting high draw weights and risk breakdowns in shooting form!

Summary

Archery is a sport of consistency. Whether one is target shooting or bow hunting, success comes from repeating the same basic shot with consistency. Shooting safely is also a matter of habit. Routinely following safety rules, without variance, and routinely inspecting equipment results in a very safe activity. Too, just like accurate shooting itself, archery safety is maximized with attention to detail. Archery instructors can send their students off to enjoy a lifetime of safe and successful shooting by teaching them the details of safe shooting and equipment maintenance and demonstrating attention to these details on a daily basis.

References

Bolnick, H., Bryant, R., Horn, M., Phillips, R., Rabska, D., Williford, H., & Wilson, L. (1993). *Archery instruction manual* (4th ed.). Dubuque, IA: Kendall/Hunt Publishing.

Haywood, K. M., & Lewis, C. F. (1997). *Archery: Steps to success* (2nd ed.). Champaign, IL: Human Kinetics.

Haywood, K. M., & Lewis, C. F. (1989). Teaching archery: Steps to success. Champaign, IL: Leisure Press.

CHAPTER 6

Badminton

Donald C. Paup
The George Washington University
Washington, D.C.

Introduction - Major Risks and Dangers

Badminton is one of the fastest racket sports. The shuttle speed off the racket has been measured at over 200 mph for men and 180 mph for women (Gowitzke & Waddell, 1979). Opponents usually have less than a second to return an opponent's shot. In doing so, one must run, jump, or lunge to reach the shuttle for an average of about eight hits per rally. In games with players of similar skill, the shuttle is in play between 30-40% of the time.

With these play characteristics, it is not surprising that most injuries are muscle strains and sprains, and blisters on the feet or racket hand. Hamstring and quadriceps strains and sprained ankles are the most prevalent injuries in school classes. Compared to tennis, there are very few rotator cuff and other shoulder injuries in badminton, and "tennis elbow" injuries are relatively rare (Hensley & Paup, 1979). This difference from tennis is probably due to less stress from the light racket and shuttle. A fairly equal number of forehand and backhand overhead power shots hit in badminton may also balance muscle strength and flexibility of opposing muscles and thus reduce shoulder injuries in badminton, even though the frequency of badminton hits is much higher.

The most serious injuries in badminton are eye injuries. In Malaysia there are more eye injuries from badminton than there are industrial ocular injuries (Chandran, 1974). In school badminton, eye injuries generally occur when a smash is hit from the forecourt to an inexperienced player just on the other side of the net. The player getting hit doesn't realize he/she is about to be hit in the eye, and the person hitting the smash doesn't have enough control to direct the shot away from the opponent's face. Ocular injuries also happen to international players who are not expecting a smash at close range in the forecourt.

As skill and fitness levels increase, the physical demands of badminton increase significantly, and Achilles tendonitis, plantar fasciitis, bursitis, and other injuries of attrition become more common. Dislocations and ligament injuries of the knee (particularly the anterior collateral ligament) are more prevalent in females than males.

Injuries also occur due to players running into one another or from a player running into a non-player who is walking near a court or who wanders onto the court. A player moving backward to return a deep clear is generally unable to see a person entering the back of the court. In competitive play where children are in the gym, it only takes a couple of seconds for a child to put him/herself in danger of being struck by the player moving to return a shuttle. Classes require close supervision when there are several players on one side of the court doing drills. Racket injuries can occur because the player loses grip of the racket and it is, in essence, thrown across the gym. Similarly, a racket head may fly across the gym and strike somebody if the racket breaks. In these cases, most injuries are cuts and bruises. Players may also strike their partners with their racket, or follow through with their swing and hit themselves. This is most likely to occur with beginning players who have not yet developed a sense of their partner's position on the court.

Supervision

Necessary Skills and Knowledge of the Supervisor

Proper supervision of badminton requires adequate planning, risk management strategies, prudent judgment, and elimination of environmental hazards. The class should receive warnings of the inherent dangers of the activity and any specific hazards in the gym. Initially, pre-activity warnings should be followed by regular verbal reminders and posted visual aids containing safety measures presented at the eye level of the players.

The badminton curriculum should be educationally sound. Identification and provision of learning progressions are characteristics of good teaching. The students should demonstrate both physical and psychological readiness in the appropriate developmental areas. Physical readiness should include proper warm-up routines, satisfactory health, demonstrated fitness levels, demonstrated performance in prerequisite neuromuscular skills, and proper post-activity cool-down routines. Psychological readiness refers to the student's ability to act responsibly in competitive situations, to enjoy the participation, and to grow from positive interactions with partners, opponents, and teachers.

Organization and Control

Quality supervision by professionally trained teachers is needed to observe the playing area and determine that class conduct and safety rules are followed. Planning is required to set up reasonable participant/space ratios and practice formations to provide adequate space for racket swing and follow-through and shuttle flight. In badminton, care should be taken to ensure that inter-court space is adequate to run the necessary drills. Space between courts should ideally be at least five feet. This will allow students to pass between courts and space for the instructor to move to advantageous teaching positions at courtside. Players seldom move outside of the court side boundary lines in badminton, so the danger at the sides is from players wandering onto the court when moving from one end to the other. However, at the court ends, players often move behind the baseline to return a singles serve or high deep clear. This also occurs in smashing clears where players often move 2-3 feet beyond the baseline. The distance between the baseline and the back wall should be at least eight feet. This will allow for students to pass safely behind the court during play.

In reality, the space between courts is often only about 2 1/2 to 3 feet, due to the size and position of many badminton standards. In this case, play on both courts should be halted for players to pass from one end of the court to the other. Students should be cautioned about passing around the standards so they won't trip over wheel protrusions or knock down portable standards, causing the nets and standards on adjacent courts to fall. It is generally best for teachers to rotate players from one court to another rather than move them to opposite sides of the net. This will allow players to practice against a variety of opponents and reduce the risks they encounter when crossing between courts. With this rotation scheme, it is possible to use the five-foot area between courts to have students play some drills. However, this should only be done with intermediate or advanced players who have good basic skills and control of where they are hitting the shuttle.

The ideal badminton net setup is to have 5'1" standards inserted in holes drilled in the floor right on the sideline. Thus there are no net cords or pole standards to cause a hazard between courts. Unfortunately, most gyms are not ideal, and the nets are often tied together and attached to a ratchet mounted on a wall at either end of the gym. This makes for an easy setup for badminton, but presents some risks as discussed above. Figure 1 depicts ideal spacing and net standard options and some typical formations that have potential risks. The playing environment is of primary concern for the badminton instructor. The courts need to be free of all extraneous equipment, including maintenance and sports items. The playing surface should be dry and not slippery. The court layout should provide a safe playing area, adequate inter-court space, and an ample baseline area off the court as discussed above. There should be a plan for players and observers to move to and from the playing courts. Facility guides provide court dimensions and suggest court layout patterns with the necessary inter- and off-court space *(ACSM's health/fitness facility standards and guidelines,* 1997).

Gym lighting is very important for badminton visibility. The courts should be arranged in such a manner that when one looks over the net into the opponent's court the background is a solid wall without large windows. Light entering from behind the court makes visibility very difficult. Poor visibility not only makes play difficult, but also increases the chance of ocular injury because players can't see where the shuttle is hit. Outside lighting coming from the sides or ceiling does not present as severe a problem. Where sunlight from the outside can shine directly on the court, it is best to use these courts for running specific drills and to use the other courts for game play or competition. The use of yellow shuttles is often a good remedy for play in facilities with white or light-colored walls. They increase visibility and can generally be purchased from the same dealers where other badminton equipment is purchased.

Written policies and procedures should include the court maintenance procedures, safety inspection procedures, use policies, equipment procedures, and maintenance procedures. Gymnasium maintenance forms containing an itemized maintenance checklist should be

Figure 1.

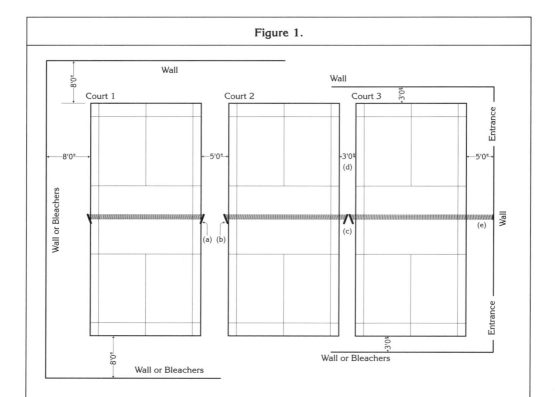

Figure 1 shows badminton court spacing and net standard arrangements that can be potential risks for injury. Court 1 depicts ideal spacing between sidelines and wall or bleachers (8') and between courts (5'). Standards are mounted on the court sidelines and have no (a) or minimum (b) interference for players and students passing between courts. Nets are attached to the anchored standards and do not cross the area between courts. Court 3 depicts a typical court spacing and standard usage with potential risks. Standards placed between Courts 2 and 3 (c) interfere with safe movement between these courts, and the net cord passes between courts at a 5' 1" height, which creates another risk. Court spacing of 3 ft (d) is less than adequate for teaching or student passage. The distance between the outside sidelines and wall (5') is inadequate for efficient entrance into the gym and passage around courts. Net cord attachment to the wall and a ratcheting device for pulling the nets tight (e) are potential risks for people passing in this area.

used to record and verify cleaning schedules. The safety inspection procedures should include a timetable, key element precautions, and the personnel responsible for safety in the area. Use policies should indicate eligible users, conditions, risks, hours of use, and user responsibility.

The equipment should be checked regularly for deterioration and damage. In badminton, from a safety point, this is primarily a racket inspection. Visual inspection may not always reveal a loose racket head or damaged racket. Thus, the students should be assigned a racket and be instructed to report to the instructor any malfunction of the racket head, twisting or squeaking, or the grip coming apart during a class session. These factors could lead to a racket head coming off during a swing or the entire grip coming out of the player's hand during a power shot. Both of these cases could result in a preventable and potentially serious injury. Badminton racket grips and broken strings can easily be repaired by the instructor. If the racket head is loose, the racket should be replaced—loose racket heads are not repairable.

The instructor can learn to repair racket strings by attending in-service classes or workshops run at teacher conventions such as the American Alliance of Health, Physical Education, Recreation and Dance (AAHPERD) at the national level or state or district conventions. These workshops are also ideal for the teacher to learn new teaching techniques, drills, age group and school competition, and rule changes.

Selection and Conduct of the Activity

Beginning badminton classes and camps are appropriate for junior high and high school instruction. Due to vast differences in skills and maturity, the teacher should try to organize class instruction and drill activities to match the size, strength, and skill development of the students.

The following factors should be considered when conducting badminton classes. Badminton is a non-contact sport in which skill is as important in playing success as strength and agility. Basic instruction is needed to teach students to serve the shuttle to the opposite backcourt and to hit the shuttle from one backcourt to the opposite baseline. Once this is achieved, players can practice or play with and against one another with very little chance of injury.

It is well worth the time required to teach students proper grip and stroking techniques. If this is not achieved, the students will not be successful, will lose interest and be embarrassed, and, generally, not have much fun.

Being able to skillfully hit serves allows students to successfully put the shuttle in play for running drills. Shot sequences can then be played that allow the students to practice their stroking skills. Unfortunately, there are no shuttle setting machines (like ball machines for tennis) in badminton. The instructor can teach students to toss the shuttle in the forecourt for some drills, but the students need to learn to hit serves to various areas of the court to begin more advanced drills. If the students or instructors are not consistently accurate, they may hit the shuttle into a court area where another drill is going on, and the players could hit one another with a racket or run into each other. To prevent injuries, students must be instructed to stay in their own part of the court for drills. If a shuttle is errantly hit into the playing area of another drill, the players must wait until that rally is over before trying to retrieve their shuttle.

Class sizes are best kept to a maximum of 4 players per court. Thus, a gym with 8 courts can accommodate a class of 32 students, whereas a gym with 4 courts can handle only 16 students. Some gyms may have space where courts are not marked on the floor; thus, space may be available for practicing footwork drills, shuttle runs, stroking drills, observation of instructional videotapes, or drills hitting the shuttle against a wall. Under these conditions, the gym could accommodate more students.

Instructors should have lesson plans that reflect learning progressions and drills. This will insure good organization and management and help promote student interest and class control. It is good practice to have badminton films to show if activities need to be moved into a classroom due to the unavailability of the gym.

Students with medical excuses or injuries should not be allowed to participate in drills and games but should participate in lectures and watch drills and games to learn the lessons of the day.

Students without appropriate gym clothing and tennis or other appropriate shoes should not be allowed to participate in class activities because this could lead to injuries as well as marking up the floor. Running shoes are not recommended for badminton because they generally have higher heels and less lateral mobility than court shoes. Cross-training shoes have a similar mobility problem. Both shoe types could increase the risk for Achilles tendon injuries and sprained ankles.

Teachers need to be present and attentive for all class activities. A class can quickly get out of hand if the instructor is not present, and injuries could be the result.

Teachers should develop a method for students to pick up rackets and shuttles and a storage container in which to return them. It is best if rackets are numbered (on the butt of the handle) and students are assigned to a specific racket for all the classes in their badminton unit. They are then responsible to help identify equipment failures that might lead to a broken racket and possible injury.

Environmental Conditions

Equipment
Students who wear glasses should wear eyeglasses containing non-breakable lenses. Although the shuttle is unlikely to break a lens, being hit by a partner's racket in a follow-through or by a thrown racket (from a slippery grip) could shatter a lens. Polycarbonate lenses are lightweight, very strong, and can be purchased with prescription lenses if desired. Although most players do not wear eye guards, the teacher should help students avoid drills and situations in which students hit hard smashes at opponents just a few feet away (i.e., in the opposite forecourt).

In classic mixed doubles, the female typically plays the forecourt and the male the backcourt. An inexperienced female in the forecourt is at risk for being hit in the eye from a powerful smash or drive from close range. Beginning players like to hit hard kill shots at the net and do not realize the opponent might not know when and how to protect him/herself. It is recommended that classic mixed doubles not be taught to beginning classes. Mixed doubles can be played using the regular side-by-side or rotation doubles formations.

If a student sustains an eye injury, it is important to not move the injured player until medical personnel examine the student and evaluate the injury. Plans for calling the school nurse's office in case of any injury should be discussed with the class ahead of time. School district guidelines should be followed for reporting injuries, and the students should know their roles as designated by these guidelines.

Temperature and Humidity

There are two risk factors when playing in high temperatures and humidity. First, the racket handles may become very slippery and slip out of a player's hand. Second, players may sweat profusely and be in danger of heat stress if they do not replenish their water loss by frequent drinks (about every 15 minutes). Teachers should be aware of the temperature and humidity in non-air-conditioned gyms and make provision for frequent water breaks.

It is recommended that badminton teachers attend clinics, workshops, and/or in-service education programs designed for teachers. They should also read professional publications or teaching texts for information on safety, equipment, and teaching strategies (Paup & Fernhall, 2000). When opportunities arise, the teacher should communicate with colleagues about badminton, how it is taught, and how to prevent injuries.

To ensure a safe badminton class, teachers should use a badminton checklist such as the following:

Safety Checklist - Badminton

Equipment
Check rackets
    Safe grip
        Tightly wound
        Tacky/not slippery
    Frame
        Cracks in head
        Cracks or bent shaft
Strings intact
Check shuttlecocks (feather or nylon)
    Cork or base is firmly attached
    Balanced shape (proper flight symmetry)
    Proper weight for environment

Check nets and standards
    Net secured properly
    Standards adequately weighted or anchored
Check courts
    Floor clean and dry (adequate traction)
    Lines clearly marked (replace worn areas if taped down)
    Playing area free of extraneous equipment

Practice
    Allow adequate space between players for swing formations
    Allow for safe distance in stroke practice
    Use fleece balls when appropriate (wall drills)
    Warm up and stretch all major muscle groups

Game Situation
    Match players by ability
    Provide recommended space around the court
    Make eye guards available for those who desire to use them
    Assist players in fitness training for badminton

References

Gowitzke, B., & Waddell, D. (1979). Technique of badminton stroke production. In Juris Terauds (Ed.), *Science in Racquet Sports* (pp. 17-41). Del Mar, CA: Academic Pub.

Hensley, L. D., & Paup, D. C. (1979). A survey of badminton injuries. *Br. J. Sports Med. 13,* 156-160.

Chandran, S. (1974). Ocular hazards of playing badminton. *Br. J. Ophthal. 58,* 75-76.

ACSM's health/fitness facility standards and guidelines. (1997). Dallas, TX: Human Kinetics.

Paup, D. C., & Fernhall, B. (2000). *Skills, drills & strategies for badminton.* Scottsdale, AZ: Holcomb Hathaway.

CHAPTER 7

Basketball

James E. Bryant
San Jose State University
San Jose, California

Introduction

Basketball is an American game and has earned a reputation as an easy, safe game that everybody knows how to play. In reality, there are countless students who really don't know how to play the game skillfully, and that situation creates potential safety problems.

The game requires physical stamina, speed and quickness, strength, explosive leg power, agility, and grace. It is a sport with the potential for extensive physical contact. Playing on a hard surface, in a confined space, always involves a certain degree of risk. The extent of that risk is determined in part, however, by the instructor's skill in supervising students as they engage in basketball activity. The ability of the instructor to select appropriate skills and experiences for the student is essential. An appropriate class lesson with logical learning progressions must be developed and implemented. Finally, the environmental conditions must be controlled to minimize risks.

It is imperative that the physical education instructor has both a knowledge of the mechanics associated with the game and a perception of potentially dangerous situations associated with basketball. The instructor must be in a position to anticipate safety problems and to plan strategies that will eliminate or reduce potentially serious situations.

Supervision

A typical basketball class will consist of 25-40 students of various skill levels and experience, confined to one or more basketball courts, each with a space of anywhere from 3,700 sq. ft.

(50' X 74') to 4,700 sq. ft. (50' X 94'). The facility can further be divided to accommodate game play by using the width of a court rather than the length, yielding court sizes even more cramped and small. The challenge to the instructor is to provide safe supervision of each student within a confined space. Strategies associated with the skills and knowledge necessary for supervision, as well as the form of organization and control required, are identified below.

Necessary Skills and Knowledge of a Supervisor

The quality of supervision of a basketball class requires that the instructor have knowledge of the following:

1. **Mechanics of basketball.** The instructor should understand how correct execution helps establish a safe participation experience for all students.

2. **Skill progression.** The instructor must be knowledgeable enough to place skill acquisition experiences in perspective through a well-designed and thought-out progression.

3. **Skill analysis.** The instructor needs to be knowledgeable and analytical in viewing skill performance. Incorrect mechanical skill execution can lead to misuse injuries.

4. **Student readiness.** The instructor must comprehend the wide variety of readiness levels of students and be able to place each student in a safe and productive learning environment.

5. **Student capabilities.** The instructor must understand the student from a physiological, psychological, and psychomotor perspective.

6. **Student behavior.** The instructor must be able to perceive and cope with student behavior in a manner that will enable the class to operate safely and efficiently.

7. **Injuries associated with basketball.** The instructor should have a background that permits insight into the prevention and treatment of the following injuries, their causes, and their seriousness:

blisters	eye injuries
calluses	overuse injuries
sprains	trauma injuries

Awareness of injuries requires additional mention. Basketball is a contact game. When students of various skills levels and sizes participate at the same time, the risk of injury increases. The most common injury in basketball is the ankle sprain. Usually this happens when a player lands on another player's foot or the ankle rolls too far outward. Knee injuries in basketball are usually serious injuries. Knee sprains and the tearing of the meniscus or a ligament are common knee injuries that require considerable medical attention.

Traumatic injuries, caused by a sudden forceful occurrence, are also common. Jammed fingers, muscle pulls or tears, and contusions are the more common traumatic injuries. Other common injuries include what are termed overuse injuries (injuries caused by stressing an area over and over until it is damaged). The most common of these injuries are patellar tendonitis ("jumper's knee") and Achilles tendonitis. All injuries cannot be prevented, but a reduction in injuries can take place if students are physically fit, skill grouping is done effectively, and students are made aware of potential injury. This allows them to, at the very least, recognize the seriousness of an injury when it happens.

In addition to the seven knowledge-based supervision categories and understanding the injury element associated with basketball, quality supervision in a basketball setting requires that the instructor sense the "messages of the gym." An example of this would be recognition of potential for an altercation between students due to frustration levels associated with the contact that occurs in basketball. The ability to "see" unacceptable physical contact during play, such as using the body to move an opponent, hand checking by pushing off the hip of an offensive player, and using elbows indiscriminately, is critical to effective supervision.

Good supervision includes organizing teaching stations in a logical manner and creating, enforcing, and identifying structure based on the physical, psychological, and emotional readiness level of the students.

Organization and Control

The organization and control of a basketball class centers on the skills of the instructor. Following are requirements for maintaining this aspect of supervision:

1. The instructor must always maintain a visual and physical presence with each student. It is not acceptable to simply be in the area. There must be interaction with the students in the class, and the instructor must establish a physical presence in the instructional area so that the total class can be observed even when the instructor is working with a single student or small group.

2. The instructor must develop a set of safety rules to be distributed as a class handout and posted. In addition, these rules must be conveyed verbally to students on a regular basis. These rules include the following:

   - No one may engage in a basketball activity unless the instructor is present.

   - All basketballs are to be removed from the playing court area and placed on the ball storage rack after use.

   - Basketball shoes only are to be worn during a basketball class.

   - Abusive use of elbows and other forms of illegal contact will not be tolerated.

   - An opposing player is never to be "undercut" (forcefully fouled while in midair).

Selection and Conduct of the Activity

The instructor's ability to select proper class content and develop the safest experience for the student is dependent on several variables. These variables are based on the students' maturation level, ability level, and readiness.

Basics

Maturation level is of extreme importance in a basketball class environment. In a class with a variety of physical differences (height, weight, strength), the potential for injury increases. It also increases when there is variance in age and playing experience.

It is important to select instructional experiences that meet the maturation level of the student. Inserting a drill that requires students to exceed their physical capabilities can result in injury (e.g., placing a 5'2" student in a rebound drill situation with a 6'1" student who has a 40-pound weight advantage is putting both students in jeopardy). Grouping can be based on factors like age, experience, skill level, and height and weight. An effective form of grouping is to establish groups based on combined weight, height, and age. Then, through a devised component system that assigns a point value to each of the three factors (e.g., all students with a combined component value of 20-24 are placed in one group, those with 25-29 in a second group, etc.), students can be grouped in such a way as to provide a balance at least based on physical size and age.

The ability of the student is also important and needs to be considered when planning a basketball class. Mixing highly skilled with low-skilled students can create a safety problem. Again, grouping is of assistance in dealing with a variety of skill levels. Two methods of reducing safety problems associated with ability levels are as follows:

- Ability group by balancing the skill level of each group during drills and/or play situations.
- Ability group by separating skill levels of each group (i.e., highest skill level in one group, next highest skill level in another group, etc.).

Within any ability grouping, the instructor needs to instill in the students an attitude of responsibility for their classmates. Highly skilled players need to be aware of their peers who are less skilled, and they need to learn to serve as mentors during instruction rather than attempt to dominate a learning situation. Mentoring in this fashion can lead to enhanced learning for all as well as reduced potential for injuries.

Student readiness is also important. On a practical level, a basketball class may consist of students not only with a variety of skill levels but also with a variety of motor readiness, interest, and motivation. Safety concerns associated with motor readiness include the following:

1. **Stress body awareness.** Basketball requires extensive jumping and movement skills. Students must be taught to be aware of their individual motor abilities. They also need to be made aware of their surroundings, where they are on the floor, how close they are to other players physically, and where they are supposed to be positioned during a given circumstance.

2. **Stress how to fall properly.** Basketball is a high-speed sport where players are darting, jumping, and running. Falls are common in the game. Since falls are inevitable, an understanding of safe falling techniques helps to reduce the potential for injuries.

3. **Emphasize being "under control."** Part of motor readiness development is to be "under control" when moving on the court. Players who dribble at a high speed and then jump before knowing whether they are going to shoot or pass provide a good example of being "out of control." When a player is "out of control," both the player and the opponent can be injured.

4. **Be aware of student fitness levels.** Highly fit students and students with low fitness in the same environment create potential for injury.

Safety concerns related to student interest or motivation must also be considered when teaching basketball. These considerations include the following:

1. Help students deal with fears associated with basketball. The fear of failure, for example, can result in tentativeness on the court. Fear of being hit or tripped are other fears that create tentative movement on the court. When students play tentatively, they don't move in a predictable way, thus contributing to the potential for injury to both the tentative student and others.

2. Help students reduce pressure. There is a common misconception that "Everyone knows how to play basketball." Therefore, it can be embarrassing for a student to not perform successfully. Try to minimize the pressure by discussing performance and evaluation expectations in a positive light. Understand how important it is for a student to experience success.

Planning and Progressions

Planning a basketball class is crucial to the safety of all students. Planning should include a detailed lesson plan for each instructional class. The plan should relate directly to that day's lesson and should specifically identify safety strategies related to the class period.

The lesson plan should reflect an effort to provide a well-supervised situation that includes the following:

- Organized teaching stations that include supervision and assistance for students practicing skills.

- Logical progression. For example, shooting a continuous jump shot should be preceded by learning how to shoot free throws.

- Proper warm-up and cool-down activities based on recent exercise physiology research.

- Organized drills that are designed for the particular age and skill level of the class. These drills should be designed to eliminate situations that would create a frustration level leading to physical altercations.

- An instructional experience designed to enhance learning without fear of injury. Drills that place students in unreasonable jeopardy are contraindicated (e.g., loose ball drills have a potential for injury beyond the norm and should be controlled or eliminated. Rebound drills and playing five-on-five half-court basketball may also have injury potential, depending on how students are grouped regarding size and skill level.).

- Specific instruction on the execution of a drill or play situation. An example would be the need for definitive directions to describe the path players should run during a drill in order to avoid collisions (e.g., running a fast-break drill downcourt and then returning to the start in an organized fashion by running on the outside of the court sidelines.

Environmental Concerns

A variety of environmental conditions, related to the facility and the equipment being used, affect the safety of a basketball class. Being aware of these environmental conditions and eliminating those that have potential to be a safety problem is of extreme importance.

Facilities

A gymnasium, on the surface, appears to be a relatively nonthreatening facility. It has four walls, a ceiling, and some kind of hard playing surface. However, what is contained within the gymnasium may well provide for concern. Blacktop playgrounds also may seem to be harmless, but when basketball is part of the activity, there is the possibility for harm. Adjustments to meet safety standards for gymnasiums and playgrounds are listed below:

1. There must be buffer zones between teaching stations and playing areas. Students who are concentrating on the game will pursue a ball into an adjacent court. A buffer zone of at least six feet must separate courts to avoid collisions.

2. There must be large, padded mats affixed to the wall behind every baseline of a basketball court. Players are often driven out of bounds behind the baseline; without padding, there is potential for serious injury. Typically, there are pads behind the baseline of basketball courts, but seldom are there pads behind the makeshift baseline of courts where play occurs width-wise. These areas are actually the sidelines of the length of a court and are usually ignored. Often bleachers are located in these areas. If so, the bleachers must be rolled back and mats need to be installed on the back of the bleachers that form walls where they are in close proximity to the sideline backboards.

3. Backboard safety padding must be attached to the bottom of rectangular backboards in order to avoid injury to those players who have excellent jumping ability and risk hitting an arm or head on the bottom edge of the backboard.

4. Breakaway rims should be installed and maintained. A breakaway rim dramatically reduces the potential of a glass backboard shattering. It also provides for safety of a player by allowing the player to hold onto to the rim and then land in a controlled fashion.

5. Rim restrainers—used with breakaway rims to prevent the rim from breaking away if the glass on the backboard breaks-need to be installed and maintained.

6. Nets for the basket must be in good repair. Nylon/cotton anti-whip nets are recommended. Chain nets for outdoor rims, although economical, do not protect the

hands, wrists, and fingers from cuts and other possible injuries, and should be replaced with cord netting. These cord nets should be replaced when broken.

7. Safety belts are a safeguard designed to prevent folded backstops that support the backboard from collapsing and injuring players or spectators. These safety belts are a required safety feature for folded backstops.

8. Outdoor basketball areas tend to lack many of the features of indoor basketball facilities. It is important to check on potentially dangerous features, including tight or bent rims, rust on the rims or backboard, and proper netting. Of particular importance is to use either gooseneck or double-poled backstops to support baskets and rims. These forms of backstops should be positioned at least three feet behind the baseline of the court to provide a buffer zone. If the backstop is closer to the baseline, it must be padded. Also, careful attention should be given to the provision of ample surfacing beyond the sidelines and baselines of the designated playing area. At the very least, the border between the court surface and the ground area must be smooth and not a drop-off (e.g., curb). In addition, the actual playing surface needs to be checked for holes or crevices; if they exist, they need to be repaired.

9. Floors must be cleaned on a periodic basis. Both hardwood and synthetic surfaces should be consistently cleaned of dirt during the day just as the floor is swept at halftime of an interscholastic game. Also, wet surfaces should be dried immediately with towels. Outdoor courts must be free of gravel or other loose materials and should be washed on a routine basis.

10. All obstacles and equipment, such as the following, should be placed away from the basketball teaching area:

    • Basketballs routinely strewn on the court.

    • Gymnastics apparatus or other physical education equipment located in proximity to the instructional area (even padded and secured apparatus belongs in an area away from the basketball court).

    • Shirts and other clothing tossed on the court in proximity to the instructional area.

Equipment

Equipment requirements or recommendations associated with instruction of a safe basketball class are designed to prevent injury and enhance enjoyment when playing the game. They are as follows:

1. Promote protection of the teeth and mouth area of students by encouraging them to wear mouth guards, a highly recommended preventive piece of equipment.

2. Promote protection to students' eyes by encouraging them to wear protective eyewear, another preventive piece of equipment that is recommended.

3. Encourage students to trim their fingernails in order to avoid scratches that could develop infection.

4. Require all jewelry that might harm the wearer or another participant to be removed (e.g., a stud ear ring probably does not present a problem, but a hoop earring clearly does).

5. Prohibit the wearing of inappropriate shoes (e.g., running shoes). Basketball shoes provide some relief from serious ankles injuries. To wear a running shoe or any athletic shoe designed for a specific function other than basketball is to invite injury. A good basketball shoe has the following characteristics:

   • A high collar.

   • A Y band, which is a leather strap around the ankle that holds the ankle in the shoe.

   • A heel counter that reinforces the ankle when it rolls in and out under stress caused by quick turns.

   • A full midsole that absorbs shock.

   • A wide base of the sole of the shoe, which provides protection against minor ankle sprains.

6. Basketballs should be cleaned on a regular basis. Balls that are dirty or worn due to extended use can be slippery and difficult to control.

Checklists

Facilities checklists can serve as useful reminders to secure the basketball instructional area. Here are two sample facilities checklists:

Indoor Basketball Court Facility Checklist

   • Buffer zones between teaching stations are established

   • Padding is located behind every baseline

   • The backboard is padded

   • Breakaway rims are installed and in good condition

   • Rim restrainers are installed and in good condition

   • Nets are in good repair

   • Safety belts for backstops are installed and in good repair

   • Court surface is clean and nonslippery

   • All obstacles are removed from the court area

   • Gymnastics and/or other equipment is totally removed from the area

Outdoor Basketball Court Facility Checklist

   • Rims are straight (not bent)

   • Rims and backboards are free of rust and sharp protrusions

- Nylon/cotton netting is affixed to the rims and in good repair
- Backstops behind the baseline are padded and positioned at least three feet behind the baseline
- Court is washed, with no gravel or loose materials on the surface
- All holes and crevices on the court surface have been repaired

Final Thoughts

With each potential hazard in basketball, there is a preventive measure that can be taken. Proper planning and anticipation of potential safety problems, along with capable supervision by the instructor, contribute to a safe environment for student participation in a basketball class.

CHAPTER 8

Climbing and Challenge Course

Anthony J. Doody
Rutgers University
New Brunswick, New Jersey

> *"Progress always involves risks. You can't*
> *steal second base and keep your foot on first. "*
> *~ Frederick B. Wilcox*

Introduction

Climbing and challenge course programs have become increasingly popular additions to secondary school curriculums over the past decade and have given teachers powerful tools for developing self-esteem; promoting a sense of cooperation, teamwork, and support; and fostering awareness and respect for cultural, social, physical, and gender-related differences. The catalyst for this powerful change is an element of perceived risk. Managing, minimizing, and preparing for these risks are essential to a successful program.

Climbing and challenge course programs are comprised of individual and group activities that typically involve a degree of physicality and problem solving and allow students to venture past their comfort zone in a safe, positive, and fun environment. Activities or "elements" are constructed of wood, cables, tires, and ropes and are connected outdoors to trees or telephone poles and indoors to steel and wood girders.

Group initiative courses (low ropes) offer an experiential approach to leadership skills, group interaction, and teamwork. A group may be asked to swing across an imaginary canyon, pass through a giant spider's web, or blindly navigate a three-dimensional minefield. The group's response to each challenge often reveals insights into their ability to work together, communicate, and creatively solve problems. By discussing what occurred during and after these activities, students can draw analogies and develop strategies for real-life situations and problems.

The confidence course (high ropes) presents a unique and often intimidating challenge to students. Students might be asked to step off a platform 50 feet above the ground or soar 200 feet on a pulley system down a steel cable. Trained staff instruct and guide individuals as they weave their way through ropes, swings, cables, and catwalks high above the ground. After developing the courage to overcome the challenge, participants often come away with a sense of personal empowerment and increased self-confidence.

> *"I hear and I forget, I see and I remember,*
> *I do and then I understand."*
>
> ~ *Confucius.*

These types of activities are often referred to as experience-based or experiential. Whether it be by watching a demonstration, listening to a teacher, reading a book, or attempting a new skill, our learning is "based" on those experiences. Thus, all learning that takes place is experience-based. Therefore, if the objective of a program is not the personal development and growth of the student, it is not experiential. To be experiential there must be reflection that takes place beyond the activity. It is this type of activity that will be addressed in this chapter.

Accidents in climbing and challenge course activities can be avoided with an effective safety program. The checklists, operating procedures and guidelines presented in this chapter are not a substitute for good judgement, common sense, and professional training. Facilitators should be proactive and attempt to recognize and minimize possible dangers and incidents that may occur.

Supervision

Skills and Knowledge of Supervisor

Climbing and challenge course activities themselves are inherently safe. Factors such as unprepared staff and failure to adhere to and enforce rules and program policy are the cause of most incidents. A school or organization should make an investment in quality instructors and provide them with the utmost in professional instruction. Any money saved on staffing and training will assuredly be small in comparison to a potential lawsuit. If budgetary constraints make it impossible to hire, maintain, and train capable instructors, consider eliminating some of the higher risk activities or scrapping the program altogether until proper resources become available.

Serious injury and death can occur as a result of improper supervision. Climbing and challenge course activities require special training by qualified instructors. At this time, there is no national certification available for adventure program staff. There are, however, many recognized organizations that can provide professional training for all levels of activity and experience. The Association for Experiential Education (AEE) maintains a list of companies and organizations that can provide training to suit specific school and course needs.

Selection of qualified instructional staff is the first and foremost step to creating a safe experience for student participants. Whereas training can be provided for sequencing and technical aspects of activities, administrators should choose staff with the following attributes:

- Possess effective communications skills
- Exhibit maturity and emotional stability
- Are sensitive to the needs of others
- Show evidence of common sense
- Are safety conscious
- Act as positive role models (e.g., if students are required to wear a helmet, are instructors also wearing them?)

One effective method for selecting staff is to require an apprenticeship program regardless of past experience and training. Becoming a safe and effective instructor is an evolutionary process that requires a broad range of knowledge and skills that could take months or years to develop. Pairing a new staff member with an experienced veteran can allow safe monitoring and training to take place. The apprenticeship should be evaluated and documented by the veteran staffer. Some staff may not be deemed qualified or capable of working with a group on their own and should not advance to full instructing positions. However, they can often be used in conjunction with other instructors as a "second seat" to help supervise, control, and spot a larger group.

The following guidelines are provided as sample requirements that can be incorporated into an employee policy handbook.

Basic Low Ropes

- A minimum of three days of training for low ropes/initiative type activities
- Successful completion of CPR and first aid training
- Demonstrate ability to present and understand each event and all safety issues and features

Advanced High Ropes

- A minimum of five days of training for high ropes/confidence course activities
- Demonstrate correct knot, harness, and belay technique
- Demonstrate setup and takedown for each event
- Demonstrate a working knowledge of all safety gear, including the following:
    - Safe working load
    - Minimum breaking strength
    - Dynamic and static ropes

- Cable
- Pulleys
- Belay devices
- Static and dynamic belay methods
- Harnesses
- Helmets
- Demonstrate ability to perform high course rescues

Program Manager

Someone needs to be responsible for the overall safety and management of the program. This individual should have ample experience in leading groups and a superior knowledge of the latest standards and requirements for climbing and challenge course activities. Some sample duties of this position relating to safety might include the following:

1. Scheduling annual inspections by an outside vendor
2. Providing and recording in-service training
3. Purchasing, maintaining, and replacing gear and equipment
4. Scheduling the appropriate number of instructors for any given group size
5. Developing emergency action plans
6. Filing records of participants' waivers, medical forms, equipment logs, and incident reports
7. Evaluating and documenting instructor performance
8. Maintaining effective employee records to include the following:
   a. Employment application
   b. Record of recognized training attended
   c. Record of apprenticeship (how long, with whom, apprentice trainer evaluation)
   d. Copies of required certifications such as first aid and CPR
   e. Copies of evaluations and appraisals
   f. Record of incidents or accidents pertaining to the staff member
   g. Record of instruction (dates, times, groups), medical screening forms, incidents, and near misses

Action Plans

An effective emergency action plan is a step-by-step set of procedures designed to guide staff through potential emergencies such as a minor, serious, or fatal injury; a lost or missing individual; a criminal activity; or a situation that has potential to draw attention from the media. It is specific in assigning responsibility to individuals and assuring that information is communicated to the appropriate parties.

Safety-related operating procedures should be communicated to staff in training sessions and reinforced in writing. Action plans can be placed in a "field" handbook or "miniaturized" so that staff can carry them in a wallet or pocket while conducting activities on site.

A safety committee should be formed with essential personnel who can develop and periodically review and reevaluate the action plans. Individuals who should be consulted include the following:

- Police
- Emergency services personnel
- Program staff
- Insurance representatives
- Counselors and school psychiatrists
- Legal advisers
- Public relations professionals

Organization and Control

Prior to conducting a climbing or challenge course activity, an assessment should be made of the group's needs, abilities, and demographics so that adequate instructors are assigned and appropriate activities are planned. If the group is a familiar class or group of students, an extensive assessment may not be necessary. However, if the composition and disposition of the group is unknown, a needs assessment is a good first step in preparing a lesson plan.

The following are some sample questions that can be asked:

- What is the name of the group?
- Is it a new or established group?
- What is the approximate age range of the group?
- What is the gender breakdown?
- Are there any significant cultural, physical, social, or racial differences among the group?
- Are there any potential safety or emotional problems or issues within the group or an individual?
- Has everyone functioned together as a group before? If yes, in what capacity?
- Does everyone in the group know each other's name?
- Is there a group hierarchy?
- Is there a group mission?
- What are some group goals? What do you or they hope to accomplish?
- Are there any specific issues that should be or need to be addressed?
- What are the group's strengths?
- What are the group's weaknesses?

Another common practice is to screen participants to assess whether they have medical or psychological issues that could present potential problems or incidents during a program. Integral to the screening process is warning students (and parents) in advance of possible dangers so that they can better understand the activity and protect themselves. Some participants may not be able to participate in some or all of the activities. Facilitators can find alternative roles for these individuals such as scoring, timing, cheering, and/or coaching.

Suggested screening components include the following:

Health History

    Allergies

    Medications

    Dietary restrictions

    Required immunizations

Other Information

    Address and phone

    Who to contact in an emergency (name and phone number)

    Medical insurance provider

    Permission for medical treatment

    Equipment needs

    Special needs such as food or access

It is also imperative to inform students of the risks and their responsibilities with regard to adventure activities. The participant and a parent or guardian should sign a statement acknowledging these risks and assuming responsibility for protecting themselves from them. Participants (or their parents) who are unwilling or unable to assume this responsibility should not be allowed to participate in the program.

Basics and Progressions

Prior to conducting a program, participants should reach a mutual agreement about basic rules, guidelines, and code of conduct. They should be informed that failure to agree to or abide by safety rules could mean an end to the activity or program itself.

The instructor should state the objectives and emphasize the safety procedures and hazards of each activity. Any unsafe actions such as hanging upside down, diving, jumping, throwing people or objects, or overexerting should be stopped immediately.

Instructors should ask that objects in pockets or around necks and fingers like earrings and rings be removed and eyeglasses secured.

Although students are encouraged to safely push beyond their preconceived limitations, the responsibility and the ultimate choice as to whether to participate in any given activity MUST lie with the individual. They must take responsibility for their own actions and recognize to some degree their own limitations. Following a thorough explanation, description, and/or demonstration of an element, individuals will have to decide for themselves whether they are comfortable participating in any given activity. If they are not comfortable for any reason, they should inform either the group or the instructor that they choose not to participate. This is an important safety consideration and requires that the instructor develop a group atmosphere where such admissions are not seen as socially stigmatizing.

Activities and related skills should be presented in a progressive manner to encourage group trust and support and to minimize and prevent injuries. Staff should select activities with consideration of the emotional, physical, and psychological state of the group. When in doubt, it is best to make a conservative decision. There will be times when group dynamics will force a change in plans. Knowing when to call it a day should not be viewed as a failure but as a safeguard against potential injury.

An effective organizational and safety tool is to write lesson plans for each population and age group that outline the progression of objectives and activities. A single sequence may not be appropriate for every group due to the group size, dynamics, mood, or skill level, so instructors need to observe body language and listen for signs from the group as to their readiness before advancing to the next level. Flexibility and a large "bag of tricks and activities" are essential. Some groups may need to spend more time in a given area before moving on. Some groups may never graduate to the higher level activities. Instructors should not push a group toward the "main event" at the cost of physical and emotional safety.

Instructors are always encouraged to add new activities to their repertoire but should be careful about experimenting when safety is a concern. Students will often come up with new unforeseen and untested methods of accomplishing a task that could raise spotting and/or safety issues. New strategies and activities should always be carefully evaluated prior to implementation.

Spotting

Falling from a moderate height (below six feet) is a reasonable expectation in climbing and challenge course programs. Teaching students correct spotting techniques will minimize injuries that can result from such a fall. Spotting is usually taught in simple introductory activities so students become comfortable supporting, touching, and trusting one another before moving to more complex situations. Activities such as a partner trust fall, a three-person trust fall and a circle trust fall ("willow in the wind") are easy to manage and relatively safe. Spotting techniques and the number of spotters are unique for each activity. The instructor should be cognizant of the requirements and possible fall scenarios for each situation.

The purpose of spotting is simple. It is a way to soften a fall and/or provide a safety net for students participating in an activity and to protect and support their head and upper body in the event of a fall. It is not designed to literally catch a falling body but merely to slow the descent to the ground. It is imperative that students understand that although the spotter and/or the participant may both wind up on the ground, it does not necessarily mean that the spotter has not performed his or her function. Falls do occur, and minor abrasions and bruises are unfortunate but realistic occurrences.

The following are some suggestions for effective spotting:

1. Spotters should stand balanced and centered with their knees flexed to absorb impact and with hands up, elbows bent, and fingers together reaching toward the participant.

2. Spotters should keep a close eye on participants and try to anticipate the potential fall. They should make adjustments in their stance and reposition themselves to better and more quickly respond.

3. Spotters should move with participants as they traverse an activity or element and attempt to avoid crossing their feet (so as not to trip over themselves).

4. Spotters should try to absorb force, not stop it. Giving with the body through the use of bent arms and knees and rolling in the direction of the force will provide a cushion for the fall.

5. Explain to participants that this is serious business and that injury can take place as a result of poor spotting technique. This is not the time for joking about not catching someone.

6. Be sure to closely supervise spotting and correct technique as necessary. Don't be afraid to remind lazy spotters of their responsibilities.

7. Rotate spotters so that everyone has a chance to spot.

8. Factors such as height, weight, size, and potential fall distance will necessitate adjustments to the number of spotters.

9. If you are uncomfortable or unsure of the group's ability to spot, you may need to stop the activity and regroup by taking a step backwards in the progression. The group may not be physically or mentally ready, or they may need more skill reinforcement before attempting more advanced, spot-intensive activities.

10. Spotters should be prepared for forward and backward falls.

11. Spotters and participants should talk with one another to communicate readiness and their current state. Phrases such as "ready to fall," "spotters ready," "falling," and "fall away" are effective tools in promoting confidence for the participant and making an instructor aware of a group's attention, focus, and readiness.

12. Position yourself near the potential fall so that you can intervene if necessary.

    NOTE: Spotting does not mean assisting or helping an individual with an activity. Participants must be allowed to succeed or fail on their own!

There are some challenge activities such as "the wall" that will require lifting and elevation of participants for successful completion of the element. A good rule of thumb is to disallow more than three levels of participants stacked vertically at any one time. Good hoisting technique includes standing with the back straight, knees locked, fingers interlocked, and arms straight to minimize back strain and injury. Under no circumstances should an individual be allowed to step on the middle of a lifter's back. Prior to teaching this skill, instructors should ask students if they have a bad or injured back, elbow, or knee and find alternative roles for those individuals.

Belaying

Climbing and challenge course programs sometimes promote a perceived risk by adding an element of height. Activities that are too high to be safely spotted from the ground require a safety system referred to as a belay. It is essentially a lifeline between two individuals, and its function is to reduce the possibility of injury in the event of a fall and to provide psychological reassurance to the participant. The basic system uses rope, carabiners, a harness, and other hardware specific to the activity.

Some programs will elect to have only professionally trained adults perform the belaying duties whereas others will teach and test students and allow them to belay with adult supervision. Having a student or trained professional in the position of backup belayer is a wise safeguard.

Static or self-belays use a short length of rope or webbing that is connected from an anchored point to the participant's harness. This type of belay is effective in allowing several participants on a high course at one time under the close supervision and precise instructions of one facilitator. There are times when participants on a static or self-belay will "fall" a few feet below an element and be unable to reposition themselves. Facilitators should be ready for this eventuality and have contingencies to assist and/or exact a rescue.

Dynamic belays involve a participant with a belayer on the ground. Rope is taken in or let out according to the movements of the participant. In the event of a fall, the belayer can control the rope, prevent a fall, and lower the participant in a slow and gradual descent. A dynamic belay tends to put less strain than static belays on individuals and gear due to the built-in stretch of the rope.

Dynamic belays are controlled by a system of friction where the rope is slowed or stopped through the actions of the belayer. It is possible, if properly taught, to use one's body and gloved hands as a method of braking. However, a body belay has potential to produce rope burns, muscle strain, and smoking gloves. The alternative is to use a mechanical device such as a figure 8, a sticht plate, a munter hitch, or a self-arresting belay device.

A third belay technique, called an Australian or group belay, is sometimes used in adventure programs. Several members securely attach themselves to the belayer's end of the rope, and, as the climber climbs, the team of belayers back up, reducing slack in the rope. If the climber falls, the combined weight of the belayers prevents the fall. The belay team simply walks forward to lower the participant to the ground.

Here are some suggested guidelines for belaying:

1. Only well-trained, competent, and tested belayers should belay.

2. Before allowing the participant to move, check to make sure the harness is worn correctly, appropriate knots are tied, and carabiner gates are locked and in the down position.

3. Under no circumstances should the braking hand of the belayer ever be removed from the climbing rope until the climber is safely on the ground and off belay.

4. Keep full attention focused on the climber at all times. The belayer should not take his/her eyes off the participant.

5. Belayers should keep up with the movements of the participant. There should not be excess slack on a rope. If a participant is moving too fast, the belayer should tell him/her to stop or slow down.

6. Make sure the belayer is securely anchored so he/she does not become airborne during a fall or descent.

7. Keep even with any participant who is moving on a traversing element. Move at the participant's pace and be ready to catch a fall at any time.

8. Stay aligned with a laterally moving participant. Stand as close to an element (without standing directly underneath) as conditions permit.

9. Clearly communicate with the participant at all times.

10. Carefully monitor and supervise any belay passes or switches so that the participant is never off belay at height.

11. Secure the assistance of another belayer to back you up.

    NOTE: Sometimes stopping the fall can cause the participant to inadvertently swing into the element. Without allowing a free fall, try slowly letting out the belay rope so that the participant moves safely below the element before stopping them.

A high ropes rescue is a possibility that must be trained for, practiced, and planned. When these elements are being taught, an individual who has been properly trained on rescue techniques should be present. Before attempting an advanced "cut-away" rescue, participants should seek alternative solutions, including self-rescue, use of a ladder, and attempting to remove the hazard or load on the safety system.

Regardless of the activity, it is always a good idea to conduct a debriefing session with other facilitators after a class or day of programs. A short debrief can expose common problems or issues that may be improved or solved through group discussion and the group's collective experience. Any safety concerns should be addressed and reported to the appropriate individual(s).

Environmental Concerns

Climbing and challenge course programs are a high-risk business. The condition and construction of a course and the equipment used could mean the difference between life and death for instructors and participants. A sample inspection checklist can be found in Table 1.

Facilities

In response to the growing field of climbing and challenge course construction, the Association of Challenge Course Technology (ACCT) was formed in the summer of 1993 to develop practices and standards in challenge course construction, inspection, and operation. Their standards cover everything from aircraft cable and pulley specifications to tree and pole diameters.

Climbing and challenge courses should be constructed by recognized professionals, organizations, and companies according to ACCT standards. If professional construction is not economical or feasible, the course should be inspected by a reputable professional or an outside peer who is familiar with current standards and can provide written documentation as to the condition and safety of the course. Factors such as tree health, cables, trail conditions, element integrity, and equipment such as ropes, harnesses, carabiners, pulleys, and helmets are some typical items included in the report. Never use any course, activity, or gear deemed unsafe after an inspection.

The many ropes, swings, ladders, cables, and platforms that make up an adventure course present an "attractive nuisance" to individuals when the program is not in session and directly supervised. With this in mind, every attempt should be made to prevent unauthorized use of potentially dangerous equipment and elements. "No trespassing" or "No unauthorized use" signs should be clearly posted and visible throughout a course. Elements should also be constructed or modified so that they are out of reach without the aid of a ladder, mechanism, or other structure. If ladders are to be left in the open or on a course, they should be secured with a lock and key.

There are many hazards in the general environment of climbing and challenge courses that can be minimized or eliminated by inspecting the area prior to use. Indoors, that means removing potential obstacles that students could slip on or fall or run into and providing a mat or some other medium to help absorb their fall during "height" activities. Outdoors, it means checking trails for new growth, loose branches, and poisonous trees and plants and making sure that trails and activity areas are well-covered with mulch, wood chips, or the equivalent to prevent tripping on roots and to provide a cushion for any falls that might occur.

Climbing and challenge course programs typically run in a variety of weather conditions, including snow, rain, extreme heat and ice, and thus present a unique set of challenges and potential problems to participants and instructors. Students should be informed prior to their day of arrival to dress appropriately for any weather. If conditions are deemed poor and there is a significant risk of slippage (especially with belaying in the high ropes arena) due to rain or ice, activities should be postponed or brought inside if feasible. Instructors should always have a backup plan for inclement weather.

One of the most dangerous and frequently encountered weather hazards in climbing and challenge course programs is lightning. Approximately 100,000 thunderstorms occur in the United States each year, resulting in an average of 750 injuries and 200 deaths. Blue skies and the absence of rain are not an assurance that lightning will not strike. Lightning can travel up to 10 miles from cloud to ground. The area and composition of most adventure courses (i.e., trees, steel cables, metal hardware) is not the place to be when lightning strikes. Many schools and organizations have begun to adopt a lighting safety policy for all of their outdoor sports and activities.

There are two ways to measure the distance of lightning. Battery-operated, handheld, commercially available lightning detectors can detect lightning as far as 40 miles away and inform the user if a storm is moving towards, away, or parallel to their position. They cost between $75 and $200. Another method is to use the "flash/bang" technique. Every count of five from the time of seeing the lightning stroke to hearing the associated thunder indicates that lightning is one mile away. A "flash/bang" count of 10 seconds represents two miles; a "flash/bang" count of 30 seconds represents six miles. If possible, err on the safe side and suspend all activity when you first hear thunder. Do not resume outdoor activities until 20 minutes have passed from the last observable thunder or lightning.

The National Lightning Safety Institute provides the following recommendations when lightning is nearby:

- If possible, get indoors or inside a car.
- Avoid water and all metal objects.
- Get off the high ground.
- Avoid solitary trees.
- Stay off the telephone.
- If caught outdoors during nearby lightning, adopt the Lightning Safety Position (LSP). LSP means staying away from other people; taking off all metal objects; crouching with feet together, head bowed; and placing hands on ears to reduce acoustic shock.

Insects like bees, wasps, and ticks are another environmental nuisance that can pose a serious health hazard and present unwanted distraction from safety-dependent activities. Be sure to check areas such as tires, platforms, and trees prior to a day of activity for nests or insect activity. If they cannot be safely removed, activities should be relocated or eliminated from the program until the problem is corrected.

The dramatic increase in the reports of Lyme disease over the last decade, particularly in the Northeastern and North-Central United States, has made tick control and prevention a top priority. Removing leaves and clearing brush immediately surrounding trails and activity areas can reduce the number of ticks that can potentially transmit the disease. There are chemicals that can be sprayed that are toxic to ticks, but their effectiveness and environmental safety are still in question. The Centers for Disease Control and Prevention recommend the following precautions for personal protection from tick bites:

- Wear light-colored clothing so that ticks can be spotted more easily.
- Tuck pant legs into socks or boots and shirt into pants.
- Tape the area where pants and socks meet so that ticks cannot crawl under clothing.
- Spray insect repellent containing DEET on clothes and on exposed skin other than the face, or treat clothes (especially pants, socks, and shoes) with Permethrin(tm), which kills ticks on contact.
- Wear a hat and a long-sleeved shirt for added protection.
- Walk in the center of trails to avoid overhanging grass and brush.

After being outdoors, remove clothing and wash and dry it at a high temperature; inspect your body carefully and remove attached ticks with tweezers, grasping the tick as close to the skin surface as possible and pulling straight back with a slow steady force;

Table 1. Sample Inspection Checklist

Administrative Questions

☐ Are background records checked on all prospective employees prior to hiring?

☐ Do staff possess appropriate and current certification and training? Are they filed?

☐ Are there written action plans for emergencies?

☐ Are staff trained in emergency procedures and rescue?

☐ Are staff trained and knowledgeable in program policies and procedures?

☐ Are staff training and evaluations documented and filed?

☐ Are periodic in-service training programs and meetings conducted and documented?

☐ Are there written lesson plans or curriculums?

☐ Is the course inspected by an external source at least once each year?

☐ Is equipment retired and disposed of according to manufacturers' recommendations?

Environmental Checklist

☐ Check for cracked wood and splinters.

☐ Check for rotten or loose wood.

☐ Check for excessive rust and fraying and loose cables, bolts, cable clamps, and serving sleeves.

☐ Check for tree or pole damage caused by disease, high winds, or lightning

☐ Check for broken glass and other ground or floor hazards.

☐ Check for loose nail heads.

☐ Make sure all the nuts, bolts, and cable clamps are tight.

☐ Inspect gear for wear.

Pre Checklist

☐ Review all medical and screening forms.

☐ Review needs assessment.

☐ Schedule appropriate staff for group size and composition.

☐ Make sure all participants have filled out and signed (and gotten their parents to sign) a waiver or informed consent form.

☐ Check the weather report and make backup arrangements if necessary.

Day of Checklist

☐ Check first aid kit and restock if necessary.

☐ Review emergency procedures with staff.

☐ Check phone or two-way radio for function and battery strength.

☐ Verbally remind participants of inherent risks, hazards, rules, and guidelines.

☐ If applicable, distribute tick spray and/or inform participants of precautions.

Post Checklist

☐ Conduct a safety debriefing with facilitators.

☐ Properly store and secure all equipment.

☐ Complete and file all log books.

☐ File all incident or near miss reports.

Rescue Bag List

It is always a good idea to carry a rescue pack that you can purchase commercially or piece together and place in a backpack.

Suggested Rescue Pack Contents

120' 11mm rope

30' 9mm rope

5 steel locking carabiners

1 figure 8 descender

1 belay device

1 set of "lobster claws"

2 8' piece of 5.5.mm spectra cord

2 twistlock carabiners

1 safety knife

1 utility scissors

1 pair belay gloves

1 first aid kit

Some courses have also begun to use this technology:

Cell phone or two-way radio (with someone else on the other end)

Portable Automated External Defibrillator (AED)

Table 2. Sample Breaking Strengths of Climbing and Challenge Course Components

Participants often inquire as to the strength of the different gear they will be relying on while "dangling" high above the ground. An instructor who doesn't have a general idea of equipment strengths does not instill a sense of confidence in the student.

The following statistics are approximations only and come mostly from manufacturers' technical information. Differences will exist between various compositions, diameters, and designs.

GEAR	APPROXIMATE BREAKING STRENGTH (in pounds)
Carabiners	
Aluminum carabiners 11mm	5,000-6,000
Autolocking carabiners 12mm	5,000-6,000
Steel carabiner 12mm	6,000-8,000
Aircraft Cable	
7 x 19 class 5/16" galvanized cable	9,800
7 x 19 class 3/8" galvanized cable	14,400
Webbing	
1" tubular webbing	4,000
1" flat webbing	6,000
2" tubular webbing	7,000
Rope and Cord	
11mm dynamic rope	5,000-6,000
KM III static 7/16" kernmantle rope	10,000
KM III Static 1/2" kernmantle rope	10,000
5.5 mm spectra cord	4,000-5,000
Miscellaneous	
Sewn harness	4,000-5,000
Pulleys	7,000-9,000
Figure 8 rescue device	12,000

avoid crushing the tick's body. In some areas, ticks (saved in a sealed container) can be submitted to the local health department for identification.

Equipment

There are many types and brands of equipment used for climbing and challenge course activities. Some props such as yarn balls, hoops, and rubber chickens require little or no maintenance or inspection. Other gear designed to bear weight or support participants must be carefully selected, maintained, inspected, stored, and used according to the manufacturer's instructions.

Helmets are typically worn by both instructors and participants while on and in the vicinity of a "high ropes" course. Aside from protection from falling debris and branches, helmets protect participants from bumping their heads into branches, wires, and equipment as they climb and traverse activities. Helmets identified as meeting the Union of International Alpine Association (UIAA) standards are the most common types used for adventure activities. Helmets, like other gear, should be properly fitted to the participant so that there is no wobble front to back or side to side. A four-point chinstrap and a method of venting to prevent heat buildup are other desirable features.

A harness is a rope or straplike device that serves to connect other equipment to the body. It is possible to wrap and secure webbing and rope around participants' legs and waist to provide them with a safe and secure attachment point. Commercially sewn harnesses, however, are generally more comfortable and easier to use. Most commercial harnesses meet minimum standards for strength and construction and are designed to fit different body types.

Make sure all manufacturers' directions and procedures are followed because adjustments and buckling differ from harness to harness and affect both fit and function.

A carabiner is an oval-shaped aluminum alloy or steel link with a spring-loaded gate in one side. It is used as a universal connector and needs very little in the way of care and maintenance. Impact (especially from a high ropes height), can damage a carabiner internally and weaken it. Dropped carabiners should be retired. Visual inspection does not always reveal damage.

Ropes serve as the lifeline between participant and belayer. There are many compositions and diameters that are used in ropes course settings; minimum standards are set by UIAA and CEN (European standard). Be sure to check manufacturers' ratings, recommended usage and care, and approximate lifetime of ropes before using them in a program. To get the most life out of your rope, take the following precautions and suggestions:

- Do not step on a rope. Stepping can grind grit into a rope that can work its way through the outer sheath and into the inner core, making it more susceptible to shearing and breakage.
- Do not wash, rinse, or soak ropes prior to initial use.
- Keep ropes out of direct sunlight whenever possible. Ultraviolet radiation can deteriorate nylon.
- Loosely coil, gather, bundle, or bag rope for storage and transportation.
- Mark ropes with either commercial labels or colored marking pens as to their length, assignment (to a particular activity), and age.
- Clean dirty ropes to maintain and extend their life.

Ropes can be cleaned easily and cheaply with a nylon scrub brush and a hose. There are also commercial "T"-like PVC devices that hook up to a garden hose and provide quick and thorough cleaning. Another method is to loosely bundle rope into a mesh bag and place it in a front-loading washing machine. Rope placed in top-loading machines can knot and break the central agitator. Some detergents can affect the waterproofing of the rope, so be sure to check with the rope manufacturer's care recommendations before using a mild soap.

All ropes course belay and weight-bearing ropes should undergo a thorough inspection prior to use. Carefully run the length of the rope through your hands and fingers and look and feel for the following:

- Soft or hard areas
- Stiffness
- "Fuzzing" or "puffing"
- Cuts, kinks, or other damage
- Variations in thickness

Any rope found to have one or more of these conditions should be retired and labeled or discarded accordingly. Breaking-strength illustrations for carabiners, ropes, and other weight-bearing equipment are presented in Table 2.

Good record keeping is advisable for all safety-related equipment and construction. Inspection checklists can be placed in three-ring binders or clipboards in the storage area and updated each time the course or equipment is used. Records should be monitored so that equipment is retired and replaced in a timely fashion. Good documentation includes keeping the following:

- Files on the construction of elements, including who built them and when
- Records of daily, weekly, and yearly inspections-both internal and external
- Records of periodic maintenance routines and repairs
- Logs documenting purchase date, source, hours of use, and element designation for ropes, harnesses, helmets, carabiners, etc

Take calculated risks. That is quite different from being rash.

~ *George S. Patton*

Conclusion

Conducting climbing and challenge course programs requires proper training, experience, and attention to detail. The effect these experiences have on participants are often powerful and memorable. If managed properly, they can have a lasting positive impact on facilitator and student alike.

Improvements in facilitation technique and equipment have made initiative problems and low and high ropes course activities safer than most conventional sports. Instructors can stay abreast of the latest information by attending conferences, reading books, subscribing to related organizations and newsletters, and utilizing the power of the Internet. Facilitators and administrators who plan ahead and ask "What if?" can maximize the quality of the experience while minimizing their liability.

References

"Center for Disease Control and Prevention." (October 4, 2000). *http://www.cdc.gov/ncidod/dvbid/ lymeinfo.htm*

Gass, M. (Ed.). (1998). *Administrative practices of accredited adventure programs.* Needham Heights, Association for Experiential Education and Simon and Schuster.

Gass, M., & Williamson, J. E. (Eds.). (1995). *Manual of accreditation standards for adventure programs.* Boulder, CO: Association for Experiential Education.

"National Lightning Safety Institute." (February 24, 2001). *http://www.lightningsafety.com/nlsi_pls/ ncaa.html*

Rohnke, K. (1989). *Cowtails and cobras ll.* Dubuque, IA: Kendall/Hunt.

Rohnke, K, Tait, C., & Wall, J. (1997). *The complete ropes course manual.* Dubuque, IA: Kendall/Hunt and Wall's Outdoor Associates, Inc.

Padgett, A., & Smith, B. (1995). *On rope: North American vertical rope techniques for caving, search and rescue and mountaineering* (5th ed.). Huntsville, AL: National Speleological Society.

Wade, I. (1990). Safety Management. In John C. Miles and Simon Priest (Eds.), *Adventure Education* (pp. 299-307). State College, PA: Venture Publishing, Inc.

Webster, S. E. (1989). *Ropes course safety manual.* Dubuque, IA: Kendall/Hunt.

CHAPTER 9

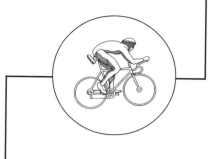

Cycling

Gary L. Wilson
The Citadel
Charleston, South Carolina

Cycling is a popular activity around the world, and most individuals in the United States will learn to ride a bicycle during their childhood. However, few individuals who learn to ride a bicycle have formal education or training concerning proper riding skills. Many schools offer bicycle training via bicycle rodeos and formal class presentations, but too often the training is limited and lacking in continuity. Mastering proper skills can be fun and can be done efficiently in the classroom setting and the gymnasium.

Common Injuries

The United States Department of Transportation keeps precise statistics on automobile and cycling accidents; most cycling injuries occur when the cyclist encounters obstacles other than automobiles. Environmental hazards such as wet pavement, leaves, sand, gravel, drain grates, dogs, and potholes all cause more accidents than encounters with automobiles. Although these hazards may not be as dramatic as an encounter with an automobile, they can still cause death and injury. Falling from a bicycle often causes the head to fall and strike the surface from a height sufficient to generate forces that can and do cause skull fractures and brain trauma. During these falls, the upper limbs and hips are also at risk of serious injury, and if the rider has an accident involving an automobile, his changes of survival are limited. Because of the potential for injury to the head, it is mandatory that a helmet be worn each time a bicycle is ridden, no matter how short the trip.

The following guidelines concerning supervision, conduct of the activity, and environmental management can assist teachers in the successful conduct of cycling classes free from injury and accidents.

Supervision

1. Cycling experience of the instructor can vary. It is not necessary that the instructor have extensive racing, touring, or commuting experience. If the instructor has good riding and classroom management skills, he or she can conduct an effective course.

2. Students should be adequately supervised in a cycling class, with the ratio being no greater than one instructor for every twenty students. Fewer students would be more desirable, but this may not be practical in physical education classes.

3. During classroom activities, every skill should be selected based on safety, and all class activities should reflect an attitude of safety and respect for others. Proper hand signals should always be used, and correct spacing must be maintained between riders so that no accidents occur in the class.

Selection and Conduct of the Activity

After the teaching area has been selected (gym, school parking lot, church parking lot, or playground), the instructor can develop a logical progression for teaching the activity.

The primary attitude and skill that must be taught is respect for other vehicles and safety. A rider can ride in a community with minimal skills if an attitude of respect for other vehicles is the over-riding guide. Following are guidelines for conducting a safe cycling class.

1. Follow the school administrative process to have cycling adopted as part of the school district's physical education curriculum. This will help gain support for the activity and insure that proper organization of the activity will take place.

2. Plan the bicycle unit as any other unit would be planned. Suggestions for skills activities and classroom discussion are as follows:

   • Riding skills for straight line riding

   • Hand signals

   • Agility riding through cones

   • Braking and proper use of brakes

   • Basic bicycle maintenance

   • Proper bicycle selection

   • Traffic law (local police can help)

   • Bicycle security

   • Repairing a flat

   • Evaluation of a riding area for safety

   • Proper clothing

3. Be sure that all students have the proper background to learn new skills in the class. This will help prevent injuries and will keep the students interested and motivated.

4. Teach students the necessary skills that will allow them to ride safely. They should be taught how to evaluate a situation to determine if it is safe to attempt to use their bicycle for transportation.

5. The instructor should attempt to keep students together, but there will always be situations when students will need individualized instruction. Be sure all students are ready before moving to each new riding skill.

6. The instructor must always stress using the rules of the road when riding. That is, when on a roadway, bicyclists must follow the same rules as automobile drivers and must always use proper signals to let other vehicles know their intentions.

7. *Never* allow a student to participate without a helmet.

8. In large classes with limited instructional area, allow only a small number of students to participate at one time. Other students can serve as course monitors until it is their turn to participate.

9. Teach students to conduct their own bicycle safety checks.

Environment and Equipment

1. Site selection for conducting the class is most important. You must have a large area to properly teach riding and safety skills. The gymnasium and/or the playground make ideal areas for instruction, but if the playground is grass, gravel, or dirt, the area cannot be used due to the narrow tires on some bicycles. The school parking lot would be ideal, but most will be filled with automobiles belonging to teachers and school personnel.

2. Be sure that the instructional area is safe. Parking lots and playgrounds with holes or unusually rough surfaces should not be used as instructional areas.

3. Be creative when selecting the instructional area for cycling. A street around the school can be ideal, with some traffic control assistance, and a hard-surfaced playground area such as a basketball court also can work well.

4. Do not allow too many students to participate at one time. The larger the instructional area, the more students can safely participate.

5. Traffic should be avoided during instructional time until all students are prepared to ride with the instructor.

6. If students use their own bicycles for the class, each bicycle must be checked for safety and proper fit. The instructor must decide how each bicycle is to be checked. It is highly recommended that students take their bicycles to a bicycle shop for this check, although the most convenient method for the student is for the teacher to check the bikes. If the teacher decides to be the mechanic, he or she should be prepared to spend a great deal of time conducting the check.

The following should be checked on each bicycle:

- Trueness of wheels
- Cone adjustments
- Tire wear
- Brake function
- Handle bar adjustment
- Seat adjustment
- Gear function
- Pedal function and tightness
- Crank function and adjustment
- Chain wear

Cycling is a reasonably safe activity when proper skills are taught. If teachers follow reasonable progressions and use safe instructional areas, accidents in class can be avoided. Careful planning and proper instruction can assure that students will be safe both in the class and on the streets of their community. Good instruction in the class can assist students develop a lifelong healthy activity for transportation and recreation.

References

Bull, A. (1992). *Learn mountain biking in a weekend.* New York, NY: Alfred A. Knoph.

Chauner, E., & Coello, D. (1992). *Mountain bike techniques.* New York, NY: Lyons Burford.

Forester, J. (1994). *Effective cycling.* Cambridge, MA: MIT Press.

Henry, S. (Ed.). (1994). *Bicycle magazine's complete guide to bicycle maintenance and repair.* Emmaus, PA: Rodale Press.

Matheny, F. (1998). *Bicycling magazine's complete guide to riding and racing techniques.* Emmaus, PA: Rodale Press.

Plevin, A. (1992). *Cycling: A celebration of the sport and world's best places to enjoy it.* New York, NY: Ballantine/Byron Preiss Books.

Van der Plas, R. (1993). *The bicycle touring manual.* San Francisco, CA: Bicycle Books.

Seidler Productions. (1994). *Effective cycling video.* Crawfordville, FL: Seidler Productions.

Sloane, E. (1988). *The complete book of bicycling.* New York, NY: Simon and Schuster.

Whitt, R. R., & Wilson, D. G. (1995). *Bicycling science.* Cambridge, MA: MIT Press.

CHAPTER 10

Dance Education

Barbara Lorraine Michiels Hernandez
Lamar University
Beaumont, Texas

Introduction

Dance is a physical performance art and lifetime sporting activity. In dance education, students are actively involved in a universal, nonverbal form of cognitive, affective, and psychomotor development. Dance education also develops discipline, perseverance, and critical thinking. All students need opportunities to transfer skills and knowledge into creative processes and expression, which increase their rhythmic ability, movement skills, and fitness levels. A variety of progressive dance experiences also provide students with a broad understanding of cultures and traditional forms of artistic dance. Therefore, a comprehensive dance program or unit of instruction enriches the growth and development of the total student.

Curriculum

The dance curriculum provides for a comprehensive and balanced dance program designed to meet the national, state, or local (school district) standards and mandated curriculum guidelines. It ensures that the physical education and dance experience is disciplined, focused, comprehensive, and age- and ability-appropriate. This includes the goals and objectives, skills, choreographic elements and compositional forms, and assessments of each lesson in each of the required forms of dance education for quality instruction. All students deserve access to dance education regardless of race, creed, age, sex, or ability.

An appropriate, quality dance curriculum assures the safety and accountability of the dance education program.

The National Association for Sport and Physical Education (NASPE) and the National Dance Association (NDA), the state department of education, and the local school district's physical education and dance education standards are developmental resources for your curriculum, unit, and lesson plans. The NASPE standards list the accomplishments for students taking a dance course as part of the physical education curriculum. The NDA standards state what students accomplish when enrolled in a continuous dance education program as a separate core curriculum class. These two documents are exemplary nationwide efforts endorsed by the U.S. Department of Education that formulate the goals, objectives, and assessments of a dance education program.

Curriculum guides provided by your state or local school district that include dance education units of instruction are incorporated, along with the above standards, into the yearly curriculum. This ensures a learning environment based on scientific content and processes. Curriculum guides provide a comprehensive; sequential; knowledge-, skills-, and process-based model for quality dance education.

The standards and curriculum guides together are the basis for the goals and objectives, skills, choreographic elements and compositional forms, and assessments expected of the students. From these resources, the instructor can develop lesson and unit plans based on a physiologically sound, standards-based, instructional format with health-related fitness components and correct training principles. Appropriate standards, curriculum, and safe practices provide lifetime student competencies.

Structure

For skills, safety, and reduction of physical stress, injuries, and liability, the instructor can incorporate the following into the dance education curriculum:

1. The curriculum is described and outlined in a series of sequential, articulated, and developmentally appropriate units and plans.

2. The repertoire includes a diverse background with representation from all dance forms.

3. The curriculum develops and presents exemplary works from the structural, cultural, social, technical, and historical dimensions of dance.

4. Equal opportunities in dance education are available to all students regardless of gender, ability, or special needs.

5. Proper dance attire standards are assigned for the class, rehearsal, and performance activities.

6. The pupil/teacher ratio per dance class is appropriate for the dance instruction and space.

7. The staffing for the school dance program includes certified physical or dance educators (certified and/or degreed) by state or national accreditation agencies in those disciplines.

8. The dance unit is 20% of the curriculum, and the class meets at least three days per week.

9. The environmental dance concerns (facilities, audiovisual equipment, and materials) are adequate.

Safeguards

Know what is accepted practice for dance education instruction that is legal, safe, and appropriate. Use prudent care and provide the minimum requirements for a safe dance environment. For the protection of both the student and the instructor, the following procedures are recommended:

Legal and Liability Implications - Courses in school law or reference books for self-education are available. Know the legal responsibilities assumed, precautions to take, and responsible activities for your students' ages and ability levels in dance education classes. Purchase liability insurance, available through most educational organizations, for financial and legal protection.

Proper First Aid Procedures and Referrals - Recognize emergency situations in a dance education class and act quickly. Become certified in CPR and first aid. Know what health care professionals are on duty at your school and how to contact them in case of any accident or injury, not matter how minor. Ice should be available at all times in close proximity to the instructional area in case of accidental injury. Know the health care referral procedures for students.

School Accident and Injury Forms - Know the school and district policies for reporting and recording injuries. Report all accidents and injuries in a dance education class. Adhere to standard school policies and written forms. Document what happened, your reaction, and the witnesses, and keep in a file. Indicate how you provided reasonable and prudent care to avoid the injury in the class. You will need a written recollection of events if legal litigation occurs.

Health Records - Obtain access permission to the school's health records that are on file. This information is vital for dance instruction. Know each student's health history and concerns, illnesses, acute or chronic conditions, health problems, and physical limitations for dance activities before instruction begins. Observe students with specific health concerns for warning signs and symptoms and avoid stress to vulnerable areas for students at risk for injury by using adapted dance. Consult with a health professional for recommended corrective exercises.

Screening - In addition to obtaining health and injury records, instructors are advised to screen and test students for fitness before class. Two faculty members (of the same sex as the student) must be present during these exams for protection and liability purposes. Ensure each student's privacy and confidentiality. Check for problem areas and deficiencies. Measure height and weight in the school nurse's office or the training room. Calculate fitness tests for body composition, flexibility, posture, muscular strength and endurance, cardiorespiratory endurance, and body type. Evaluate the feet, ankles, knees, hips, spine, and overall posture. Relate this information to the specific dance activities planned and adjust accordingly.

Medical Conditions - Diabetes, epilepsy, asthma, and chronic diseases require direct supervision. Know the warning signs and symptoms of medical conditions or injuries that require medical referral and learn the proper first aid procedures for students with known medical conditions. Make necessary referrals to the school health care professionals. Use adaptive dance activities as appropriate.

Medical Care and Rehabilitation - Avoid dance activities that put undue stress on an injury. Use recommended activities that work around the injury or modify the activity. Do not allow students to perform dance movements that aggravate the condition. If weight bearing is impossible, a floor class (lying down) or water exercises (in the pool) are possible alternatives. Above all, follow the recommendations of the health care professionals.

School Emergency and Disaster Procedures - Learn the school policies and procedures for emergency situations and keep them with you. Take roll daily to account for the number of students in each class, in case of an emergency. Know what to do in an emergency and act accordingly. Inform the students of responsibilities in case of an emergency and post them. Have a buddy and a backup buddy system for accountability.

Waivers and Participation Agreements - Waivers or release forms for school activities generally are not legally sound, but a permission slip or participation agreement ensures consent and awareness. This signed document states that the participants and parents know and understand the rules, procedures, possible consequences, and risks or dangers involved in the activity. This is a requirement for after-school dance education events, performances, field trips, etc.

Parental Excuses - When a student brings a note from a parent or health professional that limits or restricts physical activity, adhere to it. Respect the parent or health professional's request for no physical activity. Recommend some limited or adapted dance when appropriate, but obtain signed permission.

Contracts - A student contract is a binding, signed agreement between the student and the teacher stating the expectations for the dance class and student outcomes, grading criteria, and class objectives. It specifically outlines student responsibilities and accomplishments in a dance education class. Students are accountable and responsible for their actions. Contracting assures communication of the required level of accomplishment.

Class Supervision - Never leave a dance class unattended or unsupervised at any time for any reason.

Facilities - Always secure and lock dance facilities and equipment upon exiting.

Student Images - Secure and lock away photos, videotapes, slides, etc., for class/performance evaluations. Obtain copyright permission from parents if images are used outside of class.

Prevention of Common Dance Injuries

Dance education classes must provide proper and accurate instruction and protective devices for students. Movements must be appropriate to the age, development, and ability levels of students. Enforcement of safety principles in class is of the utmost importance. Classes must emphasize scientific body placement and alignment, and proper technique.

Proper feedback and corrective techniques are necessary, as well as adherence to class safety rules and regulations.

Safety Procedures - Establish a written class safety plan. Share and review it with the students before each lesson. Post and refer to it when instructing stressful or higher risk dance activities. Recommend safety factors in executing skills and warn of risks in difficult, airborne, and impact activities. Instruct students how to avoid risks or injuries caused by another student's action, whether deliberate or not. Use proper, firm warnings and restrict students who pose a threat or danger to others.

Rules and Regulations - Share class management and organizational procedures with students on the first day of class and review them often. Post these in full view of the students.

Appropriate Attire - Proper attire reduces injuries. Instruct students about proper clothing and footwear for the dance activity. Encourage them to layer clothing and remove it as the body becomes warmer. Hair should be pulled back from the face, and any dangling or large jewelry must be removed.

Appropriate Dance Activities - All classes should be developmentally appropriate, sequential, comprehensive, and designed to prevent injuries. Know the technical dance level of your students. Promote correct execution of techniques and use kinesiology and biome-chanics to improve skills. The instructor needs a working knowledge of the content of the dance class and dance standards appropriate for instruction. Avoid having students perform controversial activities that stress a joint or muscle excessively such as double-leg lifts, hyperextension, ballistic stretching, etc.

Props - These are checked and inspected, if used, before the dance class. Give clear safety rules regarding props.

Accidents and Injuries - The majority of dance injuries in class fall into two categories-those due to accidents or injuries and those due to overuse syndrome. Although the choreography and step patterns are different in many different forms of dance, the injuries are similar. Report and refer all injuries, however minor, to the health care team at the school for treatment. Know the procedures for immediate care of injuries. Learn the common dance symptoms, conditions, or injuries that require medical referral. Know the appropriate modified dance activity programs for students with medically identified injuries.

Overuse Syndrome - This condition occurs with continued stressful physical and repetitive movements. Employ safety factors to reduce physical overuse of the body. Avoid overtraining and improper technical execution of dance skills. Refrain from working a student too soon after an injury.

Alignment - Constantly check for misalignment of the feet, knees, hips, spine, shoulders, and posture in all dance activities, especially pliés. Misalignment leads to improper weight bearing, poor posture, improper techniques, and an increased risk of injury.

Stress - Recognize the emotionally stressful triggers for students in dance education class and reduce them. Reduce the effects of stress on students by proper class management and organizational procedures. Refer students to the school counselor for stress reduction techniques when necessary.

Landing Techniques - Provide proper instruction and teach correct preparation and execution in jumps and weight-bearing dance activities. Avoid improper landings from jumps, leaps, turns, and combinations. Stress the proper flexion of the ankles, hips, and knees in a smooth and continuous landing for safety, proper technique, and lightness of movement.

Heart Rate - Instruct students how to calculate and monitor their heart rates after warm-up, low-intensity activities (center floor), conditioning (combinations), creative, and cooldown (culminating) portions of each dance class are completed. Determine their target heart rate zone and monitor their progress. Look for inconsistent or high rates and take appropriate action.

Hydration - Dehydration can be a problem in physical activity. Encourage students to hydrate regularly and bring water to drink any time they feel thirsty in dance class. Never restrict water "breaks," especially on hot and humid days.

Nutrition - Observe dance students for signs and symptoms of dietary problems, vitamin deficiencies, and anorexia nervosa or bulimia. Report at-risk students to the health care professionals and school counselor. Know the warning signs of nutritional problems. Recognize and report inadequacies.

Fainting - This is often caused by the student not having eaten, having taken medication on an empty stomach, or other health problems. Avoid it by instructing students on proper diet and nutrition before a strenuous dance class. Know proper first aid procedures for fainting. Report fainting because it could be symptomatic of something more serious.

Physical Limitations - The effects of the size and shape of a dancer in relation to the movement potential must be considered. Different levels of flexibility, strength, and endurance and various body proportions can limit participation in dance activities. Perform careful screening and fitness testing. Access records (with permission) of health histories, medical conditions, and injuries. Supervise and observe students' dance capabilities and limitations. Avoid encouraging students to overstress if they are not physically adapted or able to perform certain activities.

Stress Fracture - This condition should always be supervised by a physician, including diagnosis, treatment, and follow-up.

Tendonitis - This is the inflammation of the tendons. Direct students to avoid activities where the muscle strength is inadequate to meet the physical demands made on it, and instruct them to stretch out muscles following intense dance exercise.

Sprain - This is an injury that involves a tearing of the soft connective tissue (ligament, tendons, etc). Avoid over-movement of joints, improper landing from jumps (the foot rolling towards the outside and twisting), stubbing the toe, and inadequate rehabilitation of a previous sprain.

Strain - This is a joint and soft-tissue injury. It is a tearing of muscle fibers along a joint or tendon. Instruct students to avoid over-movement of the joints when landing, airborne, and stretching.

Turnout - Proper turnout is never forced. This is the external rotation of the femur, at the hip joint, so that the knees and feet face as close to the side as possible with the rest of the leg in alignment. The range of motion is determined by anatomy. Progress slowly for beginners. Have a proper understanding of the biomechanics and know the dangers of turning out too much. Improper turnout leads to stress on the back, hip, knees, ankles, and feet.

Spine, Back, and Posture - Most dance injuries involve the lumbar region, although other areas are also common. Improper posture and technique can exacerbate an injury. Avoid dance activities that require overarching of the back and rolling the shoulders forward. Stress proper dance alignment and execution of techniques. Incorporate knowledge of the principles of anatomy and biomechanics of the spine during dance activities to decrease back and spinal injuries. Posture is the alignment of the body parts to each other and is the basis for effective dance movements and everyday life. Constantly check the students for incorrect posture. Proper posture and body alignment for dance education include the following:

1. The head sits directly on top of the neck and is not protruding or sinking.

2. The neck stretches up from the back or spine.

3. The shoulders are relaxed but not dropped, are slightly back, and are on a line with each other.

4. The sternum is lifted but relaxed.

5. The pelvis is centered and balanced below the spine to create tight abdominals and lengthen the lumbar spine.

6. The knees are in a direct line with the bone on the inside of the ankle, hips, and shoulders.

7. Body weight is in the center of the feet when standing.

8. The body line is adjusted slightly forward for relevés and movements on the balls of the foot.

Feet and Ankles

1. *Supination and Pronation* - This is an improper distribution of the weight on the foot. Avoid allowing students to roll the foot inward or outward when standing and landing.

2. *Blisters* - Blisters are fluid under the skin. Avoid stress to tender areas of the foot in positions such as demi-pointe, and relevé. Corns and callouses are caused by pressure over a bony prominence. Sometimes improperly fitted dance shoes can rub against the skin. Gauze, lamb's wool, and moleskin padding protect bony or blistered areas. A preventive foot soak of one tablespoon of vinegar or alum to a quart of water twice a day toughens the skin.

3. *Sickled Foot* - This is an improper point where a portion of the foot is turned instead of stretched. Observe students pointing the toes and look for signs of a turned foot.

4. *Footwear* - Use of the feet and ankles are different in various dance forms. Attention to the particular foot function and shoes fitted properly for that function avoids injuries such as blisters, corns, etc. Tap dance requires footwear with a good arch support for reducing the impact of weight-bearing activities. In ballet and jazz dance, the dance shoes serve little protective function, so students must use care in

airborne activities such as jumps and leaps. In modern dance, no footwear is used. Consider the floor surfaces and use caution for airborne activities.

Leg Problems

1. *Cramp or Charley Horse* - This is a muscle spasm, contraction, or cramping, particularly in the lower leg. To prevent this condition, avoid overuse of the leg in dance warm-ups.

2. *Turnout* - See previous entry.

3. *Knee* - This is the most often injured area for dance participants. To prevent knee injuries, avoid improper external rotation of the hips, improper pliés, or a forced turnout.

4. *Shin Splints* - This is pain in the middle of the leg. To prevent shin splints, avoid overuse of the foot flexors and high-impact activities.

Supervision

Use prudent care in instructing and supervising dance classes. Use appropriate dance practices, within the ability levels of the students, for a safe and risk-free environment. Physical educators need exposure to each of the forms of dance for proper instruction and supervision. Knowledge of the human anatomical and kinesiological principles involved in performing certain skills is also necessary, as well as knowledge of common dance student injuries. For proper supervision of dance education classes, the teacher understands the following:

1. The use of kinesiology and biomechanics to create illusion in dance (such as soft landings) and improve dance technique.

2. The effects of the size and shape of a dancer in relation to the movement potential and the importance of emphasizing correct body alignment and mechanics.

3. The techniques to prevent injuries, the attire to reduce injuries, and the minimum requirements for a safe dance environment.

4. The anatomy of the body, including the major muscles and bones of the body, major muscles in various dance movements, and the interrelationships among the nervous, muscular, and skeletal systems in dance education movements.

5. The types of instruction for each type of dance, including techniques, skills, musicality, accompaniment, and rhythmic instruction.

6. The qualitative aspects important for the affective domain, artistry, and aesthetics in dance.

Management

Have a plan for managing the students in each dance education class. Institute management procedures, including rules for entering and leaving, taking roll, recording daily participation, evaluations, and assessments. Ensure the class size is appropriate for the lesson and the available dance space. Consider the length of time for each lesson, the number of days per week, and the length of the entire dance course for the specific type of dance instruction. Block scheduling for schools presents new challenges in dance education by increasing the activity time for classes and the student's physical workload. Supervise and monitor students carefully in block classes.

Administration

Determine the dance education ability level of each class. The class should begin at a level where the students are successful, progressing logically from warm-ups to complex techniques. Provide for measurable objectives with at least a 75% student success rate. Adapt instructional activities for the level of the students. Include various dance activities that work all body parts as well as the mind. The lesson design and organization should provide for proper skills progression and appropriate technique levels and should empha-size technically correct work habits. Some specific methods for proper dance class administration are as follows:

1. Know the developmental dance ability of the learner and the class.
2. Use the state or local dance standards or curriculum guides, the NASPE standards for dance, and the National Standards for Dance Education.
3. Construct and teach exemplary dance education lesson and unit plans.
4. Spend an adequate amount of time on each activity. Include goals and objectives, skills (knowledge and techniques), choreographic processes and compositional activities, and assessments and evaluation
5. Use audiovisual aids for cognitive and affective development.
6. Provide exposure to live dance performances or dance in films or videos.
7. Know and require the correct attire for various types of dance.
8. Include the subject matter, story, or theme for choreography.
9. Use appropriate accompaniment.

Selection and Conduct of Activity

Planning

Construct a dance unit and lesson plans that include accepted, sequential, comprehensive, and age- and ability-appropriate teaching methods. These are research-based pedagogical, psychological, and kinesiological principles. Include the basic components of health-related physical fitness. These are cardiorespiratory endurance, muscular strength and endurance, muscular flexibility, and body composition. Consider the basic training principles of intensity, duration, frequency, and consistency.

Use a pedagogical focus, hands-on orientation, and problem-solving and critical-thinking skills. When performing predetermined dances, teach the basic steps in the center floor techniques and perform them in the combinations section. Leave class time for the choreographic elements. Below are sample elements for a lesson and/or unit plan.

Organization

Sample Dance Education Unit or Lesson Plan

I. Goals and objectives

    A. Goals and general objectives

    B. Specific objectives (these overlap)

        1. Cognitive-knowledge

        2. Affective-choreographic processes

        3. Psychomotor-techniques

II. Skills (these overlap)

    A. Knowledge

        1. Evolution-social, cultural, historical, personal

        2. Dance classifications

        3. Terminology

        4. Dance accompaniment

        5. Dance attire, costumes, footwear

        6. Dance artists, noteworthy performances, and choreographers

    B. Techniques

        1. Warm-ups

            a. Positions-feet on floor and sitting

            b. Arm positions

            c. Warm-up techniques

        2. Center floor

            a. Basic movements

            b. Nonlocomotor

            c. Locomotor

        3. Combinations

            a. Traditional dance movements

            b. Turns

            c. Falls and recoveries

        4. Choreographic elements and compositional forms (see below)

        5. Cooldowns

        6. Adapted activities

III. Choreographic elements

    A. Creating-concepts of space, time, and energy

    B. Performing-improvisation and compositional forms

    C. Responding-evaluate, analyze, and interpret performance

    D. Compositional forms

        1. Stage floor classifications

IV. Student assessments
    A. Written
    B. Oral
    C. Observation
    D. Self- and peer evaluations
V. Instructor evaluations

Strategies

The instructor should employ logical progressions using standards-based education. Close supervision, a supportive attitude, and development of sound dance techniques by the instructor are critical factors for successful dance education. It is also important for the dance instructor to have critical eyes, a vision of dance education, and a progressive attitude. A quality dance educator inspires good work habits and helps students learn and improve dance techniques in a challenging and inspiring environment. The following specific strategies for before, during, and after you teach can effectively keep you on task and improve dance education skills for all students.

1. Before You Teach

Determine your specific objectives for each class and write appropriate lessons plans with standards-based dance education content and assessment techniques.

Be prepared. Use a well-organized, sequential, developmentally appropriate written dance education lesson plan and refer to it often to keep on task. Stress the knowledge, training or skills development, and the performance aspects of the dance class.

Cue your music for each activity. Bring the musical recordings to class. If an accompanist is available, discuss the accompaniment before class. Count the music accurately with students.

Wear the proper professional attire and shoes for the specific dance class.

Ensure the sound system is adequate and in working order.

Prepare warm-ups for specific body parts that are conducive to proper class execution and performance.

Ensure that the physical environment, facilities, and equipment are safe for dance activities.

Obtain knowledge of the health, physical limitations, and developmental and psychological characteristics of the student in each grade level.

Know the basic steps, patterns, sequences, and accompaniment before instruction.

Employ a serious commitment to student learning and aesthetics in dance.

Understand the relationship between the dance movements and the musical accompaniment.

Research and be prepared to provide the relevant historical context of the lesson, choreography, and choreographer, etc., to students.

Arrive and dismiss class on time, be appropriately attired, and bring all of your accessories and shoes.

2. As You Teach

Make sure your starting and stopping signals are clear and consistent.

Make sure class management, supervision, and organizational procedures are developmentally appropriate.

Use developmentally appropriate disciplinary techniques.

Use positive reinforcers and feedback when students are performing new dance education skills, when students need assistance or correction, or for exemplary technique.

Give directions clearly, simply, carefully, and by using correct dance terminology.

Demonstrate posture, alignment, anatomy, and proper body placement in dance techniques.

Observe any physical discomfort in students and use appropriate measures immediately.

Recognize emergency situations and be prepared to act quickly.

Analyze each dance activity and choreographic piece carefully for succinct, specific instruction.

Monitor student learning and performance carefully. Supervise generally at all times. Specific supervision is necessary for students needing assistance.

Give positive, objective corrections for improper physical, rhythmical, or aesthetical movements.

Use logical progressions in techniques from easiest to hardest, with carryover and transfer.

Reverse all exercises and combinations and perform on the right and left sides.

Give specific teaching cues and refer to them often with appropriate dance terminology.

Reinforce proper technique often and provide verbal reinforcers and safety reminders.

Observe technique for proper execution and monitor student learning. Make constructive corrections immediately. Caution against improper technique and give corrective exercises.

Review dance combinations carefully and distinctly. Break difficult steps into parts and then demonstrate and practice them with the students.

Encourage students to perform the dance activities accurately and listen to the musical introduction, sequence, and tempo. Review the proper tempo, musicality, pacing, and rhythm.

Note the musical changes and nuances to the students.

Analyze and demonstrate each movement accurately and technically correct each time.

Answer students' questions and review the combination or demonstrate it again.

Encourage the artistic and expressive element in dance as an art form.

Space the students in staggered lines to maximize teacher observation and student visibility.

Ensure there is adequate room to move. The teacher must be able to see each student.

Rotate rows or formations, if necessary, to observe each student carefully.

Allow time for the students to enjoy creating their own dances and the dance performance experience! Let students appreciate dance as an aesthetic art form.

3. After You Teach

Make written notes on your lesson plan for a review of knowledge for the next class.

Pay attention to problem areas in dance technique and re-teach in the next lesson.

Prepare for the next lesson by building on the dance skills and knowledge from previous classes and addressing problem areas and material not covered.

Stay abreast of new teaching techniques and participate in continuing professional development opportunities, workshops, and seminars.

Join professional dance education organizations and attend professional conferences.

Student Assessment

Proper documentation of dance education assessment techniques is an instructional and legal necessity. Accurate, up-to-date records of student progress, attendance, scores, and assessments earned must be properly recorded, filed, and available to the student and/or parent. This provides proof that a student did or did not fulfill the contract and grading requirements. Provide progress reports required by the school district.

Environmental Concerns

An adequate dance environment is a key factor to accomplishing your goals and objectives. The annual school budget provides for purchase, upkeep, and maintenance of the facilities. An annual departmental budget provides for purchase, upkeep, and maintenance of audiovisual equipment, materials, supplies, and annual production costs.

A safe, appropriate environment is a necessity for dance education. Adequate facilities will comply with federal, state, and local construction codes and safety guidelines essential for all dance-related activities and will be accessible to the handicapped. Facilities guidelines are as follows:

1. The dance studio or gymnasium floor should be at least 40 feet by 40 feet. The recommended minimum space is 65 square feet per student. A minimum ceiling height is 16 feet.

2. The floor should be a sprung or resilient wood floor (floating sub-floor) that provides a safe, adequate surface to perform the required movements. It must be free of cracks, chips, holes, nails, and splinters. It must be kept clean and not sticky or slippery.

3. The dance area should be free of obstructions. Be sure that all clothing and audiovisual equipment are kept well out of the way of all dance activities.

4. Wall-mounted mirrors, though not required, are desirable. Recommended measurements for mirrors specify that they be at least 25 feet long and 6 feet high for self-evaluation.

5. Barres should be available for warm-up and stretching activities. They may be either securely fastened to the walls or freestanding (portable). Portable barres

must be heavy enough to withstand pressure by the students and have a wide support base. Space at the barres must be adequate for every student.

6. Lighting must be adequate and safe.

7. The ventilation system (heating and cooling) should provide for proper air circulation. Provide proper room temperature. Use caution and warm up students properly in cooler and warmer weather.

References

American Red Cross. (1993). *Community first aid and safety.* St. Louis, MO: Mosby Lifeline.

Gilbert, Anne Green. (2000). *Creative dance for all ages* (6th ed.). Reston, VA: National Dance Association.

Giordano, Gus. (1992). *Jazz dance class-beginning through advanced.* New Jersey: Princeton Book Company.

Goals 2000: Educate America Act of 1994, PL 103-227, 20 U.S.C. 5801 et. seq.

Hanna, J. L. (1999). *Partnering dance and education-intelligent moves for changing times.* Champaign, IL: Human Kinetics.

Harris, J., Pittman, A., Waller, M. (1994). *Dance a while.* New York: MacMillan Publishing Company.

Hays, Joan. (1991). *Modern dance, a biomechanical approach to teaching.* St. Louis: C.V. Mosby Company.

Hernandez, Barbara (Ed.). (2001). *Dance education, what is it, why is it.* Reston, VA: National Dance Association.

Minton, Sandra Cerny. (1986). *Choreography: A basic approach using improvisation.* Champaign, IL: Human Kinetics.

National Association for Sport and Physical Education. (1995). *Moving into the future: National physical education standards: A guide to content and assessment.* Reston, VA.

National Dance Association. (1994). *National standards for dance education: What every young American should know and be able to do in dance.* Pennington, NJ: Princeton Books.

Schrader, Constance A. (1996). *A sense of dance: Exploring your movement potential.* Champaign, IL: Human Kinetics.

Sherbon, Elizabeth. (1990). *On the count of one.* Chicago Review Press.

Solomon, R., Minton, S., & Solomon, J. (1990). *Preventing dance injuries: An interdisciplinary perspective.* Reston, VA: American Alliance for Health, Physical Education, Recreation and Dance.

Shipley, Tutterow. (1992). *Tap talk dictionary from vaudeville to now.*

Warren, Gretchen. (1989). *Classical ballet technique.* Florida: University of South Florida Press.

Resources

Dance Magazine
Dance Research Journal
Dance Teacher
Journal of Physical Education, Recreation and Dance

CHAPTER 11

Flag Football

Maryann Domitrovitz
The Pennsylvania State University
University Park, Pennsylvania

The popularity of the game of football is reflected not only by the attendance at high school, college, and professional games, but also by its frequent appearance in the physical education curriculum. Although in physical education classes the game appears in a modified version, such as flag football, the skills and strategies inherent in football, exclusive of physical contact, apply equally to flag football.

Prior to participation in this activity, it is imperative that students differentiate between the game as played with protective equipment and that played with flags. Further, because some aspect of the game can appear from the elementary level through the senior high school level, it is critical that the students are kept in mind when designing the unit and lesson plans. When the activity classes are coeducational, this must also be a consideration for selecting and programming skills, progressions, drills, lead-up games, and the regulation game.

The attention to appropriate equipment must also be deliberate. The size, weight, and composition of the football will vary from the modified equipment appropriate for the elementary level to the regulation football appropriate for the high school student.

Because students may be unaware of or ignore the potential for injury in this activity, it is imperative that a safe learning and playing environment be maintained. Although the correct execution of the activity skills and their application in practice or game play is a priority, enforcement of the rules of the game is of the utmost importance. Inconsistency in officiating and rule interpretation or enforcement, particularly with the noncontact rules, has the potential to contribute to a wide range of injuries. Supervision must be of the highest quality.

The impact that daily use and the weather have on the activity area must also be taken into consideration. An inspection of the playing field to determine its suitability for class must be regularly scheduled. Bare spots, rocks, holes, glass, and obstructions near boundaries are hazards to safe playing conditions and must be removed before approval for use is issued.

Although attention to each of the aforementioned is essential, perhaps the most important ingredient is the selection of a qualified and conscientious physical educator who is knowledgeable and qualified to teach the activity and who will devote the time and effort necessary to provide a safe and enjoyable experience for the students.

Conduct of Activity

Prior to designing a unit for flag football, it is essential to identify the skill and ability level of the students for whom the unit is planned. This is a consideration that must be dealt with not only in the preparation of the unit plan but with each daily lesson plan as well. The important question to ask is, "Do these students possess the skill necessary to allow them to safely and successfully participate in this lesson?"

The following checklist will assist in the development of a safe and successful plan.

1. Assess the abilities of the class. Do they possess the skill level to allow them to participate in the day's activity?

2. Assess the physical attributes of the class. Organize the assignment of participants for equitable practice and competition. Do not permit unequal competition.

3. Develop your unit plan and lesson plans with cognitive, psychomotor, and affective objectives.

4. Develop content appropriate for the age and skill level of the participants.

5. Stress fundamental skills prior to competitive activities. Do not progress until fundamentals have been acquired.

6. Prepare the class physically—provide proper and adequate warm-ups.

7. Organize practice activities so that all directional flow is similar. (Example: all students throwing in the same direction.)

8. Allow adequate distance between drill groups when accuracy and execution may not be consistent. (Example: punting.)

9. Consider the direction of the wind in drills when the ball will be thrown and kicked.

10. Be aware of the location of the sun in drills involving catching and tracking the football.

11. Emphasize to students the rules interpretation for the day's activity.

12. Demonstrate, describe, and teach the correct skill technique and provide feedback to the students regarding their execution.

13. Remind students of boundaries and limitations of the drill, lead-up, or regulation game.

14. Review your expectations for the lesson.

15. Emphasize the lesson experience and not the outcome of the game.

To help develop and organize a unit or lesson plan, prepare a chart of class ability levels, like the one shown in Figure 1. The three levels can be interpreted as beginning, intermediate, and advanced skill or knowledge. The use of such a chart for each activity class should enable you to evaluate the class and modify your lessons accordingly.

Figure 1. Form to Record Class Ability Levels for Reference

CLASS ABILITY RECORDS

Class (Grade & Period)_____

Number of students: Female _____ Male _____

Overall Ability Level: I _____ , II _____ , III _____

Skills/Knowledge	Level			
	I	II	III	Safety Rules
1. Rules				
2. Body Control				
3. Blocking/Screening				
4. Passing				
5. Receiving				
6. Place Kicking				
7. Punting				
8. Centering				
9. Tagging				
10. Lead-ups				
11. Ball Carrying				
12. Ball Handling				
13. Regulation Game				
14. Team Offense				
15. Team Defense				

Skill Exceptions: (List students of extreme levels of skill)

High	Low
1.	1.
2.	2.
3.	3.
4.	4.
5.	5.

Supervision

The importance of proper supervision cannot be overemphasized, particularly with an activity such as flag football. To ensure the needed supervision for the lesson, the physical educator must be well organized and prepared. The following checklist will assist the planning and preparation of the lesson with particular emphasis on supervision.

1. Specify the area where the class should meet.

2. Establish a procedure for dispensing equipment.

3. Organize the warm-ups, drills, lead-ups, etc., so that all the activity will be within your field of vision.

4. Establish a pattern of rotation so instruction and specific supervision can take place without hindering your vision of other activity areas.

5. Determine if the student behavior in the activity is what you had intended and initiate corrective action where appropriate.

6. Establish specific rules of safety and acceptable behavior. Immediately correct an unsafe situation.

7. Assign only competent student officials who have successfully completed an officiating clinic or workshop. Observe and evaluate their performance.

8. Observe the officiating and correct any interpretation or enforcement of the rules as necessary.

9. Specify a procedure for dismissal. Check to see that the area has been vacated by all students.

Environmental Safety Conditions

Prior to any activity, a procedure must be established for inspection, maintenance, and reporting of hazards. Inspection should occur on a regular basis, and any reported hazard must be attended to before granting permission for resumption of the use of the facility or equipment.

The following checklists will assist in the inspection of the facility, the equipment, and proper activity attire.

Equipment Checklist

1. Inspect the condition of the flags and belts; make repairs or replace when necessary.

2. Inspect the condition of the footballs.

3. Order a variety of sizes and types of footballs to accommodate the various levels of ability.

4. Inspect all markers and determine whether they are safe for the activity.

5. Gather and place unused equipment off the field of play and a safe distance from the activity area.

6. Collect all equipment at the conclusion of the class and store it in a secure place.

Facility Checklist

1. Inspect the fields for holes, glass, poles, stones, sprinklers, and obstructions.

2. Inspect the turf for suitability of play.

3. Lay out adjacent fields with enough space between fields to minimize the potential for collision between participants on neighboring activity areas.

Participant Checklist

1. Check for proper footwear. Do not allow metal cleats.

2. Check for students wearing glasses and provide appropriate glasses guards.

3. Stress the rules governing play for the day's activity. Reinforce the noncontact rule.

4. Assign appropriate stretching exercises for the weather conditions and the activity to be presented.

5. Establish a procedure for the reporting and treatment of injuries sustained in the activity.

CHAPTER 12

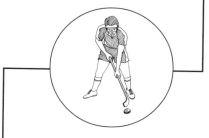

Floor Hockey

Gary R. Gray
Iowa State University
Ames, Iowa

The game of floor hockey is a popular activity in school physical education and intramural programs. For many students it is a novel activity, particularly for those who live in areas where ice hockey is uncommon.

It is extremely important that careful planning goes into the development of a floor hockey unit in a physical education program. Because many students lack prior hockey experience when first introduced to floor hockey, it is critical that stick and puck control be taught in an effective manner. Furthermore, because floor hockey is not a body contact sport as is ice hockey, constant physical control is an important safety factor.

When the teaching of floor hockey is carefully planned and conducted, students are able to master the skills necessary to be successful in playing the game and can participate in a safe and enjoyable manner.

Common Injuries

Research related to the playing of floor hockey in elementary, junior high, and high school physical education and intramural programs has determined the various types of injuries that can occur to participants (Gray, 1991). In floor hockey, as in other physical activities, almost any type of injury could occur to almost any specific part of the body. However, research data show that three major categories of injuries are most prevalent.

The category of injuries most common to floor hockey, as reported by teachers, are scrapes, bruises, and/or cuts on the extremities, such as the knees, shins, ankles, feet, hands, wrists, and arms, as the result of being struck by a floor hockey stick. Contact between a stick and another player's extremities result from two main causes. The first, and one that should be earnestly prevented by teachers, is high sticking. Teachers should strive to have all students consistently keep their sticks below waist level. High sticking is most common during the follow-through phase of a shot. Students must be taught that, when another player is within close proximity, even a waist-high follow-through could cause serious injury. The second cause of injuries to the extremities is due to the stick following through too long when the shooter is closely guarded by another player(s). Even if the stick is kept low, a long follow-through could result in contact with the opponent's feet and/or ankles.

The second category of injuries identified by teachers involves those resulting from being hit by a stick or puck in the head area, including the face, eyes, mouth, and nose. Here again, it must be stressed that the stick should be kept low at all times. Also, players should be taught to keep all shots either on or close to the floor.

The third category is injuries caused by collisions between players. These collisions can result from illegal acts of body checking and other acts of aggression as well as poor control of the body when stick handling, attempting to take the puck from an opponent, and other similar situations.

The following guidelines concerning supervision, selection and conduct of the activity, and environmental conditions can assist teachers and supervisors in successfully managing the risks related to the game of floor hockey.

Supervision

1. Provide an adequate number of supervisors who are familiar with the game of floor hockey and who know what to look for in attempting to prevent injuries. The number of supervisors needed may vary based on the circumstances present in any given situation, such as the age and maturity of students, previous floor hockey experience, ability levels, amount of equipment, size of playing facility, etc.

2. Maintain visual contact with the students being supervised. The supervisor should not allow his or her attention to be diverted. This is particularly important when students are practicing shooting drills where several sticks and pucks might be active at any one time.

3. Maintain a position of immediate accessibility to all students and inform students to locate the teacher/supervisor any time assistance is needed.

4. Develop and consistently enforce all necessary safety rules. These rules are designed to prevent injury but cannot do so unless enforced. Be sure to post and explain the rules to students and answer any questions they might have regarding them. Students are often very helpful in formulating important safety rules and are usually quite willing to offer their input if given the chance.

5. Stop all unsafe acts immediately. Certainly it is preferred that unsafe acts never occur, but if they do, immediately curtail them before an injury occurs. Be constantly alert to activities that could develop into dangerous situations if not stopped.

Be especially alert for inadvertent high sticking. The teacher/supervisor should observe the students as they practice floor hockey drills and play floor hockey games; stop dangerous acts that could lead to foreseeable injuries; and explain to students why it is important not to repeat the unsafe act.

6. If more than one supervisor is deemed necessary, have them spread out in logical formation with overlapping fields of vision. If only one supervisor is present, remain near the most "dangerous" locations to provide specific supervision while still providing general supervision to the rest of the group. For instance, one might position himself/herself near a shooting drill while other students are working at other stations, such as stick handling, passing, etc. If the use of stations presents a supervisory problem to a given teacher, it might be that all students will simply have to participate together in the same drill.

7. Inform students of the risks inherent in the game of floor hockey and what to do to avoid injury from those risks. Give specific examples and demonstrations of situations of particular concern. For example, demonstrate what might happen as the result of a high stick follow-through after a shot. Then show students how to properly and safely complete that follow-through with the stick in a low position. Discuss in detail the rules prohibiting body checking, cross checking, tripping, etc.

8. The supervisor should always maintain control over the students. Discipline where necessary so that a potentially dangerous situation does not turn into an injury-causing one. Develop "withitness." Be constantly aware of what is going on within the area of supervision. "Lifeguard" the group of students as would a lifeguard at a public beach. Supervise actively by being mentally and physically alert and active. One cannot actively supervise merely by virtue of his or her physical presence alone.

9. Attempt to anticipate the acts of students before they occur, especially when an accident appears "ready" to happen. Be particularly concerned about rowdy behavior that might lead to body contact or dangerous use of the sticks. Although a teacher might not be expected to prevent a sudden, spontaneous outburst by a student, the teacher is expected to prevent reasonably foreseeable occurrences.

10. Complete a well-designed injury report form or determine that one is completed by an authorized person. Be certain that the information recorded is factual and is recorded as it was reported to the individual in charge. Obtain enough information regarding the injury to be useful. Study the injury report forms on a regular basis to search for patterns in the nature of injuries sustained by students as the result of playing floor hockey.

11. Constantly observe the students' floor hockey play patterns and tendencies in order to note areas of concern. Discuss these concerns with other staff members and suggest changes, modifications, or improvements to decrease the likelihood of injury and to increase the likelihood of success in acquiring floor hockey skills.

12. Strive to develop a safety-conscious attitude among the students. Discuss with the students their responsibilities with regard to personal safety and the safety of others. Develop an environment where students will feel accountable for their own actions.

Selection And Conduct Of The Activity

1. Follow the local administrative process to have floor hockey formally adopted as part of the school district's physical education curriculum. This will increase the likelihood that the planning related to scope and sequence concerns has been thoroughly discussed and resolved by a curriculum committee composed of individuals familiar with the game of floor hockey.

2. Continue the written planning process with carefully prepared unit and lesson plans. Pay particular attention to the appropriate sequencing of skills from the beginning through the more advanced skills, using sound and well-placed progressions. The time spent in careful, written planning will pay off in the long run with safer and more successful lessons. Be certain that lower level skills that serve as prerequisites to higher level skills are mastered prior to moving on.

3. Always be certain that the skills presented to the students are within their physical abilities. If students are asked to execute advanced skills or maneuvers that are beyond their abilities, injuries could result.

4. Teach students the skills that are necessary to play floor hockey in a safe and reasonable manner. Merely explaining the general concept of the game prior to full competition is an invitation for unnecessary injuries to occur. As students practice floor hockey skills, the teacher will have opportunities to step in and make technique corrections that will not only increase the students' likelihood of successful skill execution but also decrease the likelihood of injuries related to incorrect execution. To do this, the teacher will need to know floor hockey skills, particularly those pertaining to use of the stick, and be able to communicate proper execution of these skills to the students.

5. To the extent that it is reasonable and feasible, instruction should be individualized. All students do not learn in the same way or at the same rate, so teachers must be sensitive to individualized learning needs. A particular floor hockey skill that is acquired quite quickly by one student might take considerably more time for another student to master.

6. Plan warm-up and cooldown activities that are designed specifically with the class period's activities in mind.

7. Be certain students understand that floor hockey is a noncontact sport, quite unlike ice hockey. Although the basic concept of the game is similar in that students attempt to score goals by shooting a puck into a net by use of a hockey stick, there is no similarity whatsoever in the nature of body contact. This fact must be clearly explained to students and consistently enforced. Students should be

taught to keep their bodies under control at all times so as to avoid collisions. Stress that all students who have the potential to collide in a given situation have equal responsibilities to avoid that collision. One cannot simply assume that the opponent will stop. It is important to stress this when teaching stick handling. Simply because a student is progressing down the floor with the puck does not mean that he or she can proceed in any direction whatsoever. If an opponent is in close proximity to the student who has control of the puck, the student with the puck must share the responsibility of avoiding a collision with the approaching defender.

8. Teachers need to stress the major importance of stick control. Students must be taught how to safely shoot and pass the puck. This includes proper back swing, puck contact, and follow-through. The most troublesome of the components of proper shooting and passing in floor hockey is the follow-through. It is absolutely critical that the stick be kept low after contact with the puck. Students who follow through with their sticks unnecessarily high pose a great hazard to opponents in close proximity. Students, particularly beginners, need to be frequently reminded of three points as part of a safe follow-through: (1) follow through with the stick forward rather than up, (2) follow through with the stick short rather than long, and (3) rotate the wrists to turn the blade of the stick down rather than up. Although these three components should decrease the danger posed by the follow-through motion of a floor hockey stick, students must still be reminded that when either opponents or teammates are very close, they must maintain control of the stick so as to prevent it from hitting the nearby player-even though this might restrict a follow-through that could be safely executed when another player is not in the vicinity.

9. Stress to students the importance of keeping the puck either on the floor or low to the floor during shooting and passing. Teach students proper puck control so that the puck is not flying around the gymnasium near head height. A high-flying puck poses a danger to opponents and teammates alike, but it is also difficult to gain control over a puck when it is off the floor. The puck should be passed on the floor where a teammate can successfully receive it. Likewise, shots on goal should remain either on or very close to the floor. High pucks will simply fly over the goal.

10. Students should be taught that when attempting to take the puck away from an opponent, they should not lean forward and thereby drop their heads toward the opponent's stick. This could result in the student being hit in the face with the stick or puck. Instead of leaning in, students should be taught to remain upright and attempt to dislodge the puck by proper use of their sticks.

Environmental Conditions

Equipment

1. Look for signs of wear and tear on the floor hockey equipment and report needed repairs in writing. Some minor repairs can be performed immediately by the teacher.

Be certain to inspect floor hockey sticks prior to each use. Be diligent in removing damaged sticks from use.

2. Perform preventive as well as corrective maintenance. If a stick or other piece of equipment shows signs of wear, repair it before its condition worsens and, perhaps, causes an injury. Never allow students to use damaged or questionable equipment.

3. Do not allow students to abuse the floor hockey equipment or use it in a manner for which it was not intended. Such treatment will not only shorten the life of the equipment but could also lead to injuries.

4. Provide students with equipment that is designed appropriately for their various ages and developmental levels. For example, providing young children with floor hockey sticks that are too long or too heavy might lead to problems related to adequate control.

5. Provide students with protective eye guards and mouth guards, which could be instrumental in preventing injuries caused by a high stick or errant puck. Although students should be taught how to maintain constant control of their sticks and the puck, at one time or another a stick or puck might go dangerously high.

6. Provide students with field hockey protective shin guards or shin guards worn inside the socks, to help prevent injuries to the lower legs caused by contact with the opponent's stick. Shin guards also help to protect against bruises caused by the puck hitting students' lower legs.

7. Provide goalies with protective face gear, preferably a full face mask, to protect their face, mouth, and eyes from the puck and from sticks that might be carelessly raised when near the goal.

8. Use either the specially designed low-bounce floor hockey ball or the light, hollow puck that comes with most sets of floor hockey sticks. Do not use a heavy, weighted puck or an ice hockey puck. Some teachers even prefer to use a small foam ball.

9. Secure all floor hockey equipment when it is not being used in a supervised situation.

10. Teach students to perform safety checks on their floor hockey sticks and require them to do so prior to each class.

Facility

1. Be alert to relevant environmental conditions that might affect safe participation in the game of floor hockey. The gymnasium floor should be clean and dry to prevent unnecessary slippage by students who are making fast movements and sudden changes of direction.

2. Pay particular attention to obstacles on the floor or the gymnasium walls. Usually the game is played using all floor space inside the four gymnasium walls. Passing the puck off the walls is a common maneuver to elude opponents. However, if floor or wall obstacles or protrusions exist, the teacher might need to restrict the use of available floor space similar to the confines of a basketball court. In this situation,

there would be a buffer zone between the area of play and obstacles or protrusions that might pose a hazard to students. This would eliminate the use of the walls in passing the puck but would be necessary to prevent injuries related to collisions with the obstacles or protrusions. If this modification is employed, the teacher could either have a face-off near where the puck goes outside the floor of play or simply allow the nonoffending team to put the puck back into play as is done in the game of basketball.

3. Do not allow too many students on the floor at any one time. Remember that the movement of students in the gymnasium along with the use of sticks and pucks requires that students have ample room to maneuver. Depending upon the number of students in the class, the teacher might need to have students take turns practicing the drills as well as take turns in playing the game itself. It is not recommended to exceed the regulation six players per team on the floor at any one time during actual competition. Rather than crowd the floor with an excessive number of players, teachers should substitute players when play is stopped or at predetermined time intervals.

4. Students should be grouped and spaced appropriately when practicing floor hockey drills. Make maximum use of the existing facility but do not overcrowd it during skill practice.

5. If two or more floor hockey games are played in close proximity (e.g., two games played across the width of the gymnasium, one at either end), care should be taken to provide an appropriate buffer zone between the adjacent areas. Because players might leave their respective areas, this buffer zone is important to prevent collisions with players on adjacent floor spaces. It is also helpful to use a barrier (e.g., a dividing curtain) to prevent the puck from leaving one area of play and entering an adjacent area of play. Use of an opaque curtain, however, would require additional supervisors to guarantee the ability to maintain visual contact with all players.

6. The goalie crease should be clearly marked with tape on the floor in front of each goal to identify the area where opponents may not enter and thus interfere with the goalie's movements near the goal.

7. Students who are waiting to enter the game should be placed outside the area of play where they can be adequately supervised but do not pose a collision hazard to players in the game.

Floor hockey is a reasonably safe physical activity as long as certain guidelines are followed. If teachers carefully plan the use of their instructional time for the successful learning of floor hockey skills; carefully supervise the activity with particular attention paid to stick control, puck control, and body control; and provide adequate floor hockey equipment and a safe facility; then students can enjoy and benefit from their participation in this exciting game. Careful planning and structured control of the activity make a real difference not only in the students' enjoyment of the game but also in their safe participation.

CHAPTER 13

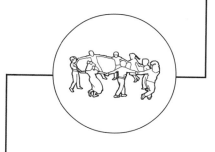

Games

Diane Bonanno
Rutgers University
New Brunswick, New Jersey

Games are a staple of most physical activity programs, especially those that are designed for elementary school age children. Their popularity is understandable— they provide a vigorous and exciting activity for the participants, and they allow the leader to accomplish a wide variety of objectives.

As an educational tool, games can be used to improve motor skills, practice sport skills, or develop desirable characteristics such as teamwork. They can also be used to help a child understand and execute simple concepts or strategies that are needed for other activities. But there is one important drawback that should be noted. Because games are a part of everyone's childhood experience, both in and out of school, they are sometimes used without much forethought on the part of the leader. The end result is that games are occasionally played without adequate supervision or conducted in a manner that can be hazardous to the participants. This is especially true when a game is used at the end of a lesson as a filler or when a leader develops or modifies a game during the course of a class. In these instances, there is very little time to consider the possible consequences of any given action. Because of this, the risk associated with playing a game increases and so does the likelihood of injury.

It is difficult for most people to believe that a game as simple as tag can create a dangerous situation for anyone. Children play tag and a number of other simple games at home or on the playground every day without adult supervision. But this observation is misleading. In a study of 175 lawsuits brought against instructional programs, games were the second most frequent source of litigation.[1] Only gymnastics resulted in a greater number

---

[1] Dougherty, N. J. (1988). Learning from the mistakes of others. *Athletic Business, 12*(8), 59.

of suits. Even sports, such as football, that are considered high-risk, were well behind games in the number of lawsuits that were generated. The reason is simple. Leaders are often lulled into complacency by the simplicity of a game. What they fail to realize is that a game has the same components as a sophisticated sport such as soccer and rugby and therefore requires the same diligence on the part of the leader.

Every game has rules, a specified playing surface, and equipment. When played in a structured environment such as a school or camp, they require supervision from a qualified leader to enforce those rules, control the pace of play, and insure that both playing surfaces and equipment are in good condition. Good coaches would never consider allowing their players to scrimmage under anything but the best circumstances. Good leaders should give their charges that same consideration when conducting a game.

This consideration should not only be extended to children, however. As our society uses games more and more to help adults learn the principles of good teamwork and sound leadership, we must remember that adults are just as vulnerable as children when asked to play a game that has been ill-conceived or poorly conducted. In fact, in some instances, they require more consideration because their bodies may not be able to cope with the stresses of physical activity as well as children's bodies can. Whether the leader is working with children or adults, there are a few important points to remember when using games as a method of achieving any goal. First, remember every group has unique needs that must be considered before a game is chosen. Because a game was used successfully with one group does not mean that it will work with another. Second, games should be dissected and modified in the plan book before they are used on the playing field. The better a leader understands a game, the more likely the game can be modified without incident. Third, leaders should never lose sight of the fact that games should be fun, but this axiom should not be the determining factor when selecting games. It should be a corollary to an educational objective. Fourth and last, never take a game for granted. Even simple games have features that place participants at risk.

Although it is impossible to eliminate all of the hazards associated with physical activity, good planning and sound reasoning can help minimize many of the problems associated with games. The following guidelines are designed to help the leader systematically review the important elements of a game where control can be exerted.

Supervision

Supervision refers to both the quantitative and qualitative control that is exercised over a group by the leader. Leaders should be sure that they do the following:

1. Establish their control as the leader of the group early in the game and insist that the group follow their directions quickly and accurately when given. This is especially important if the leader has designated someone else to direct the action of the game. Things can easily get out of hand if the group does not respect the person in charge and does not respond quickly to his or her commands.

2. Have a full understanding of the rules of the game and what they consider potential hazards that might result from certain rules.

3. Organize the activity in such a way that every person in the group is within the leader's field of vision at all times. When the group is large and more then one game is played simultaneously, the leader must be sure to move around the perimeter of the playing area so that his or her field of vision is never narrowed. If an accident occurs in one of the multiple games or a situation develops that requires the leader to move into a specific area that might cause some participants to be behind the leader, action should be stopped and the group reorganized as quickly as possible.

4. Enforce all rules consistently and quickly and never allow a situation to get out-of-hand. Poor behavior should be addressed immediately and action taken to correct the behavior or place the offender on the sidelines.

5. Control the tempo of the game so that rules can be observed and the pace does not exceed any one individual's ability to perform the skills necessary to play the game with minimum risk.

6. Provide direct supervision of every game if a game cannot be self-refereed. If students are employed to referee a game, the leader should be sure that they understand what they are to do and that they have sufficient confidence to handle the responsibility before they are placed in the referee situation.

7. Never play a game with the participants. Not only might this practice result in a mismatch between the leader and the participants, it also severely limits the leader's ability to watch the entire group and exercise the control that is needed to manage the pace and tenor of the game.

8. Have a plan that insures that if a participant gets hurt the leader can continue to provide the necessary level of supervision for the group and still get the participant the aid he/she requires.

Selection and Conduct of the Activity

As the person in control, the leader must make certain judgments about the appropriateness of an activity based on the readiness of the individuals in the group. When trying to decide what games to use and how to present them to the group, the leader should remember the following:

1. Readiness refers to more than an individual's physical ability. It also refers to his/her intellectual and emotional ability as well. The leader should never assume that an activity is appropriate for a group simply because group members can perform all of the physical skills necessary to play the game. They may not have the emotional maturity to engage in the action without getting angry or the intellectual ability to understand the rules well enough to play the game safely. If any element of readiness is missing, a different activity should be selected, or the activity should be modified to take this situation into account.

2. The method of presentation and the number of times instructions have to be repeated is directly related to the age and the skill level of the participants. If the group is young or has never played the game before, the leader must take the time to present the material in a variety of ways. Verbal descriptions followed by demonstrations and selected practice can greatly reduce the likelihood of injury when a group plays a game for the first time.

3. Games should be selected on the basis of the educational benefit they can impart—not just on the excitement they can provide. Fun and excitement are two important components of a good game, but they should never be the sole reason for choosing one. Stating that the game was selected simply because it was fun is a difficult position to defend in court if a child was hurt during the course of the activity.

4. Progressions are very useful when teaching a game that is complex. They can reduce the learning curve and accelerate the group's readiness to play the game with all of its component parts. Progressions also demonstrate a teacher's thought processes and are evidence of good planning.

5. Even children can be more responsible for their own safety if they know what can cause them injury. Be sure to take time to warn them about potential problems not just once but as many times as is necessary to insure that they have a full understanding of any danger they may encounter. Teach them to inspect their own equipment or the playing area to be sure that it is safe. Respond quickly when they point out some danger and praise them when they make a suggestion that will improve safety. Make them safety-conscious for themselves and others.

6. If a group responds poorly to a game the first time it is introduced, consider stopping play early and introducing another game. To keep pressing a group to engage in a game that they find boring or frustrating may very well end in disaster if the group decides to find alternatives for making the game exciting.

7. Get the group involved quickly in the game. Groups that are asked to sit or watch for long periods of time without any action will find ways to amuse themselves that can be very detrimental. Select games that allow maximum participation for the entire group. Relay races, for instance, may be exciting, but in a six-person file, a participant is only moving one-sixth of the time. The rest of the time he or she is free to stay involved or cause mischief. Large games where children are eliminated can also cause unnecessary problems. While children are waiting to re-enter the game, there are many things they can do to occupy their time, and some of these could easily result in injury.

8. Directions and rules should be given to the whole group when they are completely quiet and, preferably, seated so that they can see and hear the leader. Students should be given the opportunity to ask questions, and questions should be repeated so that everyone can hear them before the answer is given. Failure to hear or understand a rule can cause problems on the playing field that may be impossible to reverse in time to stop an injury.

9. Games that are considered hazardous by the profession should not be played no matter how badly the students want to take part in them. The leader should stay well-informed on these issues. A game that he or she may have played successfully as a child may now be considered dangerous because of the number of injuries that have resulted over the years. The leader should also be sure that these games are not played during the period before class begins or when it ends. These are the times when participants are most vulnerable.

10. Equipment substitutions should make sense and not be done for a capricious reason. A heavy ball should not be substituted for a lighter regulation ball, for instance, just because the lighter one is not available. A heavier ball could make the game dangerous.

Environmental Conditions

Paying attention to every detail of the teaching process will make very little difference if the playing area or the equipment is unsafe. The condition of the playing environment is the easiest factor to control, yet it is often the one that is most neglected. Before giving the signal to start the game, make sure to do the following:

1. Check the area before the group arrives to be sure that the playing surface is free of debris or any obstacles. Slippery areas should be cleaned before any activity is conducted, uneven surfaces such as holes or ruts should be fixed immediately, and equipment that is lying around should be stored in a safe place.

2. Make sure that there is sufficient distance between the playing area and the nearest obstacle to allow players to overrun the sidelines or endlines without placing themselves in jeopardy. If more then one game is being played at a time, be sure that there is a sufficient buffer zone between the two so that play in one game does not interfere with play in the other. If the game involves a ball, the buffer zone has to be greater than if the only consideration is a player who might run beyond the sideline. Care should also be taken to set up games parallel to each other rather then end to end. If there is insufficient room to play the games side by side, eliminate one of them. Playing games end to end is very dangerous.

3. Allow room for spectators that is a safe distance from the field of play. Physically mark the area where they should stay so there isn't an opportunity for them to inadvertently become a part of the action.

4. Never use a wall as a boundary line, finish line, or a safe area. Never direct participants to tag a wall in a relay race before turning around. Each of these actions can result in serious injuries. Always be sure that there is sufficient room for a participant to decelerate before reaching a permanent object.

5. If cones are used to mark the playing area, make sure that they are colorful and large enough to be seen by the players. Cones can easily become tripping hazards if they are dull, small, and unobtrusive.

6. Be sure walls are padded, especially when suggested buffer zones cannot be met or hazards such as water fountains and door knobs protrude from the wall.

7. Teach students to walk around the outside of a game and not to cut through it even if the action is at the other end of the playing field. The action can reverse itself quickly and the spectator can easily be caught in the middle of the game.

8. Try to orient the activity so that the sun is not in anyone's eyes, especially if the game requires a ball and the ball can be lofted in the air.

9. Use brightly colored balls when playing with younger children. It helps them track the ball better.

10. Store extra equipment far from the playing field so that it doesn't become a tripping hazard.

CHAPTER 14

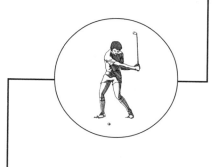

Golf

Harvey R. White
New Mexico State University
Las Cruces, New Mexico

The nature of the game of golf is relatively safe; however, it does have potential safety hazards. Swinging an implement in excess of 100 mph in an attempt to propel a solid sphere 1.68 inches in diameter and weighing 1.62 ounces can be dangerous. The manner in which the game is introduced and organized for instruction and practice can greatly reduce this danger.

The primary key to safety in golf is awareness. Awareness must be developed through the administration, golf instructor, and the student. Each has a major responsibility in regard to safety considerations.

Administration. Golf is becoming more popular in physical education curricula and in recreational programs. However, the question of whether qualified personnel are on staff to supervise and/or instruct golf is a concern that must be addressed by administrators. Often, an individual who plays golf is assigned to teach the activity with the assumption that the individual has the ability to provide effective instruction. The ability to play golf and teach golf is not synonymous. However, one's ability to play golf may add credibility to his or her teaching.

The administration must determine if an individual is qualified to teach golf. If the instructor is not qualified, adequate time must be provided for pre-service training to ensure that he or she acquires pedagogical, technical, organizational, and safety knowledge and skills.

A viable option is to employ one of the local professional golf association (PGA) teaching professionals to assist with a golf instructional unit. PGA professionals are well-qualified instructors, aware of the safety issues in golf, and dedicated to enhancing the game of golf in their communities.

Golf instructor. The greatest responsibility for the safety of the participants in a golf class lies with the instructor. Qualifications that an instructor needs to provide safe, quality instruction include, but are not limited to, the following:

- Pedagogical and content knowledge
- Organizational knowledge for structuring a safe practice environment
- Understanding of criteria for selecting and maintaining equipment
- Knowledge of appropriate procedures for the care and maintenance of facilities
- Understanding of cognitive, psychomotor, and affective needs of students as they relate specifically to learning to play golf.

When individuals are providing instruction, they should attempt to position themselves in a manner that will allow them to continue to supervise the actions of other students in the class.

Students. Students are a vital link in addressing the issue of safety in class. They should be made aware of safety concerns and be required to assume a major role for their own personal safety and the safety of others while in the golf class. This is also critical when students are practicing on their own or during actual course play.

Safety Rules

Rules should be established to help students become familiar with their responsibility in promoting safety both in and outside of class. It is important to relate the rules to class activity and to specific implications at a driving range, golf course, practice in the park or in the student's own backyard. Safety rules should specify where, when, and the direction in which clubs can be swung and golf balls hit. Once the rules are established, they should be strictly enforced. A good technique to inform students of issues relating to safety is to cover safety rules in detail and provide demonstrations to illustrate the meaning of each rule. As a follow-up to the explanation and demonstration of the rules, students should read and sign a golf risk form that includes the safety rules that were presented by the instructor (see Figure 1). Copies of the rules should be posted in areas that are clearly visible to students. If copies of the rules are laminated, they can be posted for both inside and outside activity areas.

Common Injuries in Golf

The potential for injuries during golf instruction is far greater than the actual severity of most injuries that occur. The most common minor injury occurring in golf classes is the development of blisters on the hands. This is usually the result of excessive movement of the club in the hands caused by a faulty grip technique and can be remedied by learning to grip the club correctly.

The less frequent but more serious injuries occur when individuals are hit by a club or golf ball. Being hit by a club usually occurs when an individual walks into the path of a swinging club. Such injuries can be avoided by establishing and enforcing rules that

Figure 1. Sample Golf Risk Form

EXAMPLE

GOLF RISK FORM

Department of Physical Education
Central High School

The purpose of the Golf Risk Form is to advise you of the potential for injury as a participant in a golf class. Although golf would be classified as a relatively "low-risk" sport in regards to serious injury or fatality rate, serious injuries and deaths have resulted from participation in golf. In order to make the golf class as safe as possible for all participants, your cooperation in adhering to safety rules is required. It is important that you know and observe the basic rules of safety for golf as outlined in this chapter. Please read the following safety rules before participating in a golf class.

Golf Safety Rules

1. Before you swing any club, check to see that no one is within range of your swing.
2. When someone swings a club, be careful where you stand or walk. Stay well out of range of anyone swinging a golf club.
3. You should swing a club so that your follow-through is directed toward an open area. It is not likely to happen, but the club could break or slip out of your hands.
4. You should allow a player swinging a golf club plenty of space. Similarly, when you are swinging a club, be sure you have adequate space.
5. Before playing any stroke on the course, make certain the group ahead of you is out of range of your intended shot. If in doubt as to whether you should hit the shot or wait, WAIT.
6. If you hit a ball that is traveling toward someone and may endanger that person, call "FORE" loudly to alert the endangered players.
7. Stay on the tee at the practice range. Walking ahead of the teeing ground to retrieve balls or tees is very dangerous and is prohibited.
8. When you are teaching/observing someone, stand facing the person or behind the player, looking down the intended target line. If you stand facing an individual swinging a golf club, be sure the individual behind you has space to swing the club safely. DO NOT BACK UP!
9. Lightning storms are extremely dangerous to golfers on the course. When such storms occur, the best precaution is to GET OFF THE COURSE. If that is not possible, seek shelter away from your golf clubs and large trees.
10. If you use a cart to drive around the course, drive with care and stay on the cart path.

I HAVE READ THE ABOVE SAFETY RULES AND UNDERSTAND THAT THERE IS A RISK OF SERIOUS INJURY IN PARTICIPATING IN GOLF.

_____

Signature   Date

govern where and when a club may by swung. Each swing station should have designated traffic patterns that allow students to move safely between stations.

Injuries that result from being struck by golf balls occur more frequently on golf courses with parallel fairways than in physical education or recreational golf classes. In fact, this type of injury should never occur during instruction if appropriate safety rules are followed. This is especially true if individuals are properly instructed never to retrieve golf balls prior to a designated signal by the instructor. Walking in front of an area designated for hitting golf balls should never be allowed while others are swinging a club.

Student Information Sheets

Obtaining information about students in the class is important for establishing a safe and effective environment. The following are examples of information that are particularly beneficial for constructing a safe environment for golf instruction.

1. Experiences in golf
   - Ability level of students
   - Ability of students to serve as peer teaching assistants
   - Previous instruction
2. Developmental disabilities
   - Potential equipment and technique modifications
   - Contraindications of specific drills
3. Allergies
   - Awareness to potential allergic reaction
   - Medication side effects
4. Physical Fitness
   - Flexibility (range of motion)
   - Muscle strength
   - Muscle endurance

Skill Progression

The order in which skills are taught in golf is based more on logical progression of learning rather than on safety considerations. Initially, short game skills should be taught, and the first of these skills to be taught should be putting. By starting with putting (six inches from the hole), students learn to perform a mini golf swing. Starting this close to the target allows students to have immediate success by putting the golf ball into the hole. As students move farther from the hole, the swing becomes longer and greater club head speed is generated.

Continuing to progress to a short distance off the green, students are taught the chipping stroke, which has some of the same movement characteristics as putting. As the distance from the green continues to increase and chipping is not the appropriate skill to use, the pitching stroke should be taught. The backswing and follow-through for pitching is longer than that required for chipping. The swing for pitching has many of the same movement characteristics as the full swing, with two significant exceptions. The club head does not travel as far on the backswing and follow-through for the pitching swing as they do on the full swing, resulting in less club head speed.

Moving from the pitching stroke to the full swing only requires more rotation of the hips and shoulders in the backswing and follow-through. Although there are differences among the various setups for putting, chipping, pitching, and the full swing, the initial movements to start these skills are the same. Therefore, teaching students to putt, chip, pitch, and perform the full swing is a logical progression for students to learn golf skills.

Instructional Drills

Selection of appropriate golf drills and training aids can greatly enhance the teaching/learning process. It is critical that the instructional drills and training aids selected be directly related to the specific skills being taught and that they are safe for the student. A variety of teaching and training aids are available to assist students in learning basic skills in golf.

Drills should be explained clearly, demonstrated correctly, and used appropriately. Students share responsibility for creating situations that are safe or unsafe. Dangerous situations can arise when students are unaware of one another's presence. Be sure that students understand how the length of an individual's arms and club contribute to subsequent differences in the space required to swing a club. In addition, the potential swing speed of the various clubs should be noted and compared visually and verbally when demonstrated by the instructor.

Environmental Conditions

Golf can be taught effectively in a gym or on a playing field; however, larger areas are more conducive to safety because students can be provided more space in established swing stations. Anytime space becomes restrictive, where fewer than five yards of space are allotted for each swing station, safety becomes a problem. When insufficient space is available, instructors should reduce the number of individuals allowed to swing the club at one time to provide the recommended five yards between swing stations.

Indoor Playing Areas
Designated swing stations should be marked and safety rules clearly posted. The swing stations should be free of extra clubs, bags, and ball containers.

Mats. Mats with artificial grass surfaces and rubber backing serve as an excellent surface for hitting golf balls. This type of mat provides a thick protective hitting surface, and the rubber backing creates a nonslippery surface for the student while swinging the club.

Full-swing stations, in which plastic or soft rubber balls are hit against walls, should be placed away from doorways and a minimum of 15 yards from the wall. There should be a minimum of five yards between swing stations (see Figure 2). This allows ample room for the plastic or rubber ball to bounce off the wall and roll safely back toward the mats. If the mats are placed too close to the wall, students could be hit by balls ricocheting off the wall. The physical arrangement of the stations should be checked frequently during class to insure that safe distances are being maintained between swing stations and the wall.

Traffic Patterns. Traffic patterns need to be carefully considered in the gym, particularly when various swing stations are established. Designated pathways can be marked using cones, jump ropes or chairs, etc. Students moving from one station to another should do so on a signal from the instructor, and movement should take place in a single direction.

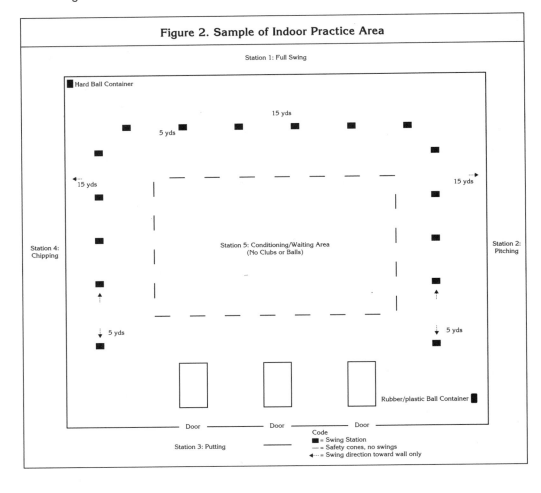

Figure 2. Sample of Indoor Practice Area

A systematic procedure of traffic patterns, under the control of the instructor, helps to assure the safety of students moving between swing stations. Once students arrive at their respective stations, activity should be allowed to begin only on a signal from the instructor.

Swing Stations. Swing stations should be marked clearly, such as for putting, chipping, pitching, and full swing. This will enhance students' understanding of the space needed to perform the different golf skills. For example, a full swing should not be made in the putting or chipping areas. Students should be informed that this is also true when practicing at a golf course.

Balls. When using plastic or soft rubber balls for swing practice and regular golf balls for putting, the containers where these balls are kept need to be clearly marked. It is also helpful to have the plastic and soft rubber balls a different color from the regular golf balls. The ball containers should be carefully checked before each class to assure that only the balls appropriate for each station are available. Students should be made aware of the differences between the balls being used and instructed to check each ball for type prior to hitting.

Dress. Students should wear loose-fitting clothing and athletic shoes during class. Tight clothing may be uncomfortable and can be restrictive when swinging the club. Street shoes are generally unsafe in that they lack the traction needed for swinging the golf club.

Cleaning up. Artificial grass mats with rubber backing create a dust film on the floor that can be hazardous to others using the gym. The area indoors, where students are practicing, must be kept clean and orderly. This area should be dust mopped each day, and preferably between each class.

Securing Equipment. Clubs and balls should be collected at the end of each class and secured in a safe place.

Outdoor Playing Areas

Hitting surface. Artificial grass mats may or may not be used for outdoor stations. A grass area is preferable to mats if at all possible. Grass provides the best learning environment and will assist in the direct transfer of the skills learned to the actual golf course. Whether artificial grass mats or grass are used, the hitting surface should be free of rocks or other obstacles that could be hit accidentally.

Swing stations. Many of the criteria for establishing swing stations and the safety considerations discussed for the indoor practice areas are equally important for outdoor practice areas. The open space of an outdoor practice area may tend to give students a false sense of security. When students are waiting their turn to practice the various golf skills, they should wait in a designated area. This area should be a safe distance away from swing stations.

Balls used outside. As with indoor practice, plastic or soft rubber balls and regular golf balls should be separated and not used simultaneously at any one swing station. A golf ball hit accidentally in a confined area could be dangerous. Golf balls are fun to hit; however, they need to be used with discretion when students are learning the full swing. Adequate space, both length and width, is needed to accommodate the novice who lacks control of distance and direction when striking a golf ball.

The grass space should be clear of debris and excess equipment and should be cut close to the ground. This will help in finding golf balls that have been hit. The total number of golf balls should be counted at the beginning and end of each class. Students should be instructed to count the number of balls they have before hitting and retrieve as many balls as they hit. Students should pay particular attention to any misdirected shots (i.e., balls that go an unusual distance or direction) and be instructed to pick them up when it is time for all balls to be retrieved. This takes time but is critical to the safety of others. Golf balls that are not found can be hazardous to others using the field. The same is true when practicing in parks or other areas.

Most secondary education facilities do not have appropriate outdoor space for safe use of regular golf balls. Training aids that simulate regular golf balls are available for purchase. When struck, these training aids have the feel and flight pattern similar to that of a regular golf ball. Advantages of using this type of training aid are that it does not travel as far when hit, requiring less time to retrieve, and it is safer to use than hitting regular golf balls.

Restrict the Area

When golf classes are in session, signs should be posted restricting traffic in and around the activity area. This is needed particularly in areas where the fields are used by community joggers or others as a thoroughfare.

Equipment

Appropriate equipment. Golf clubs that are purchased for the class should vary in length, weight, and grip size in order to best fit the needs of students. If a club is not appropriately fitted for a student, it can have a negative effect on the rate and progress of learning, and student safety can be compromised. Instructors who lack the expertise to fit clubs for their students should ask the local golf professional for assistance or request advice from a golf club manufacturer when ordering equipment.

Maintenance of clubs. The grip, shaft, and hosel are components of a club that should be checked for wear and damage. Excessive wear of the club's grips can cause the surfaces to become smooth, making it difficult for the student to maintain control of the club when swinging. This can lead to excessive movement of the grip in the hands, which leads to the development of blisters and difficulty controlling the club. Also, when clubs are used extensively, the grips tend to absorb oil from the golfer's hands, causing them to become slick. Grips can be kept clean by washing them frequently with a brush, soap, and water. Composition grips are recommended for use in most classes because they are safer on the golfer's hands, easy to clean, and inexpensive to replace.

Club shafts can bend as a result of hitting the ground repeatedly during swings, getting stepped on, or being stored improperly; therefore, they should be checked daily. When a shaft is bent, it becomes weak and could break, creating an unsafe situation. Once a shaft is bent, it should be broken completely so that it cannot be used. Depending on the condition of the club-head, including the hosel, it may be used again by having it re-shafted.

The hosel is where the shaft enters the club head, and, after extended use, it may weaken. Club heads can snap at the hosel without warning. Frequent equipment checks are needed; often weaknesses can be detected by holding the head of the club and trying to turn the shaft. Movement between the club head and shaft or a squeaking sound indicate weakness in the club structure; if weakness is detected, the club should be repaired by a club repair expert or destroyed.

Inspection. Comprehensive equipment records should be kept. As golf equipment is received, it should be numbered and the date noted that it was purchased. Equipment records should include documentation of periodic inspections of all equipment. This is in addition to the daily inspection that should be noted in lesson plans or logs of activity sessions. An ongoing record of equipment may provide information relative to the longevity of equipment purchased from various companies. Inexpensive clubs are often attractive for purchase but may not be durable or safe. Equipment records may later be used to justify budgets needed to order quality clubs.

Students should be required to play a major role in checking and inspecting their golf clubs before hitting balls. This aids in raising students' awareness of the proper care and maintenance of clubs and the importance of safety.

Summary

Safety issues in golf instruction are focused on developing awareness through classroom organization and instructional procedures. Awareness of safety in and beyond the school golf classes is critical for the students themselves and for others. The instructor's task is to establish a safe environment for learning golf skills and continued involvement beyond the school setting.

An example of selected factors that should be reviewed in order to enhance the safety of students in a golf class is provided below.

Golf Safety Review Checklist

Instructor

- Qualifications (academic preparation, teaching experience)
- Knowledge and skills to address the following:
    - Potential injuries in golf
    - Skill progression
    - Individual differences
    - Group instructional techniques and procedures
    - Appropriate drills for golf instruction
    - Criteria used for the selection/care of equipment

- Adaptation of space and facilities based on the number of students in the class and their ability levels
- Safety issues relating to golf both in and outside of class

Environmental Conditions

- Safety rules
  - Rules handouts
  - Golf risk form
  - Rules poster
- Facility (indoor-outdoor)
  - Hitting surfaces are appropriate for skills being taught
  - Instructional area free of debris and excess equipment
  - Traffic patterns established and enforced
  - Swing stations minimum of five yards apart
  - Indoor swing stations minimum of 15 yards from wall, away from doors and hallways
  - Warning signs posted around outside activity area restricting thoroughfare
  - Signal established for beginning and ending a club-swinging activity

Equipment Records and Security

- Records maintained on equipment purchase dates
- Records established for periodic equipment inspections
- Daily check for condition and repair of clubs
- Equipment secured at the end of class

Control of Balls

- Containers marked and separated for regular golf balls versus plastic and soft rubber balls
- Check containers at each station to make sure only balls appropriate for each station are available
- Direct students to check ball types before hitting
- Count golf balls and plastic and rubber balls prior to hitting and after each class

CHAPTER 15

Inline Skating

Chet Bunting
Cherry Drive Elementary School
Thornton, Colorado

Inline skating is currently one of the most popular and fastest growing participant sports in America. The participants range from cross-country skiers and hockey players who use inline skating as a form of cross training, to beginning enthusiasts skating leisurely around bike paths. Inline skating attracts adults seeking its high fitness and aerobic benefits, its low cost, and its accessibility. It also attracts young people who seek the excitement of aggressive skating or inline hockey. Millions of people have found inline skating to be a great form of exercise and a healthy workout. Benefits of skating include cardiovascular conditioning and muscle toning, particularly of the quadriceps, gluteus (buttock), and outer and inner thigh muscles. Inline skating's safety record is twice as good as that of most other sports, including baseball and basketball.

Introduction - Major Risks and Dangers

Research indicates there are two types of inline skating injuries: overuse (lower back pain is the most common) and trauma (fractures, strains, and sprains). Half of all inline skating injuries are severe. Head injuries are the leading cause of death as a result of inline skating. Many of these injuries could have been eliminated if the skaters had been wearing proper safety gear. Some of the causes of inline skating injuries are hitting an irregular surface, loss of balance, inability to stop or avoid an obstacle, and collisions with other skaters.

The most common types of inline skating injuries are fractures, road rash, strains, sprains, lacerations, and concussions. The most commonly injured areas of the body during inline skating are the wrist, elbow, forearm, head and face, and ankle. The best ways to prevent these injuries from occurring is to use common sense, always wear safety gear, learn to stop, and anticipate.

The following guidelines concerning supervision, selection and conduct of the activity, and environmental concerns can assist teachers and supervisors in successfully managing the risks related to inline skating. This author truly believes that activities such as inline skating can be implemented and instructed in a safe manner in a public school setting. Instructors should teach skill progressions and emphasize safety with every class. This is where students can learn safe habits, correct technique, and etiquette and can practice in an environment that is educational. Skate parks and skate centers are wonderful places to extend learning but all too often fall short in teaching the above-mentioned criteria.

Supervision

1. Provide a separate area for students to put on and take off equipment that is out of the way of the skating area. Mark with cones how you want students to enter the skating area from the equipment area.

2. Provide separate areas for skaters to allow for individual differences in students' skating abilities (e.g., place beginning skaters in the middle area and advanced skaters on the outside).

3. Maintain visual contact with the students being supervised. Maintain a position of "back to the wall."

4. Develop and consistently enforce all necessary safety rules. These rules are designed to provide a safe environment for all students. Be sure to post and explain the rules to students and answer any questions they have regarding them. Students are often very helpful in formulating important safety rules and are usually quite willing to offer their input.

5. Stop all unsafe acts immediately. Certainly it is preferred that unsafe acts never occur, but if they do, immediately curtail them before an injury occurs. Be constantly alert to activities that could develop into dangerous situations if not stopped.

6. Inform students of the risks inherent to inline skating and what to do to avoid injury from those risks. Always require that all students wear safety equipment, including a properly fitting helmet, wrist guards, elbow pads, and kneepads. You might even want to include hip pads (especially for beginners).

7. Provide clear and precise directions and repeat them at least once for clarity; then ask questions to check for understanding.

8. Develop the habit of writing detailed lesson plans. Address safety concerns in your daily lesson plans so that you may have legal evidence of your preparation and knowledge with regard to the subject matter. This process will also assist you in anticipating a hazard before it occurs.

9. In the event of an injury, fill out an accident report form and file it with the principal's office no later than the close of the school day. Be certain that the information

recorded is factual and secure the names of any students who may have witnessed the incident.

10. Be a lifelong learner. Gain as much knowledge as you can to become an expert in this content area. If possible, apply for certification to instruct inline skating through the International Inline Skating Association (IISA).

11. Never leave your class unsupervised. Your absence is a potential source of negligence.

12. Establish a list of emergency procedures to be followed in all accident cases. This will help prevent confusion if an accident does happen. Establish accident procedures in the same way you would prepare a tornado drill or fire drill.

13. Guide students in the development of acceptance of responsibility and safety awareness through discussions, reflection time, and modeling of responsible and socially aware actions.

14. Establish exit procedures in the event of a fire drill.

15. Always have students skate in the same direction.

16. Insist that students be aware of the stopping signal that you use. Use this signal exclusively for this purpose. Never allow students to use walls to stop. Always provide a safety barrier between the skating area and any equipment, tables, and other structures.

17. Skates must be removed prior to restroom breaks. If there is a drinking fountain in the skating area, allow only one student there at a time. Otherwise, a student may fall and hit another student while he or she is drinking. It is imperative that all students can demonstrate a proficient stop to avoid others and/or obstacles.

18. If you are using inline skates as a form of transportation to and from school, always take skates off when on school property.

19. Be a role model. Always wear safety gear when you are instructing. Be an advocate for your students by providing resources on in-line skating such as information about skate parks, magazines, websites, etc.

20. A unique program developed by Rollerblade and the National Association for Sport and Physical Education (NASPE) called Skate in School is currently in nearly 500 schools nationwide. This program offers skates and equipment at a special school price, innovative lesson plans for grades K-12, tips on fund raising and equipment maintenance, and optional in-service instruction for teachers and students by certified instructors. For more information, contact *www.skateinschool.com*

Selection and Conduct of the Activity

Procedural

1. Follow the local administrative process to have in-line skating formally adopted as a part of the school district's physical education curriculum. Many school districts

have a risk management department, and they need to have input to ensure that all safety concerns have been addressed and that teachers and students are covered by the school district's insurance policy. One of the primary goals of a quality physical education is to teach students activities that will encourage them to lead active, healthy lifestyles throughout their lives. Inline skating is an appropriate activity for students in grades K -12. Many of our National Standards for Physical Education (NASPE, 1995) can be supported through an inline skating program.

2. Send a letter home to parents regarding your inline skating curriculum. This letter should include specifics related to content, progressions, assessment, and safety concerns. Inform parents that all safety equipment will be provided by the school. If a student wants to bring his or her own helmet, make clear that the helmet must fit snugly or one from the physical education department will be issued to the student prior to skating.

3. Continue the written planning process with careful attention and detail to the progression of skills. Develop a rubric for these skills and assess students on their ability to demonstrate each skill. You can use the following fundamental skills and develop self, peer, and/or teacher assessments to work toward mastery:

   - How to fall safely
   - Posture
   - Stance
   - Stroke
   - Glide
   - Stopping
     1. Brake
     2. T- stop
     3. Y- stop
     4. Hockey stop (advanced)
   - Turning
   - Connecting turns
   - Crossover turns
   - Backward skating
   - Forward to backward skating
   - Backward to forward skating

   Determine the critical elements of all the skills you want to teach and develop assessments such as this one to hold students accountable for learning and documenting student achievement. (See Diagram 1.)

4. Use a number of teaching models for delivering instruction. These models should define the tasks clearly, provide for an ample amount of quality practice, help to

keep students on-task, and provide a solid accountability system. Direct instruction allows the teacher to provide clear goals to students, sufficient time for practice, monitoring of student practice, feedback opportunities, and student accountability. Task/station teaching is one model that can be used to create different tasks to allow for individual differences. Evaluation at these stations can be a combination of self, peer, and/or teacher assessments. Reciprocal/peer teaching is another effective method for enhancing the teaching/learning process. In this model, students are put into small groups of similar abilities where they provide instruction, feedback, and support for one another. With any teaching model, expectations must be set by the teacher regarding specific cues to improve performance, outcomes, and student responsibility.

Diagram 1. Assessing Skill Progressions

Inline Skating Assessment

Names	Fall	Posture	Stance	Stroke	Glide	Brake	T-stop	Y-stop	H-stop	Turning	Link turns	B Skate	Frd-B skate	B-frd skate

5. Listed below are some sample benchmarks for assessing national physical education standards (NASPE, 1995) #1 and #5. My students and I generated a holistic rubric and benchmarks to align with these standards. These benchmarks were developed to keep students accountable in both skill and affective domains. The criteria for these benchmarks are as follows:

4= Advanced

3=Proficient

2=Partially Proficient

1=Needs Improvement

Sample benchmarks for standard #1. Demonstrates competency in many movement forms and proficiency in a few movement forms.

1. Demonstrates the ability to maintain personal space while moving

   4. Avoids crowding and others at all times while skating

   3. Avoids crowding and others most of the time while skating

   2. Skates in and out of groups of others

   1. Skates in groups or close to others regardless of traffic

2. Anticipates traffic and avoids colliding with others

   4. Skates defensively and reacts to conditions at all times

   3. Skates defensively and avoids others most of the time

   2. Follows other skaters too closely and is unaware of potential hazards

   1. Is unaware of other skaters and does not follow safety protocol

3. Varies speed according to traffic

   4. Skates under control at all times and makes adjustments for traffic conditions

   3. Skates under control most of the time and sees traffic conditions develop

   2. Skates at a speed that is not safe for traffic conditions

   1. Skates in and out of potential hazards regardless of traffic conditions

4. Demonstrates the ability to stop on a signal

   4. Can stop under control within two seconds of a signal

   3. Can stop under control within three seconds of a signal

   2. Can stop under control within three seconds of a signal most of the time

   1. Can stop under control within three seconds of a signal some of the time

Sample benchmarks for standard # 5. Demonstrates responsible personal and social behavior in physical activity settings.

1. Uses equipment and space safely and properly.

4. Takes care of equipment and follows safety protocol at all times

3. Takes care of equipment and follows safety protocol most of the time

2. Is careless with equipment and is reminded of protocol infractions frequently

1. Does not handle equipment in a responsible manner and does not follow safety protocol

2. Demonstrates etiquette by assisting other with equipment

4. Assists another student prior to skating and assists another student after skating

3. Usually assists another student prior to skating

2. Assists another student after being reminded by the teacher

1. Tries to skate without offering assistance to anyone

6. Assess students performing the basic fundamentals and progress only when mastery of a skill is evident. Too often we make assumptions regarding our audiences without documenting specifics. It is usually surprising how many students believe they are proficient skaters who really lack the basic skills of stopping and avoiding others.

7. Develop a body of evidence that demonstrates students are meeting the benchmarks that support the standards.

8. Provide both verbal and written cues on the fundamental skills to be mastered.

Safety

9. Provide safety gear for all students and require that they always wear it (see Figure 1.) Instructors should always wear safety equipment as well. Encourage your students to purchase safety gear and wear it whenever they skate. Many injuries have occurred due to the fact that no safety gear was being worn. If you provide helmets that other students will be using, always provide the student with a barrier (e.g., surgeon caps) between their head and the helmet to prevent the transmission of head lice.

10. Have students, prior to skating, assist another student until he/she is "skate ready." This is a timesaving method for getting students rolling.

11. Teach your students how to fall safely without their skates on. Instruct them to fall to their knees (so that the plastic in the pad cushions the fall) and then slide to their hands, ending in a prone position. The plastic brace in the wrist guard, which crosses the palm of the hand, helps protect the wrist, carpals, and metacarpals. The most common injuries from skating are sprained or broken wrists. Many of these injuries would have been prevented if wrist guards had been worn.

12. Provide both verbal and written safety warnings about the risks of inline skating.

13. Teach indoor inline skating as a progression for outdoor skating. Environmental concerns can make it more difficult for beginning skaters to be successful. However, if you do not have mats, a grassy area or a carpeted area are great places to teach beginning skaters.

14. The following Rules of the Road were developed by the International Inline Skating Association. Post these rules and send a copy of them home to parents.

    • Wear safety equipment: wrist guards, knee and elbow pads, and a helmet.

    • Stay alert and be courteous at all times.

    • Control your speed.

    • Skate on the right side of paths, trails, and sidewalks.

    • Overtake other pedestrians, cyclists, and skaters on the left. Use extra caution and announce your intentions by saying, "Passing on your left." Pass only when it is safe and when you both have enough room for the full extension position of your stroke.

    • Be aware of changes in trail conditions, and hazards such as water, potholes, or storm debris. When in doubt, slow down. Do not skate on wet or oily surfaces.

    • Obey all traffic regulations. When on skates, you have the same obligations as a moving vehicle.

    • Stay out of areas with heavy automobile traffic.

    • Always yield to pedestrians.

    • Before using any trail, achieve a basic skill level, including the ability to turn, control speed, brake going down hills, and recognize and avoid skating obstacles.

15. Always have students warm up prior to skating. Proper warm-up should elevate the heart rate slightly, increase the flow of blood to the muscles, and increase temperature to prepare the muscles for exercise. Flexibility of key muscle groups can decrease the risk and severity of serious injuries by increasing the ability of the muscles to extend and improving joint motion. Strengthening exercises such as lunges, squats, toe raises, jumps, and abdominal work are critical to a proper warm-up for inline skating.

Environmental Concerns

Equipment
Inline skates are relatively low-maintenance, which is one of the appealing attributes of the sport. However, to get the highest performance and the most enjoyment out of their skates, students will need to complete a few maintenance procedures on a daily basis. It is also recommended that students be taught how to perform inspections on all of the equipment prior to skating. This system will hopefully prevent students from using any equipment that may need repair.

Bearing Maintenance

Bearings need to be kept clean to maintain their top performance. If they get wet, it is advisable to remove both bearings and the bearing spacer from each wheel and wipe them dry. Bearings do wear out with use. One indication of wear is a grinding noise coming from the bearing when the wheel is rolling. This noise is the result of breakdown of the grease that the bearings are packed in, or of sand, rust particles, or some other foreign material getting into the bearing casing. Buying a new set of bearings is not costly and is much easier than rebuilding an old set. Some bearings are non-serviceable.

Wheel Rotation or Replacement

Wheels wear down while skating. The wheels have a tendency to wear down on the inside of the foot. Proper rotation is necessary in order to get the maximum mileage. Wheel wear is influenced by many factors, including skating surface, skater's weight, skating style and activity, and the quality of the wheel. Rotating the wheels involves changing the wheel's position on the frame and turning the wheels over so that the inside edge becomes the outside edge. Wheel rotation is the most common maintenance task skaters will perform on their skates. However, sometimes the wheels are so worn they must be replaced altogether.

A wheel needs to be rotated when it starts to look worn along the inside edges. Rotate the #1 wheel to the #3 position, # 2 wheel to #4 position, #3 wheel to #1 position, and #4 wheel to #2 position (see Figure 2.) If your skates have three or five wheels, simply rotate the most worn wheels to the wheels that show the least amount of wear. Be sure to rotate the wheels regularly to prevent them from wearing out prematurely. A severely worn wheel can be dangerous because it could cause the frame of the skate to contact the ground, resulting in a fall.

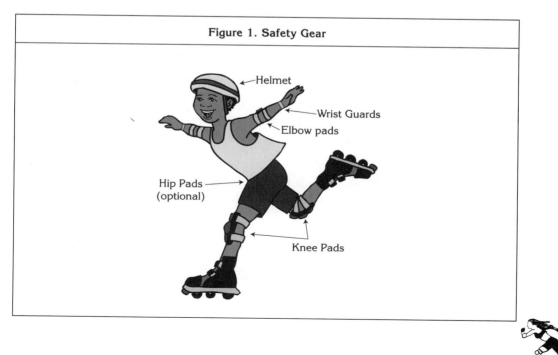

Figure 1. Safety Gear

Brake Replacement

Check the wear on your brake pad before and after every use. Brake pads have a "wear line" that indicates how much life is left in the brake. Brake pads should be replaced prior to reaching the "wear line indicator." The brake can be put on either skate; a gray brake should be used indoors. Check to ensure that the brake pad is firmly attached.

Skates

Students should always check their skates to be sure that there are no sharp edges protruding that could damage the floor (inexpensive skates tend to have sharp protrusions). Spray skates with a disinfectant after each use and require students to bring a clean pair of athletic socks every time they skate. Skates should fit snugly to prevent blisters and to improve overall performance. Mark all skates with a white permanent marker on the back so that they are quickly identified.

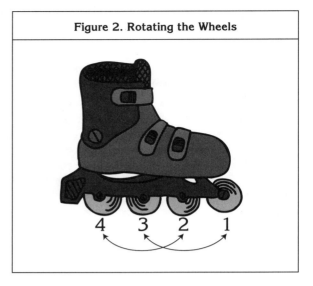

Figure 2. Rotating the Wheels

4   3   2   1

Safety gear

Helmet

There are few helmets made specifically for inline skating. Look for one that has been approved by either of the two national helmet-testing bodies, SNELL or ANSI (American National Standards Institute). Spray helmets with a disinfectant after every use.

Knee Pads and Elbow Pads

Be sure that this safety gear has the hard plastic shield over the pad and check for worn straps.

Wrist Guards

The most common inline skating injury is sprained or broken wrists. The plastic brace that inserts in wrist guards has a tendency to slip out. Make sure this brace is always in place prior to skating.

Facilities

Indoor

1. Be certain that there is a safe distance between the skating area and any walls, equipment, windows, and other structures. Provide a safety barrier like matting whenever possible to prevent students from falling into a stationary object.

2. Post written warnings and safety rules at all times.

3. Be certain that the skating surface is free from debris, water, or any other hazard.

4. Check the skating surface for any wear from a skate or brake.

5. Inspect the gymnasium floor daily for scratches or black marks. Black heel brakes leave marks on the floor that can be rubbed out. Rollerblade offers a gray brake pad specifically for indoor use. Inexpensive skates sometimes have protruding nuts or bolts that will damage a floor.

Outdoor

1. Be certain that students are not grinding on hand rails, benches, and other structures.

2. Students need to be warned of the potential hazards of uneven surfaces, gravel, and sidewalks.

3. Be aware that tennis court surfaces can be ruined by inline skaters.

4. Blocking off a flat parking area would be the ideal space. Try to avoid any area that motorists are using.

5. If students get water or dirt in their bearings, the bearings will need to be lubricated.

6. Maintain equipment when used outside. Have students help to maintain and clean skates after use.

7. Be certain that students know and understand the Rules of the Road.

In-Line Skating Resources

Safety

American Society For Testing and Materials (ASTM)
100 Barr Harbor Drive
Consohocken, PA 19428-2959
T: (610) 832-9500
F: (610) 832-9555

American National Standards Institute (ANSI)
11 W 42 Street, 13th floor
New York, NY 10036
T: (212) 642-4900
F: (212) 302-1286
www.ansi.org

Bicycle Helmet Safety Institute (BHSI)
4611 Seventh Street South
Arlington, VA 22204
T: (703) 486-0100
F: (703) 486-0576
www.bhsi.org

International Inline Skating Association (IISA)
150 South 7th St.
Wilmington, NC 28401
T: (910) 762-7004
F: (910) 762-9477
www.iisa.org

U.S. Consumer Product Safety Commission (CPSC)
Washington, DC 20207
T: (301) 504-0424
F: (301) 504-0124
Info@cpsc.gov

National Safe Kids Campaign
1301 Pennsylvania Avenue, NW
Suite 1000
Washington, DC 20004-1707
T: (202) 662-0600
F: (202) 393-2072
www.safekids.org

Protective Headgear Manufactures' Association (PHMA)
15750 Concord Circle
Morgan Hill, CA 95037
T: (408) 779-6229 x 2327
F: (408) 776-7733

Rollerblade, Inc.
5101 Shady Oak Road
Minnetonka, MN 55343
T: (800) 328-0171
www.rollerblade.com

Snell Memorial Foundation, Inc.
3628 Madison Avenue
Suite 11
North Highlands, CA 95660
T: (916) 331-5073
F: (916) 331-0359
snellit@aol.com

Sports Leagues and Associations

Aggressive Skaters Association
171 Pier Avenue
Suite 247
Santa Monica, CA 90405
T: (310) 399-3436
F: (310) 581-3552
asa@aggroskate.com

National Inline Basketball League
135 Rivington Street, #3F
New York, NY 10002
T: (212) 539-1132
F: (212) 539-1133
www.nibbl.com

National Roller Hockey LLC (NARCH)
3830 Broadway, Suite 35
Boulder, CO 80304
T: (303) 786-8764
F: (303) 546-0581
kdluff@aol.com

Roller Hockey International ~Amateur
249 East Ocean Boulevard, Suite 8000
Long Beach, CA 90802
T: (562) 628-0590
F: (562) 628-0524

USA Hockey Inline
4965 North 30th Street
Colorado Springs, CO 80919
T: (719) 599-5500
F: (719) 599-5994
usah@usahockey.com

USA Inline Racing
P.O. Box 162055
Altamonte Springs, FL 32716-2055
T: (407) 682-2328
F: (407) 682-2388
www.usainline.org

USA Rollerskating
4730 South St.
Lincoln, NE 68506
T: (402) 483-7551
www.usacrs.com

Books

Baum, Stephen. (1997). *How to inline skating flipbook series,* 24 pp. Spiral-bound pocket-sized references illustrate technique for all skating levels.

Heeley, Mark. (1996). *1st inline.* 128 pp. Full-color large-format book with excellent illustrations of equipment, technique, and maintenance.

Millar, Cam, & Curtis, Bruce. (1996). *Inline skating basics.* 96 pp. Plenty of step-by-step instructional color photographs geared toward the recreational skater.

Miller, Liz. (1998). *Get Rolling* (2nd ed.). Expanded edition of one of the first inline how-to books. Now with photographs.

Nottingham, Suzanne, & Fedel, Fred. (1997). *Fitness inline skating,* 176 pp. Book includes 48 different workouts grouped across six different training zones of increasing difficulty.

National Association for Sport and Physical Education. (1995). *Moving Into the Future: National Standards for Physical Education.* Reston, VA: Author.

Powell, Mark & Svensson, John. (1993). *Inline skating,* 127 pp. Black and white photographs, drawings, and text that introduce the reader to all facets of inline skating.

References

International Inline Skating Association (IISA)
150 South 7th St.
Wilmington, NC 28401
www.iisa.org

Rollerblade, Inc.
5101 Shady Oak Road
Minnetonka, MN 55343
(800) 328-0171
www.rollerblade.com

CHAPTER 16

Lacrosse

Kim Hutcherson
Holton-Arms School
Bethesda, Maryland

Introduction - Major Risks and Dangers

Lacrosse is a fast-paced and challenging sport. As the sport has grown in popularity, the level and intensity of the competition has risen. Because there is rapid growth in the sport, the number of injuries at all levels has also increased. Indeed, the nature of the sport involves using an implement (stick) to project an object (ball) to a teammate. This can place an inherent danger and a risk of injury to the participants. However, risks can be minimized with proper instruction and supervision.

Even though the current injury studies show that the ankle, knee, nose, and orbit are the most common areas of injury in lacrosse, the rules of girls' lacrosse and the restrictions of most physical education classes mandate only a mouth guard as protection for the field players. Therefore, proper safety planning must be implemented to help keep injuries to a minimum. At the very least, players should be instructed to mold their mouth guards properly and to keep them in their mouths at all times. Additionally, players should be encouraged to use protective eyewear.

The most obvious risk for injury in lacrosse is the ball hitting a player. Lacrosse is an aerial game based on the natural abilities of running, catching, and throwing. Because the game is played in the air, players need to be alert and aware at all times. Passers need to receive proper instruction on safe passing, and participants should not walk through a passing drill to retrieve a ball.

Players also risk injury if inappropriate body contact is made. Body contact is not allowed in girls' lacrosse or in physical education classes. Incidental contact will take place on occasion during games; however, players must be encouraged not to initiate rough play. No horseplay should be allowed during practices, either.

The stick can cause a major injury to the opponent. Risk can be minimized in this area by all players wearing a properly molded mouth guard. In addition, a coach should only allow stick checking in practice when the players have achieved a high enough level of skill to successfully control their sticks.

A fourth area of risk for injury is poor equipment or playing facilities. The teacher should inspect the playing facilities and equipment on a regular basis to ensure the safety of the students. Substandard equipment should be repaired or replaced. Any ongoing concerns should be reported to the proper authority.

Teachers of the sport can minimize the risk of injury by planning practices or lessons appropriately. If the teacher has no prior playing experience or exposure to lacrosse, he or she should become familiar with the sport prior to commencing the activity. Teachers or supervisors of the activity should be knowledgeable in the basic skills and progressions for the unit. Daily activities, focused on the age and ability level of the participants involved, should be planned in advance with a logical, sequential progression. It is important for classes to be well-organized and for teachers to have all students in their visual field. All drills should be administered with the safety of the students in mind, and proper safety guidelines must be enforced at all times.

Lacrosse is a wonderful sport and will be a safe experience for the participants if planning is done in advance. Fundamentally, it is the responsibility of the teachers/coaches, players, umpires and spectators to keep the sport as safe as possible.

Supervision

The role of the supervisor during a lacrosse unit is to provide safe competition for each student. The following is a list of the necessary skills needed by a supervisor and an organizational plan to ensure a safe experience for all students.

Necessary Skills and Knowledge of Supervisor

The coach must be a teacher, motivator, and leader who possesses good organizational skills. She/he must be able to teach the fundamentals, analyze each player's strengths and weaknesses, and make the necessary corrections. It is helpful if the instructor is able to demonstrate the various skills and concepts to the players. The following should provide a reference to educators as they plan a lacrosse unit:

1. Only instructors who have knowledge of current rules, skills, playing techniques, and ethics of the sport should supervise the activity.

2. Instructors have a responsibility to see that risks are minimal.

3. The lacrosse unit should be planned in advance of the activity.

4. The instructor should teach a logical skill progression based on the ability of the participants.

5. The instructor should be able to analyze players' skills and make corrections when necessary. He/she should know the capabilities of each student.

6. Conditioning methods should be sequential and appropriate to the fitness level of the athlete.

7. The instructor should have knowledge in basic injury prevention and first aid and should be able to administer basic emergency care if needed.

8. An emergency plan should be in place for any unforeseen injuries.

9. An organized record-keeping system should be in place.

10. The instructor should be aware of any inherent risks in the sport and make the participants aware of them as well.

11. Students must be closely supervised and rules must be consistently enforced.

Organization and Control

The following are guidelines the instructor should follow in supervising a lacrosse class:

1. Make sure each participant has a current physical examination on record. Make note of each student's medical history, prior injuries, and limitations.

2. Injured student athletes should not return to class or practice until written clearance from an attending physician has been received.

3. A stocked medical kit, ice, and water should be available at all times.

4. Arrive at the teaching area prior to the students and remain in the area until all students have departed. No students should begin the activity prior to the teacher's arrival.

5. A system should be in place for student athletes to transport equipment from the storage area prior to the activity and to return it after the activity.

6. Students should be warned of the inherent risks in the sport. Safety rules should be discussed and consistently enforced on a regular basis. Failure to do so can result in dangerous play.

7. The class should be organized so that the instructor has all participants in an unobstructed field of vision. All students should be observable at all times.

8. Try to anticipate accidents before they happen. Make sure the students are in control of their sticks.

9. The students should be made aware of the danger of balls left lying around on the playing field or gymnasium.

10. Begin and end each class with a proper warm-up that includes a stretching session.

11. Keep student athletes within the scope of their abilities. Progress from simple to complex.

12. Students should only be practicing the particular skill that is being specified. They should not be working on something different from the rest of the group unless the teacher has directed them to do so and has made appropriate organizational adjustments.

Selection and Conduct of Activity

The conduct of the activity should be based on the readiness and ability level of the participants. Maturity level, age, and size should be taken into account when developing a comprehensive lacrosse unit plan. The following should serve as guidelines in planning:

1. Develop comprehensive unit and lesson plans. There should be a logical progression of instruction and skill development from simple to complex that leads to enhanced player knowledge and ability. Goals, objectives, and assessment measures should be identified for each lesson.

2. Pair students by weight, maturity, and experience. Lessons should be structured that are appropriate for the age, maturity level, and developmental differences of the participants.

3. Post policies and regulations for good order and safety. Disallow use of dangerous techniques (e.g., stick checking). Instructors must control reckless behavior by the participants and should emphasize stick control and proper follow-through.

4. Students should be given a proper warm-up prior to the activity, and conditioning should be built up gradually. A proper cool-down should follow the activity.

5. Make your instructions clear and provide demonstrations of skills. Feedback and corrections are critical for the learning process. Consistent terminology should be used when introducing skill techniques.

6. Structure activities based on ability level. It is often helpful to group students of like ability. Make sure the activity presented is within the physical abilities of the students.

7. Stress fundamental skills prior to engaging students in more competitive activities. Try to individualize instruction as much as possible. Progress from basic to more advanced techniques.

8. Modify games or drills or adapt rules based on the level of the participants. Modifications could include using a softer ball or modifying the rules. Rules modifications could include the following:
   - No stick checking
   - No shooting
   - A three-second time limit for holding the ball
   - A certain number of passes prior to shooting

9. Students should be aware of body positioning and body control at all times. They should do the following:

- Transfer their weight when passing or shooting
- Bend from the knees and waist on ground ball pick ups
- Never attempt a ground ball pick up with the stick directly in front of the body
- Stay hip to hip when body marking
- Be under control when preparing for a stick check

10. The teaching area should be structured to ensure maximum safety for the students. When setting up drills, the instructor should carefully consider the placement of student groups. Drills should be structured in the same direction with adequate space between groups. The sun should be taken into consideration when locating groups.

11. Rules must be consistently enforced. Remind students that, in all but men's competitive play, lacrosse is a noncontact activity. Officiate games with safety in mind. It is recommended that the teacher officiate in game situations.

Environmental Concerns

Lacrosse is a quick-moving game that requires a safe environment for the participants. A procedure should be in place to create the safest possible environment.

Preparing in advance for adverse field conditions that lead to poor footing, or for extreme heat or humidity, or for other potentially dangerous weather conditions (such as rain or lightning) will foster a positive experience. The following checklists can be used to assess the condition of the facility and provide proper equipment for the activity.

Facilities

1. The instructor should walk the playing areas before activity, looking for holes, rocks, glass, or any other obstruction.

2. The playing field should be free of obstructions such as extra goal cages, benches, and bleachers.

3. Bleachers and benches should be inspected for splintering or jagged metal.

4. The grass should be an acceptable length.

5. Nonparticipants should be directed to a location that does not interfere with class activities.

6. Students should be positioned for practice so that they are not endangered by wild throws.

7. There should be adequate space between teaching stations or fields if multiple activities are taking place.

8. Drills should be positioned so the sun does not disrupt the vision of the players.

9. The playing field should be inspected for wet fields and puddles, which can lead to poor footing.

10. Facility constraints should be taken into account. If the activity is indoors instead of outdoors, care should be taken to direct the participants accordingly. If a lacrosse activity needs to take place indoors, care should be taken to instruct the students about the ball rebounding off the floor and the wall. Instructors should identify foreseeable causes of injury.

11. The number of goal cages and how they are best positioned for the activity should be considered.

12. Any conditions that the instructor cannot remedy should be reported in writing.

13. If unsafe conditions exist, make changes or stop the activity.

Equipment

1. Sticks should be inspected on a daily basis for cracks or broken strings.

2. Sticks should be a proper length for each participant. They should fit under the arm when the student is executing the overhand throw.

3. Each participant should wear protective eyewear and a mouth guard at all times.

4. If a goalkeeper is used during class, he or she must wear a helmet with a face guard, throat protector, chest protector, and mouth guard.

5. Goalkeeping equipment should be routinely sent out for safety checks.

6. The bottom supports of the goal cages must be padded the entire length with material that limits the rebound of the ball.

7. No hooks or fastening devices should be protruding from the goal cages toward the field of play.

8. Do not allow students to hang on the goal cages.

9. Damaged or outdated equipment should be discarded and replaced.

10. All unused equipment should be moved off the field of play.

Attire

1. Shoes should be properly fitted and appropriate to the activity. Tennis shoes should be used for indoor play, and rubber molded cleats or turf shoes should be used for outdoor play.

2. Clothing should be loose-fitting and comfortable.

3. Hair should be tied back and secured.

4. All jewelry should be removed.

Summary

Rules are regularly reviewed to address safety concerns. The addition of the mandatory yellow card for a check to the head and the eight-meter arc were added for safety reasons. The restraining line was introduced to limit the number of players around the goal area, reducing the chance of players getting hit by the ball.

US Lacrosse is currently investigating the improvement of safety in girls and women's lacrosse and is campaigning to get the crosse away from the head. Protective eyewear is already a requirement in some areas of the country, and US Lacrosse is working with manufacturers of protective eyewear to improve player vision on the field. They are also continuing to work on the development of appropriate soft headgear for medical needs. The NCAA has appointed a task force to examine the possibility of mandating protective eyewear in their championships. They have ruled to require the use of protective eyewear in championship play as soon as practicable.

Each educator has a responsibility for helping to keep the game of lacrosse safe for the participants, but it takes a team effort to keep the sport safe. Coaches, players, umpires, and spectators must work together. Proper coaching methods and consistent officiating will help to foster a safe and enjoyable learning/playing experience.

CHAPTER 17

Orienteering

Jeanne O'Brien
Milford High School
Milford, New Hampshire

As in every activity when students venture out on their own to practice skills, there is risk of injury. In orienteering, the risk of injury is joined by the risk of becoming lost. Careful planning by the instructor, as well as proper instruction and skill acquisition, should minimize that risk so that everyone can enjoy a day of challenge in the outdoors.

Equipment

All equipment should be checked before a group begins any orienteering program. A compass that is broken or not working properly could spell disaster. An easy way to check a compass is to ask the students to point in the direction that their magnetic north arrow is pointing. Then, have them turn 180 degrees and repeat the process. Any compass that is not working properly or that has reversed polarity should be returned to the vendor or disposed of. Older compasses often lose some of their dampening fluid. They can still be used; however, too large a bubble in the housing will affect the movement of the needle. When this happens, the compass should be thrown out.

All compasses should have lanyards attached to minimize the chance of losing them. Students should be required to wear a whistle attached to a lanyard that can be worn around the neck or the wrist. The whistle is to be used only in an emergency. Three repeated short blasts of the whistle are a summons for help; a single short blast identifies the searcher who has heard the summons and wants it repeated for location.

Before starting out, students should plan what they will take with them. A first aid kit as well as other supplies should be packed in a bright-colored daypack or a fanny pack.

Following is a list of the more essential items:

- large gauze pads, adhesive tape, and butterfly bandages for large cuts
- matches in a waterproof container
- safety pins
- a knife
- a large bandanna or triangular bandage
- water in a canteen or plastic bottle
- small mirrors made of metal (for signaling purposes)
- a candle
- nylon wind or rain pants or a poncho
- needle and nylon thread
- a small flashlight with alkaline batteries
- an extra map of the area and an extra compass
- cell phone, if possible
- a loud whistle

Preparing the map is essential to successful travel. Sometimes maps can be purchased with the magnetic north lines already in place. However, most of the time they need to be drawn by the orienteer. Instruct students that, when drawing their own lines, it is important to remember that the U.S. Geological Survey warns that the diagram pictured on the margin of their maps is only an approximation of the actual number printed next to the magnetic north arrow. This number is accurate for the year printed just below the diagram. The angle of declination may change over time and may be off by as much as one degree for every five years. The current deviation for an area can be obtained by calling the National Cartographic Information Center, Reston, Virginia. The toll free number is 1-800-USA-Maps.

As students draw magnetic north lines on their maps, they must be careful not to cover any important symbols. Whenever possible, they should use a piece of clear plastic with a straight edge to draw the lines so that symbols along the line can be seen. They should leave a break in the line where symbols occur. Further, when drawing circles for control points, students should skip a space if any symbols would be obscured. Finally, they should make sure that they draw lines and circles for control points with ink that is not water-soluble.

Supervision

The whole point of orienteering is to test skills in an unfamiliar area. Therefore, the instructor may not be able to visually supervise students during the activity. When students are first mastering the basic map and compass skills, activities should be planned so that the instructor can observe the students constantly. Careful attention should be paid to each student's ability to navigate with a map and compass. Only those students who have mastered the skills should be allowed to venture out of sight. When students are ready to progress to a course where they are out of visual contact, an area should be established where these students can find help if they need it. This base area should be in a central location near prominent and recognizable features such as power lines, roads, or on top of a hill so that it is easy for a student to find.

Conduct of the Activity

Comprehensive preliminary instruction and safety training is essential to the sport of orienteering. Students need to practice and master skills before being allowed to head out on a course on their own. Besides map and compass knowledge, it is also important that they have an understanding of basic survival techniques and safety procedures. Not only will this knowledge increase their confidence in the field, it will improve their ability to survive should they become lost for an extended period of time. An introductory survival course should include information on the following:

- How to treat an injury or sudden illness
- Building a shelter
- Conserving energy and body temperature
- Foraging for food
- Finding safety in a storm
- Signaling for help
- How to remain calm and wait for help
- How to assist in a search

One method to determine a student's fitness for a more difficult course is to use the beginner Compass Game available from Orienteering Services USA, P.O. Box 1604, Binghamton, NY 13902. This game may be played in any open area of approximately 100 x 100 feet. To play, the participant must be able to find directions with a compass. Determination of distance is not necessary. There are 90 courses, using eight labeled markers placed at exact spots in a large circle.

While playing the game, all players are contained in the circle. This game makes it easy to identify the students who have mastered the skill and those who are struggling. As students complete the game, they must report to the instructor to determine if the courses they have charted are correct. If their courses are correct, it is helpful to place those students' names at the top of a list and then ask them to help those students who are still having difficulty. When finished, the instructor will have a rank order list of most to least proficient. Orienteering teams of three can be formed by taking one person from the top, the middle, and the bottom of the list. Groups of three are the best method for sending students out on an orienteering course. When there are three in a group and one person becomes incapacitated, the second member of the group can remain with that person while the third member goes for help. Groups larger than three provide a similar safety margin, but the size may result in less involvement for some of the students.

When designing an orienteering experience, the instructor should consider the following factors: the participants' age, experience, and skill; weather conditions; and time of year. The orienteering course should be designed so that it is challenging but at the same time possible for the least skilled of the group to negotiate successfully and in a timely manner. Before allowing students to venture out on a course, the instructor should record what that student is wearing and other information to help identify them should they become lost. Boundaries for the course, return times, collection areas, and guidelines for keeping the group together should be firmly established before a group heads out. A procedure should be developed concerning cancellation due to storms or other emergencies. Students should know ahead of time how to break off the activity and head for the nearest collection area. Make sure that orienteers understand what to do in the event of severe thunderstorms with frequent lightning.

Prior to beginning an orienteering course, students should be taught to orient themselves to a larger geographic area. This can be accomplished by using a large wall map that covers an area greater than the orienteering course map. Prominent mountains with specific shapes can serve as gross reference points. Identify any off-limits or dangerous areas and the farthest limits students should go. For example, there might be a long straight road on one side, a river on the other, and a power line on the third side. Any student who travels far enough in a straight line will end up at one of these catching features or handrails. If there are no catching features or handrails available, then teach the students to trust their compass to get them close to their destination or back to where they started. Students should be instructed that if they get seriously lost, they should hike downhill if possible until they come to a stream or a trail. Water usually leads to civilization.

The sun can also be of help for a lost orienteer. Before going out, students should observe the position of the sun in the sky and the direction their shadows cast. Discuss the approximate direction the sun will be in two to three hours from the start. Even after the sun has set, the western part of the sky will remain lighter for several hours, providing a direction point.

Emergency Situations and Lost Students

The fact that students are in the field navigating with a map and compass means that they have a valuable survival skill. However, they are also more likely to go out on their own and venture farther upfield.

When students have not returned at the expected time, the instructor must take into consideration several possibilities. The students may be lost, or if they are unreliable, they may have abandoned the course. Regardless, an unaccounted-for person can create an urgent situation that requires a response in the form of search procedures. A delay of two hours instead of one in beginning a search means that the search area will be four times larger. Figure 1 illustrates the effect of time on a search.

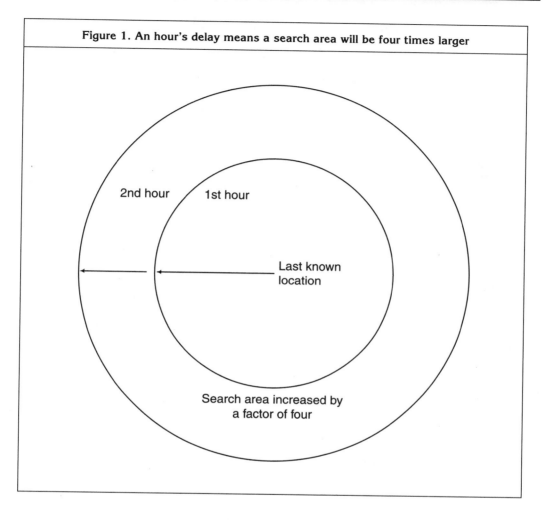

Figure 1. An hour's delay means a search area will be four times larger

2nd hour   1st hour

Last known
location

Search area increased by
a factor of four

When a search becomes necessary, the first action should be to designate the person in charge. This person stays in a central area and coordinates communication. Before sending anyone out to search, a missing person questionnaire should be filled out to assist the searchers in identifying the lost orienteer. Figure 2 is a sample questionnaire.

When beginning the search, send out a few people to patrol the perimeter of the search area. The searchers should travel in the fastest way possible, i.e., by car, boat, all-terrain bicycle, or on foot.

Figure 2. Missing Person Questionnaire

Name _____ Age_____ Sex_____ Race _____ Ht._____ Wt._____

Build _____ Hair_____ Length_____ Other_____

Shirt _____ Sweater/Jacket_____

Pants_____ Shoes_____

Hat_____ Gloves_____ Glasses_____

Raingear_____ Other_____

General Condition_____

Medical Problems_____

Psychological Problems _____

Handicaps_____ Medication_____

Smoke/Drink_____ Drugs _____

Outdoors Interest _____

Outgoing/Quiet _____ Hitchhike? _____ Ever Run Away?_____

Depression?_____ Give Up/Keep Going_____

Stop/Keep Moving _____ Other_____

Last Seen:Time_____ Place _____

By Whom_____ Direction_____

Reason for Leaving_____

Destination_____ Pickup?_____

Unusual Behavior_____

Pack_____ Tent _____ Sleeping Bag _____

Food _____ Drink_____ Map/Compass_____

Matches _____ Flashlight_____ Firearm _____ Camera_____

Other_____

Outdoor Skills _____

Familiar with area? _____

Ever out overnight? _____ Ever Lost Before?_____

Trails/Crosscountry_____

Talk to Strangers? _____ Accept Rides? _____ If Lost _____

Specific Fears/Interests _____

Other _____

Tendency to Hide? _____

Old Haunts, Special Places _____

Other _____

Anything Else?

Try to attract the lost person by ringing bells, blowing vehicle or air horns, or using whistles. This "attention getting" should be done in an open area so that the sound will travel better. Searchers should be careful not to make any sounds that could be mistaken for a series of three that would be the call for help from the lost orienteer. It is important to pause frequently to listen for a call from the lost student.

Confine the search area to as small an area as possible. If there are narrow, wooded areas where the lost student may wander through into larger, uncharted wilderness, searchers should be assigned to patrol these areas heavily.

Make certain that members of the search party understand to look for signs or clues of the missing person as well as the person. If searchers look only for the person, they may well miss the traces or other evidence that could concentrate the area of search and result in a quicker discovery.

If there is a high point from which most of the search area can be surveyed, assign at least two people to this point so that they can take turns surveying the area. It is recommended that binoculars be used only when a potential sighting has been made with the naked eye.

When someone has not been found after a reasonable search time, contact the person's home, friends' homes, favorite hangouts, and hospitals. The next step would be to contact the sheriff or police.

Once the decision to contact the police has been made, do not go into the search area again. Since tracking dogs may be used it is essential to keep the area free of extra people and scents. Further, any found clothing should not be handled so that the dogs can pick up the scent. If more than one person is lost, store their clothing separately.

When the police arrive, they will interview the instructor, scan the area, and call a rescue team. In some cases, the instructor and orienteers will be asked to participate in the search since they have the most immediate knowledge of the area and persons lost. The decision whether to allow students to participate is a difficult one. Wherever possible, students should be paired up with experienced rescuers.

For more information on search and rescue techniques, write to NASAR, Post Office Box 50178, Washington, DC 20004.

After reading this chapter, one might feel that orienteering is too risky to offer in a physical education program. On the contrary, the very skills acquired in this course develop the confidence in students to handle emergency situations. Further, properly taught skills and attention to safety procedures greatly reduce the risk for student participants. In most cases, students who lose their way have the skills necessary to find it again. As for the instructor, the knowledge and skills gained from this chapter should increase their confidence in developing a safe and enjoyable orienteering experience for their students.

CHAPTER 18

Self-Defense

Kenneth Tillman
The College of New Jersey
Ewing, New Jersey

Teaching a self-defense class in any setting requires strict observance of safety procedures. This principle is particularly true in the secondary school situation, where students are in their adolescent years and are striving for recognition. In most physical education activities, recognition comes from excelling through execution of skills and contest performance. In self-defense classes, students are learning skills, but they cannot use them with full force either in or out of class unless in a situation where their personal safety is jeopardized. Accepting this important concept is the base upon which safety in a self-defense class is built.

In self-defense classes, two components go hand in hand. One is mental preparedness and the other is the ability to perform a variety of techniques, often in a controlled manner, so as not to cause injury to another student. Therefore, an extensive amount of time in a self-defense class must be spent on developing an attitude that accepts the serious implications that this course has for every participant and the danger of many of the self-defense skills when used with full force.

A proper mind-set must be established on the first day of a self-defense class and followed at each class meeting. Students are required to be aware of the dangers inherent in many of the skills learned and must be taught how these skills can be safely practiced in class. The challenge for a self-defense teacher is to teach skills that can be utilized at some future date in a situation where personal danger is present. It is sometimes difficult for an adolescent to internalize future benefits from a physical education activity when they are not even permitted to use full force when learning the skill.

The key is to instill in each student the proper attitude toward the activity. Students should have a different view of self-defense from their view of other activities included in a physical education program, which are learned to develop competency in performing an activity for recreational and/or competitive purposes. In self-defense, it is hoped that the techniques learned will never need to be used.

Ingrain in your students an understanding of the serious consequences that can result if they approach the learning of self-defense skills in a flippant manner. They must accept the fact that the skills they are learning can cause serious injury, even death. It is imperative, therefore, that they follow all safety precautions established in the class.

As part of the instructional approach, the teaching emphasis will be that self-defense skills are to be used only as a last-resort technique. Avoidance of dangerous situations, fleeing when threatened, and discouraging an assailant must precede the use of physical force. This concept is important for students to accept if they are to participate safely. A macho attitude has no place in a self-defense class.

The tenor of the class should be cooperation in developing skills, not competing against another person. The skills are being developed for protection. Practice can be safe, even though the techniques will be damaging to an assailant if they are used in a life-threatening situation.

Classes should be structured to maximize safeguards against injury. Many physical skills such as falling, striking, and throwing are incorporated into self-defense skills. It is important for the safety of the students that they develop a good kinesthetic awareness, particularly before practicing some of the advanced techniques. Students who know how to fall properly, know basic tumbling techniques, and gain confidence in their physical ability not only will be able to better defend themselves, but also will be able to participate safely in a self-defense class.

Supervision

The possibility of injury will be significantly reduced by following appropriate supervisory procedures. Both general and specific supervision has to be present. A proper class setting has the entire class in view of the instructor. Safety procedures established for the class must be understood and followed by every member of the class. Established practice procedures must be adhered to at all times, and individual assistance must be provided when difficult skills are being learned. It is mandatory that skills of a sequential nature be learned step by step so the instructor can make corrections and assist in proper positioning and techniques throughout the execution of the skill.

Strict class control is critical for this activity because many of the skills that are being learned are designed to disable an antagonist. It is necessary to enforce practice procedures that provide safety for all participants in the class. An improperly executed technique could injure either the student practicing the skill or the student who is in the role of the attacker.

Aggressiveness must be controlled when practicing dangerous tactics. Blows, striking, and kicking must never be done at full force against another member of the class. Dummies, or other items such as pillows, should be used in a simulated attack situation when force is necessary to get the "feel" of proper execution of a self-defense skill.

Appropriate instructor supervision requires the following:

1. An instructor must be in the activity area at all times when students are present.

2. An activity area that provides an unobstructed view of all participants is important.

3. The instructor must be aware of each student throughout the class.

4. The instructor should be with students who are trying difficult skills for the first time.

5. The instructor should be knowledgeable in all the skills that are being taught and ensure that proper progressions are being followed.

6. Students should practice only the skills designated by the teacher.

7. Students should be taught how to assist their partners when practicing skills. Student understanding of the intricacies and dangers of the skills will increase overall class safety and assist the instructor in carrying out supervisory responsibilities.

8. It is important that the instructor knows the capabilities of each student in the class and adjusts class requirements to the psychological and motor readiness of the students.

9. It is important that students are comfortable with the instructor and are willing to seek assistance when needed.

10. The instructor should secure the instructional area when class is not in session.

11. Students should be permitted to practice self-defense techniques only in properly matted areas.

12. Safety procedures should be included in the class syllabus, and these procedures should be given to the students.

13. Class safety procedures should be emphasized on a regular basis.

14. Detailed lesson plans should be prepared and followed during each class period.

15. Potential dangers, both in the environmental setting for the class and in the class presentation, should be eliminated as part of the class planning process.

Selection and Conduct of Activities

Self-defense tactics are designed for protection from a violent action and to thwart an attacker; they are not governed by rules designed for safe participation. It is particularly important, therefore, that the activity be conducted using specialized safety procedures. This poses an interesting dichotomy. Skills are selected because of their potential to disable an attacker, and yet the teaching procedures must be designed to provide extra protection to make the learning process safe.

The self-defense skill that is being learned will dictate the safety procedure that should be followed. Certain guidelines apply at all times; others are specific to specialized tactics such as delivering a blow or throwing an attacker.

General

1. Each session should begin with warm-ups. Many self-defense tactics require explosive action and sudden movements. Warm-up is important to prevent muscle pulls and ready the body for strenuous activity.

2. Students must be physically capable of handling the rigors of executing self-defense techniques. A physical fitness unit is a good preliminary step to starting a self-defense class.

3. Incorporate physical fitness into your self-defense unit so the students will have strength, flexibility, and muscle suppleness to minimize the possibility of injury.

4. Competency in basic tumbling skills is a prerequisite to learning falling and throwing techniques. Students should, at a minimum, be able to do forward, backward, shoulder, and forward dive rolls.

5. A key ingredient for successfully defending oneself when confronted with an attacker is to have confidence in one's mental and physical abilities. It is, therefore, important to spend class time on psychological preparedness as well as on developing physical skills. Many students have limited understanding of either their physical or mental capabilities. By incorporating motor skill and physical fitness activities, students will gain greater confidence in themselves and their ability to survive in a dangerous situation.

6. Tapping is the universal signal to stop. This signal must be respected by all members of the class and the hold broken immediately if a participant taps the mat, partner, or herself/himself.

7. Establish safety rules and make sure the rules are understood and followed.

8. Emphasis should not be on trying to prove that moves work, but rather on learning the techniques.

9. Proper progression is important. Start with basic skills and use these as the basis for more advanced techniques.

10. Regularly review basic skills to develop a firm foundation for the more difficult self-defense tactics.

11. Demand that students follow instruction consistently. Horseplay cannot be condoned.

12. The only techniques that should include contact with a partner are those that do not involve inherent risk of injury.

13. Practice in a large area on surfaces having at least the resiliency of a wrestling mat.

14. The instructor should be able to demonstrate each skill that is being taught. It is important that the instructor know the dangers of each skill and be able to effectively impart this information to the students.

15. Work slowly when learning techniques. The skill must be learned before fast movements can be controlled during practice. Speed should be increased only as control is developed.

16. Never force a student to attempt a skill. Be sure the student has the necessary background before moving to new skills.

17. Do not permit the wearing of jewelry or other accessories during a self-defense class.

18. Comfortable physical education clothing that does not have buckles, snaps, or other items that can cause injury should be worn. Sneakers are the recommended footwear.

19. Safety and emergency procedures must be established and understood by the students. There should be access to a telephone, and emergency numbers should be posted.

Blows

1. Do not allow physical contact with a partner. This includes hand and foot blows.

2. Use padded dummies and other safe substitute targets such as rolled sleeping bags and playground balls when practicing blows.

3. Use imaginary opponents when using full force.

4. Make extensive use of simulation drills when practicing the various blows.

5. Emphasize the destructive nature of the blows that are being learned and the importance of treating dangerous techniques with respect.

6. Never try to prove that a disabling blow works. Emphasize learning correct techniques for maximum effect.

Holds

1. Never allow students to apply full force to a hold.

2. Do not allow the use of fast or jerky motions on an unsuspecting partner.

3. Be sure the partner is aware of the hold and knows how to react to prevent injury.

4. Instruct the class members to always go with the leverage when a hold is being applied.

5. Stop immediately when one partner taps to indicate pain.

Falling

1. Be sure that the students know how to do forward, backward, shoulder, and forward dive rolls before teaching falls.

2. Practice on thick mats to protect from injury.

3. Develop proper form by practicing each fall slowly. Speed up as the proper technique is learned. Learn the correct procedures to minimize impact when landing on the mat.

4. Follow proper progression when learning to fall.

5. Start falling from a low position (kneeling or squatting) and gradually increase the distance until the fall can be executed from a standing position.

Throws

1. Students should be thrown only after they have learned falling techniques and are able to fall correctly.

2. Simulate the throws many times before using a partner. Learn proper throwing techniques thoroughly.

3. Partners should be of a weight that the student can safely control when learning a throw.

4. Gradually increase the size of opponents as a student's skill increases.

5. Control skills are exceptionally important when making throws. Participants must be able to control their partner's body when throwing her/him to the mat. Throws should be executed gently and never with full force.

6. Instruct students as to when they should release their grip to prevent a partner from falling incorrectly.

7. Gradually increase the pace of the throws.

8. Make certain that there is a minimum of 75 square feet per pair of students when practicing throws. Other students must stay away from this area when throws are being practiced.

Environmental Conditions

Self-defense is a combative activity that requires an environment that will protect the participants when they fall or are thrown. Due to the vigorous nature of the activity, special consideration must be given to the floor surface that is provided. It is also valuable to have sufficient space so all members of the class can be practicing at the same time when the skills are being taught and practiced. Having a safe surrounding is the major consideration, but having a pleasant, clean class area also makes an important contribution to establishing a positive learning environment for self-defense.

Physical surroundings

1. An unobstructed matted area is needed. It is recommended that the mat have the resiliency of at least a wrestling mat.

2. The size of the class will determine the mat size that is needed. It is recommended that there be 45 square feet of mat surface for each student in the class. A minimum

of 75 square feet per pair of students is needed when practicing throws. Class members and/or room size may necessitate rotating groups to provide appropriate safety parameters.

3. Ten-foot circles, such as those painted on some practice wrestling mats, are ideal to use to keep satisfactory space between groups when practicing.

4. Wrestling rooms that have padded walls make good locations for teaching self-defense classes.

5. It is best to have one complete mat with the different sections taped together. Do not have small individual mats placed on the floor.

6. Any obstructions in the self-defense practice area should be matted.

7. Extra mats, including those of 6" and 8" in thickness, should be available when practicing falls and throws.

8. The mat area must be cleaned regularly.

Equipment

1. Partially deflated volleyballs and playground balls with target areas marked on them should be available for practicing various blows.

2. Punching bags, hand pads, blocking shields, tackling dummies, pillows, and rolled sleeping bags are examples of equipment that should be available for students to use when practicing.

3. A collection of items that are commonly carried or available in emergency situations should be available for demonstration purposes when teaching self-defense. Examples would be rattailed combs, car keys, purses, belts, flashlights, and books that can be used effectively as a defensive weapon.

4. A storage room or section of a room is needed to permit the accumulation of equipment that can be used when teaching self-defense.

5. Appropriate videotapes, films, and slides are effective aids to use when teaching self-defense.

6. Check all practice equipment, including floor and wall mats, on a regular basis to make certain they are in good condition and safe to use.

7. Rules of conduct and safety and emergency procedures should be clearly posted in the practice area.

Self-defense techniques are valuable skills for students to learn. Even though the emphasis of this class is different from other physical education classes, which emphasize developing skills that can be enjoyed competitively or recreationally, self-defense instruction makes a significant contribution to students' educational programs by incorporating an advanced level of kinesthetic awareness, which translates into an expanded level of self-confidence. This confidence prepares them to handle dangerous situations through mental preparedness as well as specific physical skills. It is important, however, that the safety guidelines covered in this chapter be followed so this physical education experience will be safe and beneficial.

CHAPTER 19

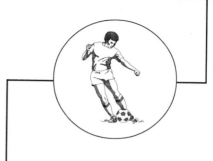

Soccer

William T. Weinberg
University of Louisville
Louisville, Kentucky

S occer is a fast-moving, exciting activity that is suitable for either sex or any age level. It is a sport that places a premium on endurance, agility, and coordination and promotes teamwork and cooperation among players. Soccer is the world's most popular sport and is the national sport of more than 150 countries. Because of its international appeal, soccer can be the ideal medium for teaching concepts related to ethnic diversity, inclusion, and respecting people from different cultures.

Soccer's popularity in the United States is increasing rapidly. The sport is now played by more than three million youths and numerous adults in both outdoor and indoor facilities, and opportunities for participation in recreational leagues, as well as on interscholastic and intercollegiate teams, abound. There are several reasons for soccer's extraordinary growth. First, the skills and tactics used in soccer are similar to familiar games like basketball, field hockey, ice hockey, and team handball. Therefore, students can quickly acquire a "feel" for the game and can begin to play modified and regulation games as they practice basic skills. Second, a person's size is unrelated to success. Ball control skills and tactical awareness are the most critical factors for success in soccer, and both can be taught to students. Third, soccer is a relatively inexpensive sport to play. All that is needed is some basic protective equipment such as shin guards, appropriate footwear, and a ball. Finally, soccer is a very safe activity when players adhere to the rules of the game and teachers take appropriate actions to minimize or eliminate the conditions that most frequently lead to injuries.

The major risks of injury in soccer are similar to those of other invasion games. Because the objective of invasion games is to score goals by advancing the ball through the opponent's territory, physical contact in the form of collisions is common as players attempt to gain and maintain possession of the ball. In addition, players often lose their balance and fall as they learn to control the ball while in motion, particularly when they find themselves pressured by defenders. Therefore, most common injuries associated with soccer are abrasions—generally to the knees and elbows—contusions, and ankle sprains.

The incidence of soccer injuries can be dramatically reduced when teachers formulate a comprehensive risk management plan. The plan should focus on competent supervision, a thorough plan for selecting and conducting instructional activities, and frequent attention to the care and maintenance of the equipment and facilities. Once teachers identify the dangers associated with participation and communicate them to students, a more positive and productive learning experience is likely to occur.

Competent supervision is an essential prerequisite for safety in a soccer unit. Teachers must know how to properly sequence and teach soccer skills and to take essential safety precautions to prevent injuries. Attending clinics, reading books and curriculum guides, and viewing videos are all suitable ways to acquire this knowledge. As the teacher's knowledge of the sport increases, it is likely that the quality of their supervision will also improve because they will be more aware of the conditions that most often lead to injuries. Teachers must also develop explicit rules and procedures for safe participation and communicate them to students at the beginning of the soccer unit.

Teachers must design comprehensive lesson plans that prescribe the proper sequence of skills and include instructional strategies that ensure the safety of students. Safety should be embedded in every activity unit, including soccer. Students must understand that commitment to safety is a prerequisite for participating in any activity, and they should be held accountable for adhering to the rules and policies for safe participation. It is recommended that beginning students first be taught the skills necessary for controlling the ball on the ground. This strategy eliminates the dangers associated with collisions that result when players attempt to use heading techniques and body traps to play balls that are kicked into the air.

Maintaining safe playing areas and equipment is a critical element of a risk management plan for soccer. Playing fields should be inspected daily for glass, potholes, or other potentially dangerous conditions, and the goals should be inspected regularly for loose bolts, protrusions, or unsecured hooks. In addition, a buffer zone around each field should be provided to minimize the possibility of collisions or of stray balls striking players. Teachers should also insist that players always wear appropriate protective gear.

Thorough planning and good judgment are critical elements for a safe and positive learning climate. The following recommendations that pertain to competent supervision, the selection and conduct of activities, and the maintenance of facilities and equipment can help teachers prudently manage the risks associated with the game of soccer.

Supervision

1. Take actions to bolster content knowledge and pedagogical skills as they relate to soccer. Soccer is a very safe sport when teachers are knowledgeable and properly

plan instruction. Injuries can be significantly reduced if teachers know how to (1) select soccer skills that are developmentally appropriate for the age or skill level of students, (2) sequence skills to ensure that students do not attempt skills that are beyond their level of preparedness, (3) structure drills and modified games that are safe, that provide opportunities to improve students' skill levels, and that maximize participation, and (4) modify the rules and equipment for the age and skill level of the students.

2. Inform students of the inherent dangers of soccer. The information should be explicit, and demonstrations should be provided as often as possible. For example, a demonstration of how the slide tackle could potentially injure both the defender and/or the dribbler is more effective than simply telling students not to use it.

3. Post, review, demonstrate, and enforce safety rules and routines. For example, if the teacher establishes a rule that goalkeepers cannot retrieve balls from the goal during a shooting drill until the teacher blows a whistle, this routine should be explained, demonstrated, and enforced by the teacher. Remember to provide positive reinforcement when the rule is consistently followed. This will contribute to a positive learning climate. Last, it is important to explain *why* each rule or routine is in place.

4. Monitor the health status of students. All school districts have policies about recording students' health status that should be followed. In addition, teachers should monitor students who have medical conditions such as allergies and asthma and restrict their participation whenever necessary. Never encourage students to "play through pain" during activities. Instead, remove them from the activity and address the nature of the injury or condition.

5. Follow the established emergency procedures in the event of a serious injury.

    (a) Have a first aid kit located close to the activity area that contains a list of important phone numbers (ambulance, police, school nurse, principal, etc.).

    (b) Be prepared to provide first aid until emergency medical personnel arrive by being certified in CPR and first aid.

    (c) Never leave the class unsupervised while you go for help.

    (d) Record the nature of each injury and do not allow students to return to activity until they have written consent from a doctor.

6. Provide both general and specific supervision. General supervision involves scanning the entire class, noting what is taking place, and providing appropriate feedback to individuals, groups of students, or the entire class. Specific supervision involves direct interaction between the teacher and one or more students who may need immediate attention because they may be experiencing difficulty learning a skill, are off-task, or require special assistance to prevent an injury.

    Suggestions for effectively providing general supervision include the following:

    (a) Stand on the edge of the activity area so that you can see the entire group. Do not stand in the middle of the group or participate in a drill or class activity

Table 1. Safety Review Checklist for Soccer

✓	**Supervision**
	Teacher has sufficient content knowledge and pedagogical skills to teach soccer.
	Students are informed of the inherent dangers of soccer.
	Safety rules and routines are communicated and practiced.
	The health status of students is monitored. Teacher is aware of physical conditions that limit students' participation and adjusts participation accordingly.
	Emergency medical procedures are understood and followed when serious injuries occur.
	All students are under the supervision of the teacher at all times.
	A variety of feedback is provided to students about their skills and behavior.
	Students' off-task behaviors are anticipated, and appropriate preventative measures are taken to stop such behaviors from escalating.
	Activities that involve an element of risk are closely supervised to minimize the possibility of injury.
	The playing rules of soccer are taught and enforced.
	Students are taught rules and routines for working safely and avoiding physical contact with other players.
	Selection and Conduct of Activity
	A well-designed lesson plan is prepared that does the following:
	Uses the school district's curricular material as the basis of progressions, etc.
	Contains goals/outcomes consistent with those of the district, professional organizations, etc.
	Lists safety rules and routines specific to the soccer unit.
	Includes an assessment of students' entry-level soccer skills.
	Describes the learning activities to be used to develop soccer skills.
	Modifies skill progressions, activities, etc., to make them developmentally appropriate for students and accommodate diverse learners. Small-sided games are frequently used to maximize participation and increase students' opportunities to learn the skills.
	Students are held accountable for knowing and following safety rules and routines.
	A warm-up routine that develops cardiovascular fitness and flexibility is employed.
	Soccer skills are taught in a logical progression. Students do not attempt new skills without first learning the prerequisite skills.
	Clear demonstrations are provided for each skill along with brief, accurate cues.
	Potentially dangerous skills such as tackling, heading, and goalkeeping are taught safely, at a basic level, emphasizing proper technique prior to being used in drills or gamelike situations.
	Basic skills are first taught with an emphasis on technique and ball control. Complexity and difficulty are then gradually increased when appropriate.
	Precautions are taken to ensure that indoor activities are conducted safely and are consistent with the goals of the unit.
	The activities used during the soccer unit are challenging and motivate students.
	There are a sufficient number of activities available to maintain students' interest.
	Activities and equipment are modified to ensure the safety of all players, particularly goalkeepers.

	Environmental Conditions
	Players are required to wear appropriate protective equipment.
	Goalkeepers wear distinctive clothing; other players wear colored vests or other clothing to distinguish teams during game play.
	Players do not wear jewelry or watches.
	Players and teacher inspect equipment regularly; damaged equipment is discarded.
	Players and teacher inspect the playing field and goals daily.
	If portable goals are used, they are taken down and locked each day and safely stored in the off-season.
	All playing fields are surrounded by buffer zones.

because both of these situations cause the teacher to lose visual contact with many students in the class.

(b) Do not stand still. Constantly move around the perimeter of the activity area in order to be as close to as many students as possible. Scan the entire class but focus your attention on students who may be misbehaving or are engaged in higher risk activities such as shooting or heading drills. However, do not lose contact with the entire class. Constantly moving around the perimeter also prevents misbehaviors because the teacher will maintain close proximity to the majority of students.

(c) Provide feedback to students located in all parts of the activity space. Feedback about behavior or skill-related progress tells students you are aware of their actions and motivates them to stay focused on the task. Try to provide frequent feedback to students who are farthest away.

(d) Develop a sense of "withitness" to show students you are aware of unsafe or disruptive behaviors. As teachers become more attuned to their students and the skills of soccer, they can better anticipate situations that may lead to unsafe or disruptive behaviors and prevent these behaviors from occurring. Use brief prompts to inform students that you are aware of their actions and to correct their misbehaviors.

Specific supervision is very important when instructing one or more students about how to execute a skill or drill that may involve an element of risk. It is a good idea to ask students to demonstrate the skill before permitting them to practice the skill in a group. Likewise, it is advisable to ask a group of students to demonstrate how to complete a drill with a " walk-through" before allowing them to disperse and attempt the drill in a distant part of the activity space. This practice will ensure that students at least understand what they are expected to do and should minimize the confusion and uncertainty that frequently lead to injuries and off-task behaviors. In addition, it is important to remember that more specific supervision will be necessary with younger or inexperienced students than with students who have practiced the skills previously. However, the need for providing specific supervision does not excuse the teacher from providing general supervision to the entire class.

7. Monitor the emotional levels of students during drills and games. When tempers start to flare, remove the players involved and give them time to "cool off." Never permit unsafe or off-task behaviors to persist; stop them immediately. If these behaviors are allowed to continue, other students will soon follow suit.

8. Teach and enforce the rules of soccer. Consistently teach the most important rules of soccer with the realization that players' safety is promoted as the rules are followed. A clear example is the "dangerous play" rule that penalizes players for either heading a ball below the waist or kicking a ball above the waist.

9. Do not leave the activity area for any reason during a class or permit students to play without supervision. Likewise, do not leave any equipment out after class because students may use it without supervision.

10. Teach students how to work safely with each drill or task. Instruct students about being aware of the presence of others, using space efficiently, and avoiding physical contact with other students. Also establish routines for distributing and returning equipment in an orderly fashion.

Selection and Conduct of the Activity

1. Design a thorough lesson plan (unit plan) prior to teaching a soccer unit. Lesson plans are critical for several reasons. First, they provide a blueprint for instruction. Lesson plans make the teacher's job of planning for each class easier and give direction and coherence to the instructional unit. Second, well-designed lesson plans provide a sound legal defense against lawsuits that stem from injuries occurring during the course of instruction.

   There are many methods of designing lesson plans. However, the following considerations should provide the basis for a written lesson plan in a soccer unit:

   (a) Use the school district's curriculum guide as a reference. Wherever possible, follow the skill progression, suggested activities, safety precautions, assessments, etc., contained in this source. Deviations from the curriculum guide should be justified on the basis of sound educational practice and should be approved by a teacher's supervisor.

   (b) List the goals and/or outcomes of the soccer unit. Be certain to relate them to the stated goals of the school district, professional organizations, etc. This will demonstrate that the soccer unit is contributing to valid educational objectives rather than simply providing students with opportunities to participate in an enjoyable activity.

   (c) List safety rules and policies that are specifically related to soccer. The safety rules should be consistent with general class rules previously established for all instructional units. Examples of safety rules for soccer are (1) no slide tackles or tackling from the rear of the dribbler, (2) no hanging on crossbars, and (3) no offensive players may enter designated areas in front of goals during indoor or small-sided soccer games (3v3, 4v4, etc.). It is important to recognize that most soccer injuries are foreseeable. Teachers should therefore anticipate the conditions that most often cause injuries and take preventative actions to eliminate them.

(d) Establish a procedure for assessing students' entry-level skills. Assessments might include a survey to determine which soccer skills were previously taught to students, simplified skill tests, checklists, etc. Entry-level assessments are important because they provide information about students' initial skill level. Teachers can then use this information to (1) plan an appropriate skill progression for each class, and (2) establish groups or teams within classes in order to individualize instruction or match students for equitable competition. **It is critical that students do not attempt skills or tactics for which they are unprepared.**

(e) Include a detailed description of the activities used to develop soccer skills. These activities include drills, small-sided games, and rule modifications of regulation games. An explanation of the purposes, procedures, and rules should be provided for each activity.

(f) Tailor the activities taught in the soccer unit to the skill level of the students. The instruction and activities included in the unit must be developmentally appropriate and should provide for maximum participation. In addition, efforts should be made to accommodate diverse learners. Therefore, it is probably unrealistic for teachers to expect a class of beginning students to play a regulation soccer game since doing so would require them to learn all of the commonly taught soccer skills and tactics in addition to knowing the playing rules, player positions, etc.

2. Inform students that safety is the highest priority when learning any activity, including soccer, and that safety is an integral part of their participation. Therefore, students should be held accountable for knowing and following all rules and policies that pertain to safe participation. Several ways to hold students accountable for this information and behavior include written tests, checklists, questioning students about safety issues, and authentic assessments (e.g., students must develop safe soccer activities, effective emergency procedures, sport-specific warm-ups, etc.). As teachers convey the importance of safety to students and hold them accountable, it is very likely that "class norms" for safety will evolve. Once this occurs, students will start to view risk management as a normal part of learning any new activity.

3. Design a comprehensive warm-up routine as a way to prevent injuries. An adequate level of cardiovascular endurance is particularly important if students are going to

play soccer safely, because skill execution will deteriorate once students become fatigued. This will cause injuries to occur more frequently. Cardiovascular endurance should be developed primarily through continuous running. Students can also dribble a ball while moving so that conditioning and ball control skills are developed simultaneously. The warm-up should also include static stretching of the lower extremities, lower back, and neck. At the end of each class, a brief cooldown should be completed, consisting of a slow jog and stretching. The cooldown will help prevent muscular soreness and cramping.

Because soccer is such a physically demanding sport, it is advisable to offer a fitness unit or other vigorous activity prior to the soccer unit in order to improve students' fitness levels. Additionally, because students frequently lose their balance and fall during a soccer unit, it is also recommended that safe falling techniques be taught and reviewed periodically (stop, drop, and roll).

4. Always teach soccer skills in a logical progression. It is recommended that students first learn to control the ball while it is on the ground before being allowed to kick the ball into the air. Therefore, the first skills introduced should be passing and trapping the ball with the insides and outsides of the feet and dribbling and tackling (dislodging the ball from the dribbler). These four skills provide the foundation for success in soccer and can be incorporated into many enjoyable activities such as small-sided games and indoor soccer.

5. When teaching any soccer skill, provide a clear demonstration of the proper technique and brief, accurate cues that are appropriate for the students' level of maturity. Be certain that students have a clear understanding of the skill before they practice it. Never force or coerce students to attempt skills they do not understand or are afraid of. Also inform students about how each skill is used in game play and how it is related to skills they already know.

6. Use smaller, lighter balls when students are first learning heading skills. This will facilitate learning the proper technique and build confidence. It is also recommended that players first head the ball from a self-toss before they try to head a ball tossed by a partner or from distances greater than a few feet away. Because several recent studies have linked head trauma to heading in soccer, it is recommended that teachers (1) avoid extended periods where players are repeatedly heading the ball during drills, (2) teach the proper heading technique (ball contacted at hairline), and (3) eliminate heading altogether for children younger than 10 or 11 years old.

7. If goalkeeping skills are taught, teach the proper catching technique first. When instructing goalkeepers on how to dive for a ball, start with the players on their knees or in a squatting position on a soft surface. Always emphasize landing on the side of the body instead of face down.

8. Teach the block tackle from the front as the primary method of dislodging the ball from the dribbler. Never allow players to leave their feet to make a tackle

or to attempt a tackle from behind the dribbler. When teaching tackling technique, first use a stationary ball positioned between two players.

9. Use the results of the entry-level assessments to group or match students, form teams of similar ability, etc. (see above). Do not permit high-skilled players to directly compete against low-skilled players during dribbling or tackling drills because this will undoubtedly damage the confidence of the low-skilled players. Also avoid obvious mismatches in size and strength during tackling drills.

10. Take precautions when students are learning to kick balls into the air. For example, when students are using the instep kick, allow a distance of at least 20 yards between the kicking and receiving lines. In addition, take special precautions when players practice shooting on the goal. Such precautions include (1) assigning only a few players at a time to practice shooting (approx. 5-6), (2) not stationing a goalkeeper in the goal when players are first learning to shoot, (3) once goalkeepers are in the goal, not allowing them to turn their backs to retrieve balls from the net until a signal is given, and (4) prohibiting players from shooting from closer than 15 yards from the goal.

11. Provide sufficient opportunities for students to develop the basic skills in controlled situations before placing them in gamelike conditions. Gradually increase the difficulty and complexity of drills. Use small-sided games as a way to maximize opportunities for players to learn skills and tactics as well as to experience the competitive aspects of soccer.

12. Thoroughly plan rainy day activities. Although indoor soccer is an excellent activity for refining the ball control skills, special care must be taken to make it safe. These precautions include (1) cleaning and drying the surface to prevent players from slipping, (2) not using a goalie unless goalkeeping skills have been taught previously, (3) designing an area in front of each goal where offensive players are not allowed to enter, (4) requiring players to play the ball on the ground, not in the air, (5) limiting the number of players allowed on the floor at any time to six or fewer per team, (6) establishing strict penalties for pushing another player into the wall or bleachers, and (7) requiring players not in the game to stand far away from the game in progress.

13. Design activities that are fun and motivating to students. Injuries are less likely to occur when students are actively engaged in an activity they enjoy because they will concentrate on the task at hand instead of getting off-task due to lack of interest. Similarly, change activities frequently instead of dwelling too long on one drill or game. Changing activities frequently maintains students' interest and provides them with opportunities to rest, thereby delaying fatigue. It is recommended that small-sided or indoor soccer games be played with a 5-10 minute time limit because players tire quickly. After this time, players can take a short rest, teams can be changed, etc.

14. Take special precautions to protect goalkeepers. In addition to teaching the goal-keepers proper techniques, teachers must be aware of the dangers that goalkeepers are exposed to and take actions to minimize their risks. First, enforce rules that prohibit offensive players from making contact with goalkeepers. Second, establish areas around the goal that are off-limits to offensive players. This will eliminate collisions between goalkeepers and offensive players and will prevent shots taken from "point blank" range.

Environmental Conditions

Equipment

1. All players should wear shin guards, protective eyewear, and mouthpieces; males should wear athletic supporters. All of this equipment should fit snugly. Sneakers or all-purpose athletic shoes must be worn for indoor soccer. Soccer shoes with molded cleats are recommended for outdoor play to provide better traction.

2. Goalkeepers should wear brightly colored long-sleeve shirts to distinguish them from field players. It is recommended that goalkeepers also wear pads on their knees and elbows and long pants to prevent abrasions.

3. The ball used should be appropriate for the age of the players. Players 6-11 years old should use a #3 ball; those older than 11 should use a #4 ball. When teaching heading skills, instructors should use lighter balls such as foam balls or volleyballs. If possible, balls that are manufactured strictly for indoor soccer should be used for indoor play.

4. Each team should wear colored vests so that players can distinguish their team-mates from the opponents.

5. Players must remove all jewelry and watches before they begin play.

6. Teachers should check equipment regularly. Teachers should also instruct students to inspect equipment before using it and to notify them of any damaged or worn equipment. Damaged equipment should be discarded.

Facilities

1. Teachers and students should inspect the playing field and goals daily. The playing field should be free of standing water, glass, potholes, rocks, or other dangerous objects. Goals should be free of loose bolts, hooks, and other protrusions.

2. Portable goals are an attractive nuisance when not in use. Therefore, they should be laid face down, chained, and locked at the end of each day's classes. At the end of the soccer unit, they should be stored in a safe place, out of the sight of students. Signs should be posted on the goal posts to warn people not to climb on the goals.

3. A buffer zone should separate the playing field from obstacles such as bleachers, benches, and fences so that players will not be injured if they run after a ball as it leaves the field.

4. If small-sided games are played, establish buffer zones of sufficient width between the playing areas. Games should be played in the same direction to reduce the number of times balls are kicked onto adjacent fields.

5. Indoor soccer creates several serious safety risks that must be addressed. If students are allowed to pass the ball off the walls or bleachers, they must be warned about pushing each other into these impediments and instructed about how to use the wall or bleachers as a tactical maneuver. In addition, the walls and bleachers must be inspected to insure that there are no jagged edges or protrusions that can cause injuries. When the walls or bleachers pose a danger, either because of structural problems or because students may collide with them, the game should be moved to a safer space.

Summary

Soccer is a very enjoyable activity that makes a number of significant contributions to valid educational objectives. Soccer is also one of the safest activities in a secondary physical education program when a well-designed risk management plan is developed and implemented. Following this plan will ensure that students receive the educational benefits of soccer in the safest manner possible.

CHAPTER 20

Softball

Lynda B. Ransdell and Darcie Oakland
University of Utah
Salt Lake City, Utah

Introduction

Softball is known as the "All-American game" because such a large number of athletes participate at a variety of levels. Over 40 million people play softball in the United States alone. According to the the National Federation of State High School Associations (NFHS), between 1988 and 1998, participation in softball by boys has increased 10% and participation by girls has increased nearly 40%. Such large numbers of participants of varying skill levels may mean a high risk of injury. Given the challenges inherent in running a safe softball program for a wide range of participants, the purpose of this chapter is to describe (1) major risks and common injuries that occur in softball, (2) skills and knowledge required of softball coaches and teachers, (3) tips for maintaining organization and control, (4) factors to consider when selecting and designing softball activities (i.e., progressions), and (5) information about ensuring the safety of facilities and equipment.

Major Risks and Common Injuries that Occur in Softball

The National Electronic Injury Surveillance System maintains that compared to other sports, softball causes more injuries leading to emergency room visits (Janda, Wild, & Hensinger, 1992). The injury rate for high school softball is 27% higher than for high school baseball (16.7 injuries per 1,000 players vs. 13.2 injuries per 1,000 players) (Powell & Barber-Foss, 2000). Millions of dollars are spent every year treating these injuries. Given the high risk involved with playing and supervising softball, the best means of avoiding liability for injuries is prevention. Specifically, the more one knows about situations where injury can occur and how to prevent those situations, the more likely it is that one will avoid major litigation.

Depending upon which article you read, whether you coach fast or slow pitch softball, and which level you coach, the injury statistics for softball are likely to vary. Therefore, this section will summarize the most common injuries in fast and slow pitch softball at the secondary level, reasons why they occur, and ways to prevent them. Specifically, injuries in softball can be divided into two basic categories: throwing injuries and collisions.

Throwing Injuries. According to a study by Powell and Barber-Foss (2000), throwing contributes to the majority of injuries that occur while playing high school softball. The windmill pitch, one type of throw, is a highly complex biomechanical skill that has not been thoroughly researched. To perform this skill, pitchers must fully rotate their shoulder-which is the most mobile but also the most unstable joint in the body. Windmill pitching requires timing and acceleration and deceleration of various body segments. One common injury reported in those who use windmill pitching is radial neuropathy. Radial neuropathy occurs when nerves become compressed, causing pain in the elbow, hand, and wrist. Another common injury that occurs in pitchers is an ulnar stress fracture. This is a fracture of the lower arm bone that extends from the elbow to the wrist on the pinky side. It typically occurs when the bone and joint are loaded repeatedly—without rest. Pitchers have also reported spine problems due to the hyperextension of the spine during the ball release. This type of movement can cause lower back pain that radiates down the legs.

The overhand throw, the most commonly executed skill in the game, is also a coordinated sequence of events that requires timing and acceleration and deceleration of body segments. The most common injury in those using overhand throws is to the shoulder. There are extreme sheer, compressive, and tensile stressors during the throwing motion. These motions can lead to rotator cuff problems and functional instability of the glenohumeral joint. The first sign of problems is often impingement (or sticking) of the rotator cuff tendons. Later, if untreated, this can progress to a rotator cuff tear. Other throwing injuries that have been reported with the overhand throw include spontaneous fractures of the humeral shaft (upper arm bone), humeral stress periostitis (a dull arm pain equivalent to shin splints in runners), and nerve compression (as described previously) (Baker, 2000).

In addition to injuries of the shoulder, injuries can also occur at the elbow. The most common injury of the elbow is a fracture of the medial epicondyle, which causes pain on the outside of the elbow. This injury is also known as little leaguers elbow.

Intuitively, the best way to prevent throwing injuries is to employ the proper mechanics of throwing, warm-up adequately before throwing hard, and perform conditioning drills that will strengthen the muscles involved in throwing. In terms of preventing pitching injuries, three things must be considered: proper pitching mechanics, pitching volume (number of pitches), and types of pitches. Clearly, coaches and teachers will be well-served to teach proper mechanics of pitching early, limit the number of pitches thrown by each pitcher (if possible), and teach different types of pitches gradually—such that those pitches that are easiest on the body are taught first, followed by pitches that are more stressful on the shoulder girdle and elbow.

Collision Injuries. Collision injuries occur when players collide with bases, bats, fixed objects, the ball, or another player. Compared to baseball, softball players are more likely to get injured sliding. This could be because more "novices" play softball than baseball (thus more novices slide into bases), because softball is played on a smaller field (which gives players less time to react), or because softball players typically wear shorts instead of pants (Hosey & Puffer, 2000). When a player incorrectly slides head first, she or he is most likely to injure the upper body (e.g., fingers, wrist, shoulder) or face. Concussions are also a possibility. When a player incorrectly slides feet first, she or he is most likely to injure the lower body (e.g., ankle, knee). Injuries due to sliding most commonly occur when the decision to slide is made late and the slide is initiated too close to the base (Wheeler, 1987). To prevent sliding injuries, supervisors should provide proper progression for teaching sliding, encourage players to start sliding 2-3 strides away from the base, and inform players that the body should be relaxed when sliding since tense muscles are more likely to get injured.

Concussions may occur when a player is hit with a ball or bat, or when she or he collides with another player. Concussions should be addressed with extreme urgency. If a player collides with a ball, bat, or another player, and is complaining of a headache, she or he should be removed from play immediately and should not play again until a professional has evaluated the injury.

When a player makes contact with a dirt surface, broken bones, contusions, abrasions, or scrapes are a common result. In rare cases, players have died as a result of being hit with a ball in the head or chest. When a ball hits the tip of a finger, a condition known as "mallet finger" may result. Mallet finger occurs when the ball hits the top of the finger so hard that the tendon is ripped from the bone and the tip of the finger cannot be straightened.

Muscle pulls (e.g., strained hamstrings) can occur when athletes fail to warm up and stretch adequately or when they practice difficult skills without using the proper progression. Therefore, coaches and teachers need to make sure that athletes warm up in a systematic fashion.

For all of the aforementioned injuries, several factors can contribute to injury risk. These include poor technique, inadequate coaching (or poor judgment), a lack of conditioning or warm-up, and faulty equipment and facilities (Janda et al., 1990). The bottom line is that injury prevention starts with emphasizing proper technique and solid coaching fundamentals. Skills should be taught in a manner that is progressive and individualized. Additionally, advanced skills should not be attempted until athletes are in adequate physical condition. In the sections that follow, additional information will be provided to ensure proper skill progressions and monitoring of facilities and equipment.

Supervision

Supervision is the monitoring, by a teacher or coach, of any activities related to softball. Effective supervision is a multifactorial job that consists of knowing the rules, skills, and strategies relevant to softball and knowing the proper progression in which to teach those skills and strategies (Bonanno & Regalado, 1993). The following section summarizes skills and knowledge required of coaches and teachers in charge of supervising softball activities.

Supervising softball play at the secondary level can be tricky. Athletes have a wide range of skills, body sizes, and experiences, and they can sometimes overestimate their abilities. Some basic principles of supervision are essential for successfully and safely leading softball activities. First, teachers and coaches should know basic behavior management skills. They should know the names of players whenever possible. This way, if students misbehave, they can be called by name and the misbehavior will be less likely to continue.

Additional behavior management skills such as "proximity control" (e.g., walking close to the area where the misbehavior is occurring) (Graham, 2001), positive and negative reinforcement, and corrective feedback are essential for controlling play. Rules should be posted, emphasized, re-emphasized, and enforced. Teachers and coaches should strive to see all participants at all times, and they should position themselves on the field such that this is possible. A technique known as "back to the wall" (i.e., against the outer edges of the playing field) (Graham, 2001) works well for maintaining all participants within the instructor's visual field.

A second essential component to successfully supervising softball play is staying current with the latest rules, skills, techniques, and tactics. This is easily accomplished by attending clinics, workshops, and conferences; subscribing to journals; and/or reading textbooks on softball skill development. As the teacher or coach, you should be the expert— if not in your ability to demonstrate, then in your ability to teach and explain skills and drills. A list of knowledge requirements for anyone supervising softball at the secondary level is provided below.

- Teachers and coaches should know the current rules of softball, relevant to the type of softball (fast or slow pitch), level of play (recreational, youth, or high school), and gender of participants. This will foster adherence to the rules and sportsmanship toward the umpires.

- Teachers and coaches should know the mechanics of the skills. Typically, skills are broken down into phases such as preparation, execution/action, and follow-through. It is especially important to know the mechanics of complex skills that have the potential for injury (e.g., sliding).

- Teachers and coaches should know the common mistakes for each softball skill performed and how to correct these mistakes. Providing corrective or instructive feedback to learners is very important for skill development and for maintaining a safe learning environment.

- Teachers and coaches should know the proper teaching progressions for the skills and strategies. These teaching progressions should consider the age and ability level of the players. For example, it is not appropriate to have beginning players learn to slide first in the dirt on a field. They should be taught first on a water slide or gym floor. Then, once their mechanics are solid, they can transfer this skill to the playing field.

- The ratio of players to supervisors should be smaller when players are beginners and/or when new and potentially hazardous skills are being taught. If groups are large and cannot be made smaller, players should be divided into groups such that more experienced players are paired with less experienced players. This enables beginners to use the expertise of the more experienced players during drills and practice situations. Players can safely perform "self-directed" activities when the teacher or coach provides written handouts (or cue cards) with instructions for groups to follow. In all situations, teachers and coaches should walk around the perimeter of the area where drills are being performed and provide corrective and positive feedback as necessary.

- Teachers and coaches should know the potential hazards inherent in the sport (e.g., common injuries) and how to prevent them (see previous section.)

- Teachers and coaches should be aware of the weather conditions during which it is NOT safe to practice. Specifically, practice should not be held during any thunderstorm with lightning. Additional "red-flag days" include those with excessively hot and/or humid weather, high winds, or any other situation in which it is hard to see the ball. Coaches and teachers should consider the time of day and length of practices or games when deciding the types and length of activities in which to participate. Lastly, coaches and teachers should always be aware of the need for water, especially on hot/humid days. Frequent water breaks should be provided.

- Teachers and coaches should know how to properly care for and maintain equipment and facilities. This information should be shared with players to ensure "double checking." Additional information on this topic is provided later in the chapter.

In addition to staying current, teachers and coaches should treat athletes as individuals as much as possible regarding their abilities. For example, readiness to learn sliding skills may be dependent on age, gender, previous experience, practice setting, and confidence in softball in general. Given that it is ideal to be attentive to individual needs and abilities, it is important for supervisors to pretest and screen athletes for their athletic abilities. This includes receiving physician clearance for participation. Additionally, coaches and teachers should keep records of all tests and progress made and should note individual progressions that may work. At no time should an athlete be forced to practice a skill for which she or he is not ready.

A third component to safely supervising softball activities is to maintain certification in first aid and CPR and to know the common injuries in softball and their treatment (as specified in the previous section). Additionally, supervisors should develop an "Emergency Action Plan" for dealing with injuries that may occur in an outdoor setting. The emergency action plan should include written information about where to go for help, who to call, and how to deal with various injuries. Ideally, it should be posted in a prominent place near the practice or game area. Given that most softball practices and games occur outdoors (and often away from phones), supervisors should have cellular phones to ensure fast action in an emergency situation.

Teachers and coaches should also have an "Accident Report Form" that requires them to write out what happened, how it happened, when it happened, and who was injured. This form should be completed immediately after an accident occurs. Failure to do so may prevent an accurate description of the injury and the conditions surrounding it. The supervisor, the injured person, and a witness should be asked to sign the form once it is completed. To ensure the safest environment possible (and to ensure that students know what to do when a teacher or coach is injured), students should be taught the procedures for an emergency action plan and an accident report form.

Organization and Control

Organization and planning are the keys to successful and safe softball activities. Proper organization ensures control of activities and enables coaches and teachers to focus on skill development instead of discipline or other issues. In addition to the principles of behavior management and drill organization mentioned in the previous section, several additional points, relevant to organization and control, will be highlighted in this section.

- Lesson plans or practice plans should be used for all practice sessions. Each lesson plan should contain measurable learner objectives, time usage plans for each segment of practice, a description of each drill or activity (including any necessary diagrams), any cues for teaching skills or drills, equipment needs, and safety considerations.

- A season or unit plan should be used to guide practices and game plans. This season plan should include the knowledge and skill/strategy expectations for the season, fitness goals, and sportsmanship and social interaction expectations.

- As has been previously mentioned, teachers or coaches should always maintain a position on the outer proximity of the playing area (e.g., the "back to the wall" concept discussed in the previous section). This enables them to see the majority of the players to provide corrective or instructive feedback. If there are stations that have variable risk, supervisors should position themselves near the area of highest risk.

- Teachers or coaches should be easy to find if any problems occur. For optimal visibility, they should wear brightly colored or distinctive clothing.

- Teachers or coaches should rotate regularly throughout the playing area. This ensures that all players are given the opportunity to interact with (and learn from) the teacher.

- Teachers and coaches should keep athletes active and participating as much as possible. Instead of having one group perform batting practice, use several areas of the field to have 3-4 groups practicing related skills. Specifically, Group I can hit off batting tees. Group II can hit plastic golf balls with broomsticks. Group III can hit "soft toss" to fielders. Group IV can hit "short tosses" to fielders. Once each athlete in the group performs the task (which should be explained and diagrammed fully on a "cue card"), the groups should rotate in a pre-specified direction. The goal is to have each athlete practice a variety of skills and make maximal use of time. *The main consideration here is to plan activities such that there is ample distance between groups to*

ensure safe practice. The goal of having athletes fully participate promotes maximal skill development and minimizes discipline problems.

- In cases where a supervisor cannot be in an area where equipment is located, that equipment should be put away immediately in a locked area. The old adage, "out of sight, out of mind," is a good credo to follow with softball equipment. Unfortunately, bats, balls, gloves, and other equipment can create an attractive nuisance for bored students.

- If possible, written policies for potentially hazardous activities should be developed. Policies should consider player abilities, type of instruction provided (and amount of supervision required), and recommended playing area conditions. Additionally, general safety rules should be discussed and, if possible, posted prominently. Some examples of general safety rules include the following: (1) starting and stopping skill practice with a signal, (2) checking before swinging a bat, (3) using the bat to hit only the ball, (4) throwing in the same direction during warm-up to avoid someone getting hit by a stray ball, (5) avoiding collisions by calling for the ball, and (6) never leaving equipment lying in either fair or foul territory.

Selection and Conduct of Activity

Readiness. One of the most important considerations when teaching a new skill is student "readiness" (Bonanno & Regalado, 1993). Readiness infers that an athlete has the physical, mental, and emotional maturity to learn a new skill. Estimating the readiness of each student within the context of your class is a challenging task. However, there are some general safety concepts to consider when estimating readiness.

First, coaches or administrators should never force athletes to attempt skills with which they are not comfortable. If an athlete expresses hesitation or fear related to a specific skill, that athlete should not be forced to perform that skill. Second, players should never be asked to play a position for which they have not received instruction. For example, if a player who has never been instructed in catching is asked to play catcher, she or he is at risk for getting injured from an errant pitch. Similarly, if a player who is a weak fielder is asked to play shortstop, that player is at risk of getting hit with a line drive. Third, players should be carefully evaluated prior to placing them in game play. *If their safety is at risk,* less talented players should not be integrated with more talented players during game play.

If players of all skill levels are forced to play together, the coach or teacher should modify the rules or equipment so the game is appropriate for all who participate. For example, to ensure that the game is safe for those of all skill levels, a softer, larger ball may be used. Additionally, rules can require that each player gets 1-3 pitches (so hitters have to learn to hit most anything). Taking the time to develop and evaluate skills and to modify rules (where necessary) is very important for safe game play. Lastly, students should be instructed in how to prevent and react to emergencies. Teachers and coaches should clearly explain the hazards of the game and any procedures for checking the safety of equipment. Any emergency procedures and phone numbers should be posted prominently.

Progressions. Making sure that players learn and practice skills in a step-by-step fashion is an important component for ensuring safety (Bonanno & Regalado, 1993). Beginning players should not start to learn how to field a ground ball by standing 10 feet from a player who is hitting the ball hard. Similarly, beginning players should not be told to slide into a base without learning the proper mechanics of sliding on a more forgiving surface. Following are descriptions of recommended progressions for catching, throwing, batting, running bases, and sliding.

Catching, Fielding Ground Balls, and Throwing. Throwing and catching practice should begin with a lightweight (e.g., whiffle ball) or large softball that is easy to throw and catch. Research has demonstrated that it is easier to see brightly colored balls; therefore, they should be used initially for most effective results. For safe practice when throwing, fielding, and catching in pairs, consider the following tips: practice on level ground with few obstacles, maintain ample distance between pairs, line up in two lines facing each other, and throw and catch in the same direction. Catching/fielding progressions should proceed as follows:

- Teacher or coach demonstrates the proper mechanics of catching and fielding ground balls.
- Athletes practice catching while tossing the ball to themselves.
- Athletes toss the ball against a wall at a variety of speeds and angles and practice catching.
- Athletes have partners toss balls to them at a variety of speeds and angles (e.g., to the left and right, moving backwards and forwards).
- Athletes have partners toss balls to them at a variety of speeds and angles. Once a ball is caught, it should be followed immediately with a throw to a target.
- Athletes field balls hit by a stationery player who is "self-tossing."
- Athletes field balls hit by a player who receives a pitch.

Instruction in throwing should follow instruction in catching and fielding. After all, one should be able to receive the ball prior to learning how to throw it. As is true when one is teaching catching, a modified ball (e.g., one that is lighter or smaller) may be used for teaching throwing. A proper progression for teaching throwing involves the following:

- Teacher or coach demonstrates the proper mechanics of throwing.
- Athletes practice throwing form without a ball in front of a mirror or coach.
- With a partner or against a wall, athletes throw short distances, emphasizing proper form and speed of mechanics.
- With a partner or against a wall, athletes throw short distances, emphasizing accuracy.
- Athletes throw with an emphasis on increasing distance.
- Athletes field or catch the ball and throw immediately thereafter, emphasizing accuracy.
- Athletes field or catch the ball from different positions on the field and throw to a designated target position.

Batting. Batting is a potentially hazardous skill because players who have not been properly trained can get hit with errant pitches, swing incorrectly and injure themselves, or release the bat during a swing if they are not maintaining the proper grip. Additionally, if batters are practicing in a non-confined area or in an area that is not supervised, other athletes run a great risk of injury. To ensure that batting is taught safely, the following should be considered: (1) the batting practice area should be netted for safety (if possible), or all persons who are at risk of being hit by a batted ball should be aware of the ongoing risk; (2) batters should wait until one ball is fielded before hitting another ball, and (3) mush balls should be used with beginning hitters and fielders. The following batting progression is recommended:

- Coaches and teachers demonstrate the mechanics of the swing for hitting.
- In front of a mirror or coach, athletes practice the swing with a lightweight bat.
- Athletes practice batting off of a tee.
- Athletes hit the ball while tossing to themselves.
- Athletes hit balls pitched to them from the side (e.g., "soft toss").
- Athletes practice batting with the teacher, coach, or experienced pitcher.
- Athletes practice batting against a live pitcher who starts out slowly and pitches faster with experience. Supervisors should remember that batting skills develop more quickly than pitching skills, so to prevent injury to the pitcher (who may not be ready for a line drive) or the hitter (who may get hit by a pitch), mush balls should be used.

Running Bases. When practicing base running, there are a few important safety concerns. First, coaches and teachers need to make sure that athletes are properly warmed up. Additionally, the area on which players will run should be carefully examined to make sure it does not contain holes or objects in the base path (such as rocks, twigs, or large clumps of dirt). There should be ample room for speeding up and slowing down. Traction should be adequate to ensure that athletes will not slip unnecessarily. Coaches and teachers should be aware that practicing running bases is very taxing. Therefore, base running should be approached progressively so that athletes increase the number of bases they run as their fitness level improves. When first learning base running, athletes should be encouraged to practice at moderate speeds. After their technique improves, athletes should be encouraged to practice at maximum speed. Some progressions for properly teaching base running are as follows:

- Practice sprinting at moderate speed with proper form.
- Practice running straight through first base at moderate speed with proper form; then, have players increase their speed as technique and fitness level improve.
- Start with a mock swing, drop the bat, and run through first base at moderate speed; speed should be progressively increased as technique and fitness level improve.
- Practice rounding bases (i.e., run from home to first to second, or from third to home) at a moderate speed; increase speed progressively.

- Start with a mock swing, drop the bat, and run as if a double were hit; next, try a triple; increase speed progressively.

- Start with a mock swing, drop the bat, and practice watching the first base coach for a signal; first base coach should vary instructions for continuing and stopping; increase speed progressively.

Sliding. Because sliding can cause numerous injuries, it is important to teach it properly. Some have recommended that sliding should not be taught to every student in physical education class. It is a skill that is primarily reserved for athletes on a competitive team. When practicing sliding, there are important safety precautions that should be considered. To prevent foot injuries that can result from catching a cleat on a base or dirt, athletes should practice first in sneakers (vs. cleats). Breakaway bases should be used to prevent injuries that result from sliding too close to the base.

When learning feet-first sliding, athletes should be encouraged to raise their hands overhead to protect them from impact. When learning headfirst sliding, runners should be encouraged to hold a handful of dirt to prevent them from extending fingers that might get caught on a base. For all runners preparing to slide, the impact with the ground should be absorbed by the maximum amount of body surface area. Specifically, those executing the feet-first slide should land first on their buttocks, thighs, and lower back. Those executing the headfirst slide should land first on their chest and thighs.

The main thing to consider when developing a progression for teaching sliding is to first have students practice sliding on a wet slide, or indoors on a gym floor with old sweat pants and talcum powder or a burlap bag. The approach run should initially be short and can be increased as the skill of the base runner increases.

Environmental Concerns

Facilities. Many instructions for properly and safely preparing fields are presented in rules manuals. When in doubt, check the rules manuals for recommended specifications for field markings, distances, and field orientation. On fields where dugouts are not provided, athletes should be placed at least 25 feet from the foul line. Backstops should be placed at least 25 feet behind home plate. If backstops are not provided, athletes (other than catchers) should not be allowed to position themselves behind home plate.

Coaches and teachers should carefully check field conditions prior to game play. Checking the field conditions includes looking for debris or rocks, wet or soft spots, holes, and other natural hazards. Players can be trained to look for such hazards during their warm-up jog prior to game play. In addition to checking the field for hazards, players should be instructed to check distances from their position to fixed objects such as fences, poles, and dugouts. This way, they have an idea where such objects lie when they are sprinting full speed for foul balls.

Field maintenance is an important responsibility of the coach or teacher. Fields should be regularly dragged (to ensure smoothness and flatness) and raked (to break up clumps of dirt upon which the ball can take nasty hops). Poles and fences should be padded to provide some protection in cases where a player runs into a fixed object. Field lines should be marked with something that is not irritating to the eyes or skin. Lastly, the use of breakaway fences is recommended where possible. This can prevent injuries to outfielders chasing fly balls. To warn outfielders of their impending approach to the fence, an area between the fence and the outfield should be a different surface than the outfield grass.

Equipment. Just as the rule books specify safe facility requirements, they also specify equipment regulations such as the minimum and maximum weight, length, and composition of bats and other equipment. This part of the chapter provides recommendations for choosing and using safe bats, balls, gloves, catcher's equipment, and bases.

The first thing to consider when selecting equipment is the size, maturity, and skill level of the players and the type of softball that will be played. Additionally, coaches and teachers should freely make recommendations for equipment selection. Although some variations may exist, the following lists will provide guidelines for selecting safe equipment.

Bats. Athletes are somewhat picky and superstitious about their bats. Most softball players use aluminum bats because the ball comes off the bat faster and travels further. Additionally, aluminum bats don't typically break during practice with normal use. To ensure maximal batting success and safety, bats should be individually selected based on the size, maturity, and skill level of the hitter. In addition, the following safety checklist should be used to ensure safe batting:

- Bats should be one-piece construction and made of hard wood or metal.
- The maximum length of a bat should not exceed 34 inches. (Fungo bats should not be used in regulation play.)
- Bats should have a safety grip made of rubber or tape that is easy to grip and designed specifically for bat handles.
- Grips should be checked regularly for tears and slippage. Those found to be defective should be replaced immediately.
- Wooden bats should be checked regularly for cracking and splintering. Bats with cracks and splinters can be dangerous and should be discarded.
- Bats should have a grip or safety knob at the bottom (narrow) end. If a knob is damaged or cracked, this can affect grip and swing pattern, so the bat should be replaced.
- Weighted donut rings are not recommended for use with softball bats.

Balls. Balls should be selected based on the size, maturity, and skill level of the athletes. Rule books will provide additional guidance as to the proper balls to use for various levels of play. Additionally, ball selection will depend on whether the game is being played indoors or out. Lastly, balls should be checked regularly to ensure that they are round and symmetrical, have intact seams, and are not waterlogged.

Gloves. Without fail, gloves should be worn any time athletes are playing softball. Failure to wear a glove can result in serious injuries to the hands and arms. The following are recommendations for ensuring safe selection and use of gloves:

- Gloves vary significantly by position. For example, the catcher and first base player may want additional padding on the heel of the hand compared to other field positions. Outfielders may want gloves with longer extension to help them when reaching for catches. Coaches and teachers should provide guidance to athletes when selecting gloves.

- Gloves should be fitted to the player's hand size.

- Gloves should be "broken in" prior to use. Gloves that are stiff are more dangerous because balls can pop out of them. A great way to break in a glove is to oil it, place a softball in it, and tie some string around it to hold the ball in place. This will shape the glove so that a ball will fit into it. Then the glove should be used continuously to make the leather more supple and easier to move.

- Gloves should be checked regularly to ensure that laces are not broken or worn, especially in the web area. Laces that are broken or worn should be replaced immediately or the glove should be removed from play.

Batting Helmets. Head injuries are the most frequent serious injuries that occur in the game of softball. Therefore, headgear is required of all athletes playing competitive softball under the rules of the NFHS. Interestingly, many physical education class settings do not require wearing a batting helmet during batting or running. Therefore, players opt not to wear helmets because they might "lessen vision" or "sit heavy" on the head. Additionally, there are sanitary concerns with switching helmets among students.

These excuses for not wearing helmets should not be tolerated because several studies have shown that requiring softball players to wear helmets when batting and running the bases can lessen injury risk. To minimize concern about the sanitary issues related to switching helmets, athletes should be encouraged to wear ball caps or bandannas during play. Face shields or wire masks can be added for additional eye protection. In situations where batting helmets are not used, coaches or teachers should modify the rules to protect the batter, runner, and catcher.

Mouth guards. An effective way to prevent dental injuries and minimize brain trauma when a blow to the jaw occurs is to have infielders wear mouth guards. Mouth guards have been proven effective in a variety of sports (e.g., football, field hockey) for preventing or minimizing mouth and brain injuries. For maximum protection, athletes can have dentists fit them with custom mouth guards. Alternately, generic mouth guards can be purchased from a sporting goods company and molded to fit individual mouths.

Catcher's Equipment. Wearing and maintaining catchers' equipment is very important for the safety of each catcher. All catchers should wear a helmet/mask/throat protector combination that fits the head snugly enough that it doesn't bobble around. Visibility should not be impeded. Chest protectors should meet published standards appropriate for each sex. Straps should be adjustable and regularly checked for wear. Straps should work so that the chest protector fits snugly without unduly restricting movement. The wire covering for the mask should not have dents or openings. If a polycarbonate shield is used, it should not have cracks. Lastly, shin guards should be used that cover the lower thigh, knee, shin, instep, and ankles. To prevent tripping over buckles, straps and buckles should be placed on the *outside* of the leg.

Bases. Unfortunately, tradition is one of the major obstacles to introducing safer equipment. Therefore, when companies introduce safer equipment (such as breakaway bases), they are often met with significant resistance. One of the best ways to change tradition (and implement a safer game) is to use some of the newer and safer equipment. For example, traditional fixed bases are up to 12.7 cm in height and must be fixed to the ground with a bolt that is sunk into concrete. Because these bases are designed to stay in place when a player hits them, they are frequently the cause of collision injuries. One of the primary ways to make a softball field safer is to use breakaway bases (Janda, Wojitys, Hankin, Benedict, & Hensinger, 1990; Sendre, Keating, Hornak, & Newitt, 1994).

Various breakaway bases are available that differ in rigidity and the magnitude of force required to cause the base to break away from its post. Because they are detached infrequently, they do not cause a "slow down" of a game. If fixed bases must be used, they should be pegged down so that the anchor pegs are placed out of the base runners' sliding path.

Other Equipment. Other equipment commonly used in softball includes batting gloves, footwear, and sunglasses. Batting gloves are worn on the hand holding the bottom of the bat, mostly to prevent slipping. Some players wear two gloves while batting, and some wear batting gloves under their fielding glove. The important things to verify when purchasing a batting glove are that it fits properly and that it is made of long-lasting material.

Footwear guidelines vary according to the level of play and the type of softball. Youth leagues require shoes with soft or hard rubber cleats, while some adult leagues allow metal soles or heel plates. League rules should be checked prior to purchasing cleats.

Lastly, sunglasses may be worn to prevent losing the ball in the sun. This is particularly important for outfielders who often stare into the sky (and sun) when attempting to catch fly balls. The most important thing to consider when purchasing sunglasses is that nonbreakable safety lenses should be used.

Conclusion

Softball has many variations, including slow and fast pitch, youth and adult recreational league, and high school and collegiate level. Depending on the size, age, maturity, and skill level of the athletes, rules, equipment, and facilities may need to be modified to ensure the safety of all participants. The best advice, in terms of conducting safe play, is to consider every aspect of play as if it were "high-risk" and to use precautions, as recommended in this chapter, to prevent unnecessary accidents.

References

Baker, M. M. (2000). Softball. In B. Drinkwater (Ed.), *Women in Sport* (pp. 626-646). Malden, MA: Blackwell Science.

Bonanno, D. & Regalado, S. (1993). Softball. In N. J. Dougherty (Ed.), *Principles of Safety* (pp. 221-233). Reston, VA: American Alliance for Health, Physical Education, Recreation and Dance.

Graham, G. (2001). *Teaching children physical education: Becoming a master teacher* (2nd ed.). Champaign, IL: Human Kinetics.

Hosey, R. G., & Puffer, J. C. (2000). Baseball and softball sliding injuries: Incidence and the effect of technique in collegiate baseball and softball players. *American Journal of Sports Medicine, 28*(3), 360-363.

Janda, D., Wild, D., & Hensinger, R. (1992). Softball injuries. *Sports Medicine, 13,* 285-291.

Janda, D., Wojitys, E., Hankin, F., Benedict, M., & Hensinger, R. (1990). A three phase analysis of the prevention of recreational softball injuries. *American Journal of Sports Medicine, 18,* 632-635.

Powell, J. W., Barber-Foss, K. D. (2000). Sex-related injury patterns among selected high school sports. *American Journal of Sports Medicine, 28*(3), 385-391.

Sendre, R., Keating, T., Hornak, J., & Newitt, P. (1994). Use of the hollywood impact bases to reduce sliding and base running injuries in baseball and softball. *American Journal of Sports Medicine, 22,* 450-453.

Smith, T. (2001). Baseball-softball: Planning, organization, and practice-Keys to diamond success. Institute for the Study of Youth Sports, *http://ed-web3.educ.msu.edu/ysi/spspr98/baseball.htm.*

Wheeler, B. (1987). Ankle fractures in slow-pitch softball: The Army experience. *Military Medicine, 152,* 626-628.

CHAPTER 21

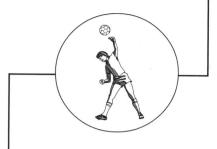

Team Handball

Mary Phyl Dwight
University of Missouri at Kansas City
Kansas City, Missouri

Reita Clanton
University of Kentucky
Lexington, Kentucky

Introduction

In 146 countries, seven million men and women and boys and girls of varying abilities play team handball. The sport uses natural athletic skills such as running, jumping, throwing, and catching. Players enjoy the game's fast, continuous pace, aggressive play, and goalie action. As with any physical activity involving a thrown object and players moving within a confined area, teachers need to carefully consider safety factors when introducing the game to students. The teacher must provide proper supervision, select suitable content, conduct the activity appropriately, and structure the environment to ensure the safety of the students.

The physical educator's team handball knowledge will help him or her construct lessons to curtail dangerous situations. Recognizing the physical nature of the game, the International Handball Federation continues to evaluate and change rules to protect the health of players. The following actions that endanger an opponent's health are penalized by immediate disqualification from the game:

- A player, from the side or from behind, strikes or pulls back the throwing arm of the opponent in the act of shooting or passing
- A player takes any action resulting in the opponent being struck in the head or neck

- A player strikes the body of an opponent with the foot or knee
- A player pushes a running or jumping opponent, causing him/her to lose body control
- A player exhibits repeated unsportsmanlike conduct

Furthermore, a player guilty of assault during the game will be excluded (the team must finish the game with one less player on the court). Most team handball injuries result from collisions with players or goalposts, ball contact, and sprains and strains due to overuse or overstress. Abrasions, blisters, contusions, jammed fingers, fractures, dislocations, muscle pulls, swelling around a joint, twisted ankles, and a player's wind being knocked out are all injuries that occur in team handball. Skillful risk management can minimize the potential risks to team handball participants. Sound planning and good judgment are important factors to an enjoyable learning experience. The following lists provide a reference for teachers as they plan a team handball instructional unit.

Supervision

1. Make sure you are a qualified instructor:
   - Have knowledge of current rules and up-to-date techniques, tactics, teaching methods, and progressions
   - Obtain certification in the American Red Cross /U.S Olympic Committee sport safety training or first aid (must be renewed every three years)
2. Prior to starting activity, complete Physical Activity Readiness Questionnaire (PARQ) to determine present physical problems and health history of the students.
3. Establish a list of emergency procedures to be followed in all accident cases. Identify location of nearest phone and keep emergency phone numbers and medical forms on-site.
4. Know where to find ice and water.
5. Maintain properly equipped first aid kit plus plastic bags for ice.
6. Write lesson plans to document supervisory procedures for creating a safe learning environment.
7. Establish a procedure for distributing and gathering equipment.
8. Never leave the class unsupervised.
9. Keep your "back to the wall" to maintain visual contact with all students even while giving individual instruction; i.e., organize the warm-up and drills so that all of the activity is within your field of vision.
10. Establish and enforce safety rules and procedures. Strictly enforce "no horseplay or fooling around" rules during all classes.
11. Students, as well as the instructor, need to take responsibility for safety when the game begins. Warn students of the risk of injuries in team handball. Specific rules

are designed to prevent injuries. State the consequences of breaking the game or class-safety rules. For example, grabbing a player's shooting arm can result in a shoulder injury. Failure to follow safety rules during a throwing activity can result in hitting a player in the head. Official team handball rules mandate two-minute suspensions for rough play or repeated minor fouls. Teams are not allowed to substitute for the suspended player. During class, players who break rules should be temporarily suspended from the game. Modify the two-minute rule and substitute a player during a suspension.

12. Complete a detailed report, including the nature, circumstance, treatment, and followup of all injuries.

13. Analyze all accidents and near misses in order to seek future prevention strategies.

Selection and Conduct of the Activity

1. Use an established curriculum guide as a comprehensive reference for course content. Make team handball a part of the official curriculum for the school and district. USA Team Handball sells the "Member School Kit for Middle and Secondary Schools." The kit contains an instructor's guide, *Team Handball: Steps to Success* by Clanton and Dwight (www.humankinetics.com), and a team handball introduction video. Their website is *www.usateamhandball.org*

2. Conduct a warm-up to help prevent injuries and mentally and physically prepare players for the game. Prepare the class for activity with a warm-up activity that raises body temperature, followed by passive stretching. Do movements specific to team handball, such as jumping, sliding, forward and backward movements, various court runs with change of direction, etc. Prepare joints and muscle groups most used in team handball: the trunk, shoulder, hamstrings, quadriceps and calf muscle, and Achilles tendon.

3. Don't allow students to wear any jewelry, hairpins, or hard protective equipment that could injure the wearer or the other players (this includes the goalie, who might come into contact with court players).

4. Never allow an injured or ill student to participate without medical clearance.

5. Assess student abilities to determine tasks and skills appropriate for the age and student level.

6. Construct daily lesson plans to show a progression of appropriate skills and tasks. Progressions are one of the most important ways to ensure safety in any sport. A proper progression minimizes the likelihood of injury during the instruction phase and prepares the player for injury-free techniques during the games. For example, proper throwing progression includes working on proper mechanics, followed by throwing short distances practicing mechanics and throwing short distances practicing accuracy. Players can then increase distance, number of throws, and speed of shot gradually.

7. Equitably group a class that has a variety of skills, ages, genders, and sizes to decrease the potential for injuries. Mismatches are a function of size, strength, skill, and experience. Gender is not a factor. Following are suggestions for grouping students:

    • Group students by balancing the skill level of the group, i.e., mix advanced, intermediate, and beginning students equally in each group

    • Group students of similar skill level, i.e., place students into advanced, intermediate, and beginner groups

    • Establish group criteria. Let students rate their own ability and choose a group, i.e., competitive, recreational, and beginner

8. Prepare a written unit plan that includes daily lesson plans with objectives (cognitive, psychomotor, and affective), tasks, teaching methods, and assessment. Stress fundamental skills, combination skills, and small group play prior to full competition.

9. In pairs, teach the fundamental skills of goal keeping to all students to assess the abilities of each student to safely play goalie. Goalie skills carry over to safe blocking skills on the court.

10. Prohibit students from climbing or hanging from the nets or goalposts.

11. Demonstrate illegal contact with opponents and warn students of the injuries that could result from the following actions along with the official rule consequences:

    • A player pulls or hits the ball out of an opponent's hand

    • A player holds, pushes, or runs or jumps into an opponent

    • A player, from the side or from behind, strikes or pulls back the throwing arm of the opponent in the act of shooting or passing

    • A player takes any action resulting in the opponent being struck in the head or neck

    • A player strikes the body of an opponent with the foot or knee

    • A player pushes a running or jumping opponent, causing him/her to lose body control

12. Unlike basketball, when the ball crosses the plane of the sideline it is out of bounds. To reduce the chance of injury, teach players not to dive for a ball crossing the sideline.

13. Design drills to teach shooters to throw around, over, or between defenders. Rules prohibit dangerous throwing, i.e., recklessly or intentionally throwing a ball at a defender that strikes him/her in the body or head or faking the ball directly at player's body or head.

14. Prepare a written evaluation of daily lesson to assist in future planning and revisions for the following year's team handball unit.

15. To help facilitate competition, include opportunities for students to officiate.

16. To ensure safety, always set up passing drills so that a) there is ample distance

between passing pairs/groups, b) each pair is throwing in the same direction, and c) throwing pairs never overlap.

17. For shooting drills, observe the following:

   • Stop a shooting drill and remove balls from the goal cage if they may interfere with the goalie's movement or are likely to cause an injury due to the goalie stepping on a ball.

   • To prevent the goalie from being hit unexpectedly by a shot, tell students to make eye or verbal contact with the goalie before taking their turn to shoot.

   • With accurate shooters, indicate a shot direction pattern on goal so the goalie will know where to focus, i.e., alternate a right high shot with a left low shot. Change the pattern frequently.

   • For each shooting drill, determine a class method for gathering balls to prevent students from being hit by a shot when retrieving a ball. Using a goalie, have students shoot one at a time and wait until the last person shoots before retrieving any ball. When shooting at goal targets, have all students shoot at once on command and then retrieve the balls.

18. If you have a substitute teacher who is not knowledgeable in team handball, plan an alternate activity for the day.

Modifications

The focus of the educational process is the student, not the activity. Plan classes to provide all students the safest and most productive learning experience. Do not force or encourage students to perform when they are fearful or unequal to the task (i.e., playing goalie). Students should receive basic goalie training prior to playing in the goalie position. If students are playing the full game early in the instructional unit, modify the rules and equipment so that the game conforms to the skill level and ability of the players. Modifications can prevent chaotic play and reduce the chance of injuries. The following modifications are suggested for physical education classes practicing skill work and/or playing a team handball game:

1. Modify game-playing time to match fitness levels of students.

2. Limit game play to smaller groups, i.e., 3 vs. 3, 4 vs. 4 or 5 vs. 5. Designate a playing area that safely accommodates the size of the teams without compromising the skill level of the students, i.e., play on half court, using the width of the gym to make two shorter full courts rather than one court going the gym's length

3. Play lead-up games that focus on skills and particular concepts being emphasized (keep away, end line handball, etc)

4. When officiating beginners, give penalty throws liberally for any rough play in addition to those called for fouling during a clear chance to score. Let the fouled player shoot the penalty throw. Increasing penalty shot opportunities will allow offensive players to score more, and defensive players will quickly learn the difference between rough play and allowable torso contact.

5. Until the teacher instructs students in basic goal techniques, have players practice shooting for accuracy, play without goalies, and place targets (i.e., hula hoops tied to the goal, towels draped over the goal crossbar, cones in the lower corners, a sheet draped over the goal crossbar that exposes only the sides of the goal, etc.) in the goal's upper and lower corners for scoring points. After a shot on goal, designate one defensive court player to retrieve any ball that lands inside the goal area and to put the ball back into play with a goal throw to a teammate.

6. For introductory team handball units or in co-ed classes, play noncontact basketball-style defense (official rules for team handball do allow torso contact). To allow torso contact in an advanced team handball unit, instructors must be able to clearly explain and demonstrate both allowable and illegal contact to students.

7. Beginners have a tendency to throw the ball at the goalie rather than to the corners of the goal. Because of the angle and close proximity to the goal, wing shots are particularly dangerous to the goalie. Until players learn to look at the goalie's position and shoot to the open spaces in the goal, use the following modifications to help players develop shooting accuracy and reduce goalie injuries:

   • Help students develop accuracy by having them shoot at targets in the goal (towels, hula hoops, or cones in the corners of the goal) or by taping a goal on the wall and marking the best corner shots.

   • When the goalie is in the goalie ready position from the wing, modify the goalie's technique to use two hands in front of the face to protect against an unintentional shot to the face.

   • Do not allow direct set shots from the wing positions. Require wings and circle runners, when they are at the goal area line, to shoot bounce shots (shots from the six-meter line must hit the floor prior to going into the goal).

   • Do not allow shots on goal from outside 10 meters (just past the nine-meter free throw line).

   • Do not allow goalies to attempt to score by throwing a long shot to the opponent's goal from their own goal area.

   • Do not allow the goalie to leave his/her goal area to intercept a fast-break pass. This avoids a possible collision with an offensive court player who is trying to catch the long, fast-break pass.

Environmental Concerns

A teacher's responsibility for safety extends beyond the actual lesson activity to the equipment and environment in which the instruction takes place. In the United States, it is unlikely teachers will have access to an established team handball court and equipment, so they may have to modify the existing facility and make use of equipment immediately available to them.

Facilities

A regulation indoor team handball court on a wood or tartan surface measures 20 meters (65'7 3/8") by 40 meters (131'2 3/4"). However, team handball may be played indoors on a basketball-size court, outdoors on the grass, on the beach, or on any even, rectangular, nonslippery surface.

1. For competition, the rules require an additional safety zone outside the court lines of at least one meter on the sides and two meters beyond the end line. Because of missed goal shots, the area behind the end line can be dangerous to spectators crossing this area. For formal competition, a large safety net is advisable behind the goal to protect spectators and also to speed up play.

2. If students must walk behind the end line during physical education class, instruct them to walk when play has stopped or the ball is on the opposite end of the court.

3. Inspect the playing area for unnecessary equipment or unsafe objects near the court.

4. To avoid collisions and protect the goalie from illegal shots inside the goal area, mark the goal area line so that it can be clearly identified by all players. Bright-colored floor tape helps players recognize the area. Most students are familiar with a basketball court and can quickly adjust to modifying the court lines for team handball. Using gym floor tape, simply extend the basketball free throw line to meet the basketball three-point line (see Figure 1). Compare the modified "goal area" created in Figure 1 to the official team handball goal area and team handball free throw line marked in Figure 2.

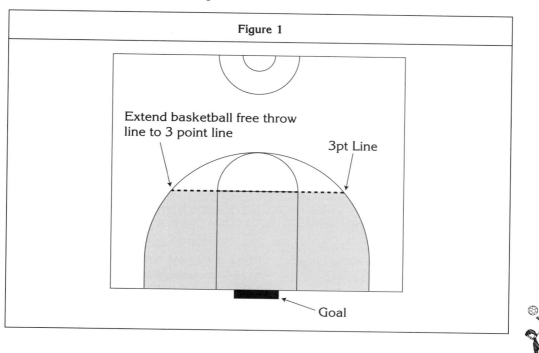

Figure 1

Extend basketball free throw line to 3 point line

3pt Line

Goal

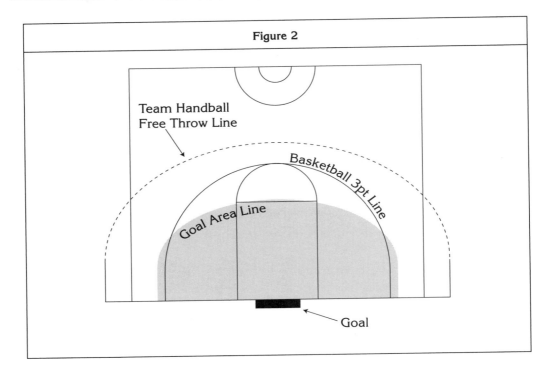

Figure 2

Team Handball
Free Throw Line

Basketball 3pt Line

Goal Area Line

Goal

5. Inspect the goal nets to insure a proper fit with no holes. A net not anchored properly may cause a goalie to get hung up in the net and trip. Velcro strips, plastic outdoor Christmas light wire holders, plastic zip ties, or plastic electric/computer wire holders work well for attaching nets easily and quickly.

6. Secure any loose bolts on goalpost joints.

7. Some practice goals may be less stable than heavier regulation team handball goals. Inside, if there is a risk of goals easily falling over, teachers are encouraged to anchor goals with sandbags. The tubes of sand used in the back of pickup trucks for traction during the winter work well. Outside in grass, "u" stakes will anchor unstable goals to the ground.

8. Prevent goal-related accidents by posting "No climbing or hanging on goals" signs and enforcing the rule.

9. Teach goalies to report problems during play with the anchor device, net, or goal structure to the instructor.

10. During a physical education class, create a reasonable buffer zone around teaching stations and playing areas or modify rules to accommodate a smaller area. For example, where space is limited, modify game rules by eliminating out-of-bounds and play all balls off the walls similar to indoor soccer.

11. For players under 12, follow recommendations to use a smaller court if possible. The International Handball Federation recommends that Mini-Handball courts be 12 -16 meters wide and 20-24 meters long (20 by 13 meters is one-third the size of a normal handball court.) The goal area is reduced to a semicircle of five meters radius from the middle of the goal.

Equipment

Similar to a soccer ball, a team handball consists of a rubber bladder and a white or orange leather, 32-panel cover decorated with a black symmetrical design. Based on hand size and individual strength, the ball varies in size and weight depending on the group participating (see Figure 3).

Follow these recommendations for team handballs in physical education classes:

1. Do not overinflate team handballs. The rules do not indicate an inflation pressure for a team handball. A simple standard is that the ball should have a good bounce when dropped from waist high, but it should not be so hard that it does not give a little when pressed with a thumb

Figure 3		
Recommendations for type and size of handballs	Metric	U.S. equivalent
*For men's competition: Leather or synthetic material Size 3 Circumference Weight	 58-60cm 425-475g	 23-24" 15-17 oz
*For under-17 males & women's competition: Leather or synthetic material Size 2 Circumference Weight	 54-56cm 325-400g	 21-22" 12-14 oz
For high school physical education classes: SuperSafe Elite (air-filled foam ball) Size 6 3/4" Made by Sportime 1-800-283-5700 Circumference Weight	 54-56cm 350g	 21-22" 12.3 oz
For middle school physical education classes: SuperSafe Elite (air-filled foam ball) Size 6 1/4" Made by Sportime 1-800-283-5700 Circumference Weight	 49-50cm 320g	 18-19" 11.3 oz
*For elementary physical education/Mini Handball: Select Ultra Light Lilliput Size 0 Circumference Weight	 48cm 290g	
*Available from USA Team Handball 719-575-4036 or *www.usateamhandball.org*		

2. To facilitate a "fear-free" game for any beginners and middle and high school physical education classes, USA Team Handball, national governing body for the sport, recommends the SuperSafe Elite 6 3/4," an air-filled foam ball with the same weight and size as an official women's competition ball.

3. For youth under 12 playing Mini-Handball, the International Handball Federation makes the following ball recommendation: suitable for children (colorful), soft, not too heavy, bounces well, easy to grasp (possibly with a textured surface), aids in a "fear free" game, and has a circumference of 44-49cm. Multipurpose dense foam balls meet most of these recommendations. Rubber playground balls are not recommended because they sting when the goalie is hit, and they are harder to catch due to the ball's bouncing capabilities.

Recommendations for court player and goalie attire:

1. Court players should wear short-sleeved shirts, shorts, socks, and court shoes.

2. Kneepads and/or elbow pads are recommended to cushion the fall of wings and circle runners in the goal area.

3. The goalie should wear a bright-colored, long-sleeved shirt or sweatshirt, sweat pants, kneepads, and a protective cup for males. The rules require goalies to wear a different color from either team uniform to distinguish them from court players. In physical education classes, use different-color scrimmage vests to help players recognize the goalies on both teams. For example, Team A court players wear red vests and their goalie wears an orange vest. Team B court players wear blue vests and their goalie wears a yellow vest.

4. It is recommended all players, but especially goalies, wear safety sport glasses attached with a strap. In physical education classes, do not allow students to play in the goal with their everyday glasses. Even with the modified softer foam ball, a misdirected shot that hits a goalie's glasses can cause injury to the goalie and damage to the glasses.

5. Rules prohibit players from wearing anything that might cause injury to another player (i.e., watch, jewelry, face mask).

Team handball is a reasonably safe physical activity as long a certain guidelines are followed. If instructors carefully plan the use of their instructional time for successful learning of team handball skills, carefully supervise the activity with particular attention to throwing in control with accuracy and body control, and provide adequate team handball equipment in a safe environment, then students can have fun and benefit from their participation in this exciting sport. A team handball unit thoroughly planned and structured with control of the activity allows students to enjoy the game and participate safely.

CHAPTER 22

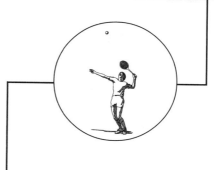

Tennis

Joanne Margaret Hynes-Dusel
Towson University
Towson, Maryland

Introduction

Group instruction in tennis, especially when carried on in a limited, crowded area, requires that certain precautionary measures be observed by the teacher and the students. An awareness of these safety rules will facilitate class organization and effective use of facilities and provide a stimulating and relaxing teaching situation. The students can be free from the worry of possible injury or harm and can concentrate on the activity.

Common Injuries

Most tennis injuries can be prevented or easily treated. Some of the more common tennis injuries include blisters, bruises, cramps, pulled muscles, muscle strains/sprains, shinsplints, back injuries, tendonitis, tennis elbow, dehydration, sunburn, insect bites or stings, and eye diseases.

Blisters that appear on hands and feet are caused by moisture, pressure, or friction. Feet that slide in a tennis shoe develop blisters; therefore, prevention requires wearing two pair of socks, with the cotton pair worn closest to the skin. The racket turning in the player's hand causes blisters on the racket hand. Players can prevent this type of blister by making sure they have the correct grip size. Usually a larger grip will prevent the racket from turning in the hand. Blisters also develop on the racket hand when the hand has not been accustomed to an extensive amount of play. The wear and tear creates a "hot spot" that results in a blister. Prevention consists of limiting playing time.

Sometimes a player is bruised when hit by a ball or racket. The only way to avoid this injury is to assume a safe position on the court so as to not be hit. For example, if the opposing player is about to hit an overhead smash in line with the opponent's position on the court, it is prudent for that player to turn and duck. Bruising can also occur when a player follows through with the racket and hits the shin when serving or when doubles partners swing at the same ball and hit each other. These incidents can cause severe bruising, called a hematoma.

In unusually warm and humid weather, when body fluid and salt are lost rapidly, a player may get cramps. A cramp consists of a muscle contracting and causing spasms, usually in the abdominal area or gastrocnemius (calf muscle). To prevent cramping, players should consume fluids in large quantities. Although water is perhaps the best choice of liquids, diluted fruit juices are an excellent alternative. Commercial sports drinks are another alternative because they replace carbohydrates and electrolytes while also replenishing liquid. The key to liquid consumption on a hot and humid day is to drink and then drink some more (Fiske, 1992).

Pulled muscles, including of the groin, hamstring, and gastrocnemius, generally occur as a result of poor stretching. They can often be avoided by going through a full warm-up.

Many tennis players sprain their ankle when they try to make a quick turn without the foot following the turn. Sometimes a player will jump to hit a ball and land on the side of the foot or step on a ball during play. Sprained ankles can be prevented by (1) coordinating effort and physical skill when jumping and landing, and (2) picking up the balls or rolling them toward the net or fence so a player does not step on one. Only three tennis balls should be available for play at any given point in a match. In addition, be aware of other courts' balls and stop play if a ball is in the court area.

Knees and wrists can also be injured when playing tennis. Knee ligament and cartilage damage can result from the same situations that cause ankle sprains. Stepping on a ball or backpeddling rather than turning a shoulder and running back to a position to return a shot are typical actions that result in these types of injuries.

Another injury associated with tennis is shinsplints. Constant pounding, running, jumping, and landing on a hard court can create an inflammation of the soft tissues of the front part of the lower legs. A change of court surfaces, or high arches, tight calves, and high intensity in workouts and playing situations all contribute to this injury. Prevention includes being aware of the causes, stretching, and using common sense regarding playing intensity and type of court being played on. Selecting the proper shoe with arch support and excellent shock absorption capabilities is also important. Recommended ways of dealing with shinsplints include rest and the application of ice (Higdon, 1992).

Repetitive twisting and trunk rotation is a part of tennis. Unfortunately, accelerating the trunk through ground strokes and executing an overhead arching motion in a serve increase the risk of back injury. Preventive measures include conditioning programs and good stroke technique (Squires, 1993).

Tennis players are susceptible to tendonitis because of the extreme pressure they place on the Achilles tendon. Players sometimes jump and land on the ball of the foot without lowering the heel. This puts pressure on the tendon, rupturing it. When the tendon ruptures, it sounds like a gunshot retort, and the player becomes immobile immediately. High-arched feet with heels angling inward or flat feet that roll inward are most vulnerable to Achilles-tendon problems.

Tennis players sometimes experience an Achilles tendon that is chronically sore because they ignore the persistent pain and continue to play. The Achilles tendon and the sheath that surrounds it become inflamed, and soreness, swelling, and more intense pain are the outcome. Ignoring these signs can cause severe problems. The only way to address the injury is to stop playing and rest. Prevention includes stretching the Achilles tendon during the warm-up. Once an Achilles tendon injury has occurred, rehabilitation is necessary. Modalities used in therapy include ice, massage, ultrasound, and/or electrical stimulation that help reduce swelling. A stiff tendon is a sign of an impending rupture, and if the Achilles tendon is ruptured, the player must go through a very long process of rehabilitation following surgery or immobilization (McNab, 1993).

The other common tennis injury is tennis elbow. There are several types of tennis elbow injuries, the main one being an inflammation of the elbow area. This injury can be prevented if a player uses proper skill techniques and strokes. Hitting with the elbow leading on the backhand or hitting numerous slice or spin serves invites the injury. Prevention requires correcting poor mechanics and using common sense regarding how many spin serves are hit. Treatment includes rest and/or the application of a support. Elbow supports and splints are available to relieve minor pain from tennis elbow, but they will not eliminate the cause.

If an injury is perceived to be serious, a physician should be consulted as soon as possible. If rehabilitation is recommended, it is advisable to seek out a sports medicine clinic. Most metropolitan areas have centers that work closely with physicians to rehabilitate injuries.

Home treatment should be limited to only minor injuries, i.e. blisters (because they usually dry up on their own). For minor injuries, some athletic trainers can develop devices that enable continuation of activity. For example, a trainer can devise a doughnut-shaped pad that will cover the blister, reduce pain at the pressure point, and prevent additional friction on the blister area.

Additional problems that occur in tennis include dehydration, sunburn, and insect bites or stings. Dehydration is particularly serious but can be resolved by drinking liquids before, during, and after a match. Caffeine should be avoided because it contributes to dehydration. Intake of beverages should begin as early as two hours before playing.

Depending on what part of the country players come from, insect bites and stings might bother them. Avoiding being stung is an obvious preventive measure. When players are around bees and wasps, they should be especially alert. When players pick up a racket, they should make sure a bee is not lurking. Bees and wasps congregate at the opening of cans containing beverages with sugar. If a player is stung, the recommended way of removing the stinger is to scrape the sac away and extract the stinger with a tweezer.

Sunburn can be avoided by applying sunscreen with a sun protection factor (SPF) of at least 15. Look for a product that blocks both UVA and UVB rays. Wearing a hat helps to prevent sunburn and heat stroke. Players often reject sunscreen because the lotion is applied by hand and then is transferred to the racket grip. By simply wiping their hands, players can avoid transferring the lotion to the grip of the racket. Some players also reject wearing a hat, suggesting that they can't see the ball on the serve toss and that it generally gets in their way. These are just excuses.

One last potential physical problem deserves consideration. Eyes exposed to ultraviolet rays over an extended time are at risk for at least three eye diseases: cataracts (clouding of the lens), pterygium (a flesh-like growth on the white of the eye near the iris), and macular degeneration (breakdown of the retina with age). Pterygium is of particular concern, as the incidence of developing this eye disease is relatively high for those who are in the sun extensively (Chen, 1995). A partial answer is to begin wearing sunglasses while playing tennis. New technology has produced a polycarbonate lens that wraps the lens around the head. A quality pair of sunglasses not only protects against the sun but also screens out peripheral light and wind while still providing clear visibility for the player.

Supervision

The following are necessary organizational and control skills and knowledge that the teacher/supervisor needs to know/have:

1. Have on file a parent's consent card and a physical examination card if required by school or department policy.

2. Make use of available netting, canvas, etc., to provide safe hitting lanes or areas for students to practice.

3. Position the students so they are not placed in dangerous situations:
   - Direct them to hit in one direction only
   - Space students far enough apart so they do not hit or run into each other
   - Make provisions for left-handed players so that they do not endanger classmates while swinging or hitting

4. File accident reports for all injuries that occur, regardless of how minor they appear to be, according to school or department policy, and keep a record of the report in your personal file.

5. Make students aware of their responsibilities for observing safety precautions and the consequences that will occur if they do not observe them.

6. Have students warm up sufficiently before starting strenuous activity.

7. Direct students to wear tennis sneakers and socks that fit properly in order to prevent blisters and stumbling. Laces need to be securely tied.

8. Require students to wear physical education uniforms or appropriate clothes for physical activity when participating in any tennis activity.

9. Prohibit jewelry.

10. Require students to listen to your instructions and follow them carefully.

11. Create a stop signal (i.e., blow your whistle) and directions to follow when the signal is sounded. For example, when the students hear the signal, they need to stand still, remain quiet, listen, and wait for the signal to start again.

12. Keep students in line, on marks, or in their own area when swinging or hitting. They should also check to make sure they are not near others when they are swinging or hitting.

13. Instruct students to refrain from showing off and participating in horseplay activities.

14. Instruct students on how to control their emotions and respect their peers, the teacher, themselves, and the equipment. For example, they cannot throw a racket or hit a ball (or a person) in anger.

15. Students should shout out a warning when there is danger of a ball hitting someone.

16. Students need to communicate with each other and must never hit a ball at someone who is not ready.

17. Maintain visual contact with all students by keeping your back to the wall, thus keeping all or most of the class in view.

18. Stop all unsafe acts immediately.

19. Allow student frequent water breaks in excessively hot temperatures.

20. Always maintain control of your class. Discipline when necessary.

21. Try to anticipate the acts of students before they occur.

22. Develop a safety-conscious attitude among students. Discuss with them their responsibilities with regard to personal safety and the safety of others.

Selection and Conduct of Activity

Teachers need to select and conduct activities, drills, skills, and games that are developmentally appropriate, that are based on a progression, and that are safe. Otherwise, they open themselves up for legal problems if anyone does get hurt. The following checklist can be used to monitor the selection and conduct of activities to make sure they are in compliance with school, district, and/or state safety standards:

1. Are lesson plans written? Do they include provisions for proper instruction, sequence of activities, and safety? Are all activities taught listed in the district curriculum guide?

2. When a new activity or skill is introduced, are safety precautions and instructions for correct skill performance always communicated to the class?

3. Are the activities taught in the program based on sound curriculum principles? Could the activities and units of instruction be defended on the basis of their educational contributions?

4. Do the methods of instruction recognize individual differences among students, and are the necessary steps taken to meet the needs of all students, regardless of sex, ability, or disability?

5. When necessary for safety, are students grouped according to ability level, size, or age?

6. Is the class left unsupervised for teacher visits to the office, lounge, or bathroom? Is one teacher ever asked to supervise two or more classes at the same time?

Environmental Concerns

The following list can be used to monitor the physical education environment (i.e., facilities and equipment). Any situations that stray from safe and legally sound practices should be corrected immediately.

Facilities

1. Be sure all first aid supplies are on hand or are easily accessible.

2. Check courts for obstacles, glass, stones, slippery spots, etc., before and after every class.

3. Post specific safety rules on facilities and near equipment (use the information printed here if you need to).

4. Courts and practice areas should be arranged so participants will not run into each other or be hit by a ball from another game. This is especially important in today's world, where many schools do not have the proper space for tennis facilities and are forced to participate in smaller areas.

Equipment

1. Make sure all the equipment (balls, rackets, nets) is in proper working order. Replace, remove, or repair equipment as necessary before and after every class. Record the inspection results on a form and send it to the proper administrators.

2. Have an assortment of developmentally appropriate rackets (i.e., different weights and handle size, etc.) and tennis balls (i.e., foam, wiffle, sponge, gator, different sizes, etc.).

3. Have a place where students can pick up and return equipment without getting hurt (i.e., away from any obstructions). Also, have a method for distributing and collecting equipment that does not allow all the students to rush in together (i.e., "if you're wearing the color..," "if you were born in the month of...").

4. When the tennis balls are not in use, make sure they are returned to the proper storage area directed by the teacher. If left on the playing area, students can get hurt.

5. As stated earlier, teach the students to respect the equipment. This includes making sure students do not abuse or use the equipment in any way other than what it was intended for.

6. Students who are waiting to enter a match should be placed outside the area of play (i.e., outside the fence) where they can still be adequately supervised but do not pose a collision hazard to players in the match.

Tennis is a reasonably safe sport as long as guidelines are followed. Teachers need to carefully plan for the successful learning of tennis skills for students of all ability levels. Teachers must constantly supervise activities with attention to the amount of space given to students to practice on the courts. They must supervise equipment distribution/collection, and equipment inspection and repair. Then students can enjoy and benefit from participation in this exciting lifelong activity.

References

The American Alliance for Health, Physical Education, and Recreation. (1972). *Tennis: Group instruction.* Washington, DC: National Education Association.

Bryant, J. E. (1997). *Game, set, match: A tennis guide.* Englewood, CO: Morton Publishing Company.

Chen, K. (May, 1995). The eyes have it. *Tennis,* 74.

Fiske, S. E. (February, 1992). Tips from the pros. *Tennis,* 83.

Higdon, D. (June, 1992). How to prevent shin splints. *Tennis,* 102.

McNab, A. (June, 1993). Protecting your Achilles. *Tennis,* 99.

Pangrazi, R., & Darst, P. (1997). *Dynamic physical education for secondary students.* Boston, MA: Allyn and Bacon.

Squires, D. (April, 1993). Oh, my aching back. *Tennis,* 10.

CHAPTER 23

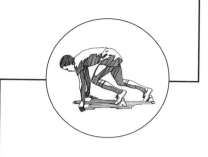

Track and Field

Nancy Knop
Ohio Wesleyan University
Delaware, Ohio

Introduction

Track and field events have always provided an avenue for comparison of human performance limits. Unfortunately, these comparisons are often a source of embarrassment for many developing junior and senior high school students and "turn them off" from the sport, from physical education, or from lifetime physical activities. Likewise, when running is used as a punishment or is implemented in a way that is unmotivating, students often learn to hate it. Track and field programs provide teachers the opportunity to support the development of lifetime physical activities by providing students opportunities and pathways to improve their physical capabilities and enjoy success in their improvement. The challenge facing physical education teachers implementing track and field is to create programs that are motivating, fun, challenging, and safe for all students.

This chapter will present an overview of the major risks and dangers innate to the various events of track and field. First, the factors influencing the selection of events into the track and field unit will be discussed. This will be followed by an overview of the types of risks teachers of track and field face. Finally, important class structure and organization issues that promote a safe and motivating environment will be discussed and highlighted for several track and field events.

Event Selection

Track and field, as a competitive sport, can include development and participation in as many as 20 different events. When using track and field in a physical education class, it is important to select only some of these events to foster a positive and safe learning environment. The following suggestions might guide selection of the several events to be included in the physical education class:

1. Consider limiting the number of events chosen to allow students enough time at each event to learn, practice, and experience a training effect. Too often, teachers spend a day on each event and then have a meet. Doing so allows little learning and no training to occur. Further, terminal competitions favor high-ability or previously experienced students and offer no opportunity for development of the lesser skilled and inexperienced students.

2. Select events for which you have enough safe equipment to allow all students equal time at each event and that you, as supervisor, can safely and competently supervise.

3. Find ways to record and reward progress toward event improvement. This may include creating lead-up competitions where students practice and then compete at a lead-up skill rather than the complete skill of an event. For example, after learning safe pit-landing skills, have a competition where students measure and record their performances from the standing long jump. This teaches and allows practice in how to measure a jump and how to perform a safe landing off a maximal standing long jump.

4. Track is both an individual and team event and is more fun, rewarding, and successful when both the team and individual experience is valued. This can be supported using the Sport Education model (Siedentop, 1995) for structuring the class. Equal teams that allow students to practice within the team unit and compete across team units provide a fun way to challenge student development. To promote individual value on teams, competitions can be supported by True Team Scoring, where all teams have the opportunity to enter equal numbers of students in each event and each student entered earns points for the team (e.g., if three students per team can be entered and there are five teams, then first place is worth 15 points, second place is worth 14, and so on to fifteenth place, which is worth one point).

Major Risks and Dangers

There are several categories of risks and dangers that must be anticipated in track and field to prevent injuries and compromised student safety. Because track and field is composed of different events that often occur simultaneously and in close proximity to other events, the potential for collisions that lead to acute injuries is a risk factor. Each event requires a unique organization of space, equipment, and student participation specific to the nature of the event. Further, to ensure student safety, teachers need to create rules and routines for spectating, participating, and entering and exiting the track or field event areas.

In addition, track and field teaches and trains students toward maximal, measurable performance improvements. Due to the exertion and effort required of students to participate and compete appropriately in each event and the repetitious nature of the activities needed to promote student learning and physiological improvement, chronic injuries due to overuse or technical faults are common. Teachers are charged with the responsibility of creating sound, sequential, and developmentally appropriate progressions that take into account both the time and repetitions needed for learning and the potential physiological impact of the repeated near-maximal activity.

A final risk consideration concerns the impact the environment can have. Track and field is most commonly taught and practiced in an outdoor environment. As a result, the weather can greatly impact student safety. As with any outdoor activity, threatening weather changes accompanied by lightning or high winds contraindicate outdoor participation. Wet conditions that might occur after a rain or a heavy dew, or hot conditions accompanied by humidity or sun also compromise the safety of student participation. Due to the nature of the different events, environmental conditions impact each event in a unique way. Once again, the teacher is charged with anticipating this impact and minimizing risk for student participation.

Safety Issues and Their Prevention for Specific Events

Each of the event areas in track and field provides unique safety issues and risk-prevention solutions. What follows is a breakdown of several track and field events a teacher might choose for a track and field unit. These specific events were chosen for several reasons. First, as a whole, they represent all the event areas of track and field-throwing, jumping, sprinting, hurdling, distance running, and relays. Second, these events tend to be the safer and more common events relative to the other events in that category. For each event, safety issues specific to that event, possible sources or causes of risk, and preventative measures the teacher should consider in creating lessons plans and class organization are described.

Shot put. Perhaps the greatest risk to competitors or bystanders in the shot put is that of being hit by a shot. Once a shot put leaves a thrower's hand it is silent. As a result, a person in the way of the shot will get no warning before impact. In addition, shot puts are heavy. A women's high school shot put weighs 8.8 pounds, and a high school men's shot put weighs 12 pounds. If either of these shots should hit a person with some velocity, the likelihood of a severe injury is great. Although a majority of the supervision suggestions below focus on creating safe environments to reduce the risk of these collision injuries, overuse and environmental injuries are also examined.

Sprinting and relays, long jump, and hurdle events. Similar to the shot put, an important risk factor in sprint events is collisions. Different from the shot put, collisions in sprinting tend to be between people or with an obstacle. Whereas the goal of a sprinter is to practice and compete at fast speeds, the results tend to be severe when these collisions happen. Again, due to the speed sprinters are attempting to attain, cold or slippery conditions can affect sprinters much more than these conditions would affect participants of other track and field events. Also, since sprinting is part of the hurdling and long jump skills, the risks identified and examined for sprinting will also apply to those events.

Shotput Safety			
Safety Issues	**Possible Causes**	**Preventions**	**Preventative Supervision**
<u>Collisions</u> -Hit by shotput	-Retrieving without looking -Thrower doesn't check sector -Thrower mis-throws -Shot hits retriever on bounce -Shot leaves sector and hits bystander	 Retrieval Path Shots Spectators & Competitors R=Retrievers	-Thrower retrieval pattern -Thrower "check sector" routine -Retriever role -Use Nonbounce shots -Retriever position well back -Stable sector boundaries -Bystander/competitor designated area
<u>Obstructions</u> -Tripping or falling	-Thrower steps on retrieved shot -Thrower trips over toe board	-Keep equipment in designated area -Teach thrower to block properly	-Create designated area for shot puts -Start student farther away from toe board in progression
<u>Acute/overuse injuries</u> of the muscle, joint, or tendon	-Improper warm-up -Improper technique or teaching progressions	-Shoulder overuse -Shoulder, elbow, wrist, hand, or finger acute injury -Hip adductors (groin) or hip flexors acute injury or overuse -Shin splints, knee soreness	-Gradual progression in number and types of throws -Supervise throws to corrector eliminate improper upper body technique -Supervise throws to correct improper hip power position -Well-cushioned shoes
<u>Environmental issues</u> -Rain or heavy dew	Wet facility -Slipping in ring -Shot slipping out of hands and hitting bystander	-Misstep causing muscle pull or joint injury -Misthrow causing shot to hit bystander	-Sweep out or dry out ring -Dry off shoes before entering ring -Dry off hands and shot

Sprinting and Relays Safety		
Safety Issues	**Possible Causes**	**Preventative Supervision**
<u>Collisions</u> with: Noncompetitors Competitors Relay personnel	-Noncompetitors in lanes -Leaving assigned lane during race or practice -Warm-up striding in both directions and across lanes -Relay personnel in way of sprinters	<u>Routine for crossing track</u> -When entering track, look both ways <u>Routine for sprint practice/warm-up</u> -Warn others of lane "Track, Lane 1" -Assign lanes for sprints at practice -Run in same direction on track <u>Exit plan for relay personnel</u> -Stay in lane or your side of lane until all runners pass -Exit to the inside of track after runners have passed
<u>Obstructions</u>	-Inappropriate track obstructions	-Check lanes before sprinting for hurdles or blocks left in lane
<u>Overuse injuries:</u> Muscle, joint, tendon (primarily shins, knee/hip joints, hamstrings/quads)	-Too much (speed, volume) too soon -Not enough shock absorption -Quadriceps/hamstring muscle imbalance or inappropriate technique	-Create gradual and age-appropriate progressions -Plan to vary surfaces (grass, track, sand, or dirt) -Teach students about and supervise for appropriately supportive and cushioned footwear -Create conditioning program focused on injury prevention of typical sprint injuries. -Progressively teach and supervise for correct technique/timing of sprint action
<u>Environmental Issues</u>	-Wet facility (rain, heavy dew)may cause slipping -Cold conditions may lead to muscle injury	-Increase traction by using spikes or decrease speed performance expectations to avoid slipping -Supervise for appropriate warm-up and clothing in cold conditions

Long Jump Safety		
Safety Issues	**Possible Causes**	**Preventative Supervision**
<u>Collisions</u> with noncompetitors or competitors (resulting in joint sprains, muscle strains, bruises, or contusions)	-Noncompetitors in runway -Jumper unaware of other jumpers in area	<u>Routine for crossing runway</u> -When entering runway, look both ways -Limit runway access to competitors only (using cones, hurdles, or other barriers) <u>Routine for jump practice/warm-up</u> -Warn others when jumping -Take turns -Start approach ONLY when pit is clear <u>Create pit exit and return routine</u> -Always exit same side of pit -Always return to take-off area on same side of runway
<u>Collision injuries</u> due to inappropriate landing surface (knee, ankle, or back-strain injuries)	-Surface too hard or too uneven, causing ineffective landing-Collision with equipment left in sand	-Ensure sand in pit is turned to provide 10-12 inch depth of clean, loose sand for landing -Rake pit level between all jumps -Remove all equipment (i.e., rakes) from pit
Injuries due to obstructions (ankle sprain, bruises, contusions)	-Tripping over equipment before, during, or after jump.	-Remove all obstacles near pit that jumper may trip over (i.e., student bags, pit care equipment, chairs, etc.) -Make sure pit care equipment is not in jumper's return path
<u>Acute-use injuries</u> (most frequently back, hip, knee, or ankle strain or sprain)	-Inappropriate landing technique	-Teach jumpers to land safely to avoid stress to back, hip, knees, or ankles -Progressively supervise jump landing at faster and faster speeds
<u>Chronic over use injuries</u> (shin stress, hip flexor or hamstring strain, or knee/hip joint stress)	-Too many take-offs or landings too soon. -Inappropriate take-off technique	-Gradually increase the number of take-offs and landings -Supervise to improve take-off form and timing -Incorporate take-off areas that reduce impact at take-off or force heel-toe roll-uptake-off (i.e. mats, boxes, or ramps)

Safety Issues	Possible Causes	Preventative Supervision
Environmental issues -Muscle strain due to wet conditions -Muscle strain due to cold conditions -Muscle strain due to muscle response in gusty conditions	-Slipping at take-off -Cooler muscles less responsive to take-off or landing demands -Muscle missteps to change in speed due to wind gust	-Try to keep take-off board and runway as dry as possible - Have students use spiked shoes to increase traction at take-off - Ensure appropriate warm-up and clothing for conditions -Educate students about effects of wind -Teach students how/when to abort attempt if unsafe

Hurdle Safety		
Safety Issues	**Possible Causes**	**Preventative Supervision**
Collisions with hurdle Types of collisions/outcome – lead foot – tripping – trail knee – bruising/tripping – trail foot – tripping – aborting attempt and running into hurdle	– Hurdle set at wrong height or distance – Inappropriate technique	– Check all hurdles for appropriate height, counter-weight setting, and spacing – Create and implement age- and developmentally appropriate progressions to teach proper form – Modify equipment when teaching skill to decrease likelihood of injury; Use shorter spacing, lower hurdles, padded crossbars
Misuse of hurdle – Tripping or falling over hurdle	– Goofing around with hurdles – Attempting to clear hurdle when hurdle is facing the wrong direction	Create and enforce hurdle rules: 1. Only hurdlers hurdle 2. Remove and stack all hurdles off track after use 3. Only go over hurdle in correct direction

Middle Distance and Distance Safety Issues. The potential for overuse injuries tends to be the primary risk facing students engaged in running activities. In addition, physical stress resulting from high exertion and hot environmental conditions provides additional risk that the teacher must manage.

Middle-Long Distance Safety		
Safety Issues	**Possible Causes**	**Preventative Supervision**
Chronic overuse injuries (shin stress; knee, hip, or back irritation; fatigue or illness)	-Too much (volume) too soon -Too little programmed rest or recovery after higher intensity or greater mileage days. -Inappropriate technique due to muscular weakness -Inappropriate footwear -Inappropriate nutrition or hydration	Create and implement -age- and developmentally appropriate workout progressions -preventative core strength conditioning to support running mechanics Teach and supervise appropriate runner footwear selection. Monitor runners for signs of overtraining – fatigue, no appetite, lethargy, worsening performance
Acute injuries (ankle sprains)	-Tripping or falling on uneven terrain	-Create preventative ankle, knee, and hip core strength conditioning (condition balance and proprioception)
Collisions on track with competitors or noncompetitors	-Runners unaware of other runners around them -Chaotic running patterns so runners can't predict who or whether someone is in their lane	Create track practice routines 1. Assign practice lanes 2. Run in only one direction 3. Warn people ("Track Lane 5!") 4. Look both ways before crossing track
Environmental issues -Hot or hot/humid conditions (heat stress, dehydration, sunburn, overexertion)	-Inappropriate clothing -Too much exposure to conditions -Too high-exertion for conditions	In hot/sunny or hot/humid conditions, promote 1. light-colored, breathable clothing 2. sunscreen and hats 3. use of shade when possible 4. frequent breaks and rehydration 5. decreasing practice intensity or volume

Conclusion

Track and field curricular programs provide a unique learning environment for students of all sizes, shapes, and abilities. At the same time, due to the nature of each of the events, track and field also presents multiple safety risks that teachers must understand and reduce. Many of the safety risks across the events can be managed by effective organization of participation patterns and space. Equally important is teaching students and holding them accountable for supporting and maintaining safety in such a complex environment.

Reference

Siedentop, D. (Ed.). (1994). *Sport education: Quality PE through positive sport experiences.* Champaign, IL: Human Kinetics Publishers.

CHAPTER 24

Tumbling and Gymnastics

David A. Feigley
Rutgers University
New Brunswick, New Jersey
Feigley's School of Gymnastics
South Plainfield, New Jersey

Risk in gymnastics is deceptive. It is not a contact sport. Moreover, with the possible exception of handgrips, gymnasts wear no protective clothing. Protective equipment in gymnastics is, for the most part, external, often leading to the perception that there is little or no risk or that whatever risk does exist can be entirely controlled via matting and spotting. Mats, especially thick training mats, may give a false sense of security, leading students and teachers to mistakenly believe that mats, spotters, and other safety equipment are sufficient for ensuring safety.

Whereas mats and spotters are often necessary and appropriate, they do not substitute for good judgment, proper progressions, and adequate safety precautions. Even specialized safety equipment such as overhead spotting belts and foam pits pose certain serious risks that the novice or intermediate gymnastics instructor might not fully appreciate[1].

The injury rate in gymnastics is comparable to the injury rates of contact sports such as football, wrestling, basketball, and lacrosse (*USA Gymnastics Safety Handbook,* 1998). However, gymnastics can be conducted quite safely, especially at the instructional level, if the predictable risks are identified and controlled by qualified instructors. For example, gymnastics involves performing in the inverted position, exposing the head, neck, and spine

---

[1] Some examples: a) arms being entangled in spotting ropes, resulting in abrasions and constriction; b) landing in foam pits in an arched position, snapping the spine at the lower back; c) forceful assistance with the belt resulting in whiplash if the gymnast's torso muscles are not held tightly.

to unsafe landings on the mats and apparatus. Thus, gymnastics requires strong attention to proper progressions to allow the student to adapt to such initially unfamiliar positions both in terms of maintaining body awareness throughout a correctly executed skill and—in the case of errors of execution—in terms of landing safely and being able to control the risk.

Landings in gymnastics often occur from significant height and include powerful rotational forces. Such combination of forces creates the potential for injury even when gymnasts land correctly on their feet. Such risks can be reduced by a) conditioning gymnasts sufficiently so they have the strength to safely absorb such forces and b) matching the skills taught to the current conditioning level of the gymnasts, especially with beginner and intermediate classes. With both advanced and beginner performers, assistance such as spotting and extra thick landing mats should be provided while they are learning new skills.

Psychological factors also introduce risk in gymnastics. Fear often inhibits attempts or causes students to display maladaptive behaviors such a shutting one's eyes during the performance of a skill or pulling on the apparatus (e.g., the high bar or the uneven parallel bars) when safe execution requires the performer to push away from the apparatus.

Another risk involves interactions with spotters. In most sports, coaches and athletes have little physical contact. In gymnastics, coaches regularly provide physical assistance to gymnasts, creating the possibility of collisions or of the coach being struck by the gymnast's arms or legs during the execution of a skill. Such a possibility requires spotters to be knowledgeable about where to stand and to anticipate where and when the gymnasts might falter. Spotters must also avoid such risks as extending their arms over parallel bars where a falling gymnast's body creates the possibility of serious injury to the spotter. An over-reliance on spotters may also lead to a false sense of security on the part of both the student and the spotter.

Research findings indicate that injuries occur most often during tumbling (approximately 35%)[2]. However, as an indicator of risk, these findings may be somewhat deceiving. The higher incidence of injuries while tumbling may reflect the fact that tumbling is typically practiced more than any other event because the skills of tumbling transfer to all other events. Additionally, tumbling typically allows many gymnasts to work simultaneously, especially if they are fortunate enough to have a floor exercise mat (approximately 40' x 40'), whereas the other pieces of apparatus typically allow only one performer per piece of equipment. Research has also found that injuries are most likely to occur in gymnastics because of incorrect dismounts, unintentional falls from the equipment, and unintentional falls onto the apparatus, especially the bars (horizontal, uneven, and parallel).

Supervision

Effective supervision is an essential aspect of providing safe and successful physical activity programs, such as in gymnastics, and is questioned virtually every time an accident is

---

[2] This pattern has been documented several times across a significant period of time (Caine, Cochrane, Caine & Zemper, 1989; Leglise & Rall, 1997, as cited in *USA Gymnastics Safety Handbook*, 1998.)

examined. Whereas both general and specific supervision are essential ingredients of all formal instruction in the schools, the need to develop deliberate patterns of teaching is of particularly great concern in gymnastics because gymnastics typically generates a greater variety of possible student responses. The teacher of gymnastics must be able to distinguish between general supervision—which is required at all times during instruction—and circumstances that require specific supervision; the teacher must be able to shift back and forth between general and specific supervision as circumstances dictate.

General supervision requires that the teacher maintain visual contact of the entire class, be immediately accessible to all students, and continuously monitor the class to ensure that safe procedures are being followed. Specific supervision is required when unsafe practices are observed and corrective action is needed or when a student is attempting a new or particularly dangerous skill. The need for specific supervision increases for beginning, immature, and lower ability students as opposed to advanced, mature, and highly skilled students. The application of specific supervision to particular students in the class does not reduce the requirement for continued general supervision of all other students. Thus, an effective supervising teacher provides individualized feedback to a single student while standing in such a position as to be able to continue to monitor the entire class.

Instructors must establish safe teaching stations, proper placement of safety matting, and appropriately matched student groupings and must assess students' abilities to work independently. Attention to these factors permits teachers to provide continuous general supervision while still providing specific supervision to those students who need individual instruction.

Effective supervision should include the following specific elements:

- The gymnasium, the gymnastics apparatus, and all gymnastics mats should be inaccessible to students unless a qualified instructor is present. Unsupervised mats and equipment should be viewed as an invitation to participants or what is often referred to legally as an attractive nuisance.

- Never leave the gymnastic area unattended while students are present.

- Policies should be developed that justify the department's position on gymnasium security and specify the steps established to ensure that an unsupervised gymnastics area is never left open to the public. At a minimum, these policies should specify the following:

  - Who is responsible for opening and securing the area.

  - The exact manner in which the area should be opened and secured.

  - The times and circumstances during which the area is to be opened and secured.

  - The placement/condition of the equipment when the gymnasium is secured.

- Position yourself so that, with a glance, the entire gymnastics area remains in view at all times. For example, individual instruction should be provided with the instructor's back to a wall or empty space so that beyond the individual or individuals receiving specific instruction, the entire gymnastics area remains in view.

- Station yourself regularly in the area judged to have the greatest need for instruction and/or supervision; for instance, when new skills are being introduced or physical assistance is requested by or required for a student.

- Students should have direct access to the instructor at all times. They should be taught to seek assistance whenever they are attempting skills of which they are uncertain, such as those that are new or difficult. They should also be taught to inform the instructor of problems and/or injuries. For example, such a referral is expected if there is a problem with equipment, if a disturbance occurs, or if someone is injured or is breaking a safety rule.

- The rules of conduct and safety should be posted conspicuously in the gymnasium to serve as a constant reminder of the expected behavior. At a minimum, the rules should include the following points regarding supervision:
  - Without exception, no one is permitted in the gymnastics area unless a qualified instructor is present.
  - Gymnastics practice may not begin without the explicit permission of the instructor.
  - Appropriate matting is mandatory for all activities at all stations.
  - Only teacher-approved spotters may be used. (Although the use of student spotters is an acceptable practice, such student spotters must be taught safe spotting techniques, tested to ensure their competency after the instruction, and regularly monitored to ensure that appropriate spotting is adhered to. Spotters—both student spotters and teacher spotters—should be matched to those students being assisted in terms of size, experience, maturity, and strength.)

- Safety rules should be reviewed with students on a regular basis to ensure that students know the rules, understand the reasons why the safety rules are required, and appreciate the consequences of violating the safety rules, both in terms of potential injury and appropriate sanctions. As a rule, the younger, the less experienced, and the less mature the students, the more frequently the instructor needs to provide formal reminders of the rules.

- All instruction should be provided in language that the participants can understand and in a tone that, while nonthreatening, conveys the seriousness of the message.

Necessary Skills and Knowledge of Supervisor

Qualified instructors should have a thorough knowledge of the following:

- Mechanics of gymnastics
- Appropriate horizontal and vertical progressions. Horizontal refers to skills of essentially the same difficulty levels, whereas vertical refers to progressively more demanding skills

- Current instructional techniques
- Safe spotting techniques and an understanding of the proper use, limitations, and risks of spotting and spotting equipment
- Care and maintenance of mats and apparatus
- Principles of gymnasium layout
- First aid and emergency procedures, including an emergency action plan sanctioned by the school
- The general physical, emotional, and cognitive characteristics of the student populations being taught
- Individual student readiness
- Safe progressions for all skills taught
- Knowledge of one's personal capabilities-both what you are and are not qualified to do

Verification of the instructor's knowledge base should be documented via gymnastics safety certification[3] or comparable training achieved through college/university courses or gymnastics-specific, in-house training programs.

Organization and Control

Lesson plans should be prepared for each instructional period. They should include not only the concepts and activities to be taught but also the strategies for ensuring safe supervision and the elimination of potential risks. They should include, at the very least, the following information:

- The difficulty of the skills to be taught, which should be matched with the skill level of the student population. In recognition that virtually all classes have a variety of abilities, such a lesson typically provides multiple teaching stations that provide for varied levels of direct supervision
- Gymnastic layout plans that include traffic control patterns and safety zones that provide sufficient room for safe tumbling lanes and landing areas for each piece of apparatus used
- The apparatus and mat placement and how such placement relates to the instructor's ability to provide specific instruction while maintaining general instruction
- Placement of qualified spotters and their responsibilities as secondary supervisors
- The efforts made to ensure student awareness of the safety rules and the behaviors expected of the students

---

[3] Gymnastics certification is available nationwide via USA Gymnastics, Inc., Pan American Plaza, Suite 300, 201 South Capitol, Avenue, Indianapolis, Indiana 46225, Telephone 1-800-345-4719.

- The procedures for securing the gymnastics area when the equipment and facilities are not in use by a supervised class
- The availability of the instructor and trained student spotters

Selection and Conduct of the Activity

Gymnastics, just as virtually every activity conducted in a physical education class, is not, by itself, a dangerous activity. However, the manner in which it is conducted can dramatically influence the risk. In general, instructors should teach skills sequentially, progressing from low to high, slow to fast, and part to whole.

In gymnastics, selection of the skills to be taught is crucial. The typical secondary class has students with a broad array of skill levels and varied physical preparation. Gymnastics skills can be tailored to the needs and preparation level of each student.

Gymnastics is one of the few sports remaining where different events have been specified for men and women. Although tumbling is central to virtually all gymnastics events, even the floor exercise has different competitive rules for men and women.[4] Table 1 specifies the competitive events and several developmental activities typically specified for competition.

Table 1. The Competitive Events for Men's and Women's Artistic Gymnastics	
Women's Competitive Events	**Men's Competitive Events**

1. Vaulting (side horse)	1. Vaulting
	     Side horse for beginners
	     Long horse for intermediate and advanced

2. Uneven Bars	2. Parallel Bars
3. Balance Beam	3. Pommel Horse Mushroom for beginners
4. Floor Exercise	4. Still Rings
5. All Around (4 events)	5. Horizontal Bar
	6. Floor Exercise
	7. All Around (6 events)

Conduct of the activity refers to the selection and development of a program of instruction as it relates to the age, ability, maturity, and readiness of the students, the type of instruction offered, the measures enacted to ensure the safety of all participants, and the warnings provided to ensure the students' understanding of the risks of the skills they are learning.

---

4   As one of many possible examples, the women's floor exercise requires music as an integral part of the routine, whereas the men's routine does not.

Care should be taken to provide instruction in a language that students fully understand. The tone of that instruction should be positive but clearly convey the serious intent of the instruction, especially where safety issues are being discussed.

Participant Readiness

Readiness is a particularly important and useful concept in gymnastics. Generally, readiness refers to the performer's potential to successfully perform the essential elements of the activity being taught. Readiness implies that the student is adequately prepared to move on in the progressions. Thus, readiness helps the instructor determine what is safe and what is hazardous for each individual in the class.

Readiness has both long-term and short-term implications. In the short term, readiness means the performer has adequately warmed up or has recovered from the fatigue of previous exertions. Readiness may also mean the performer has focused on the skill and is now ready to execute that skill with or without the assistance of the instructor. Long-term readiness typically applies to mastering prerequisite skills as well as having the required conditioning (primarily, but not exclusively, strength, flexibility, and agility) to perform the next level of the progression. Whereas long-term readiness focuses most often on physical preparedness, it also has important implications for psychological preparedness, especially in areas such as self-confidence and fear. Experiential readiness, physical readiness, and psychological readiness often interact. For example, experience in falling safely requires body awareness and strength sufficient to absorb the energy of a fall and typically reduces fear once the performer feels in control of a fall upon missing a skill.

Experiential/Motoric Readiness

- Teach proper landing techniques. These should be taught first.
- Stress body awareness with eyes open during skill executions.
- Check student competency on prerequisite skills.
- A reasonable number of successful attempts of prerequisites should be accomplished before moving to the next level of progression. The number of successful attempts should increase with the increasing complexity and risk of the skill being learned.

Physical Readiness

- Conduct a physical screening assessment before the gymnastics unit begins in order to identify any disqualifying conditions.[5]
- Physical readiness can be assessed via physical skill progressions. For example, students should be capable of supporting their body weight with their arms before

---

[5] Prior to all vigorous physical activity, a medical screening is advisable. However, this chapter was written specifically for gymnastics and assumes that the precautions appropriate for a general physical education class have already been carried out.

attempting inverted skills where the body weight passes directly over the head and neck. Assessments of strength can be made by having students kick to a partial handstand where their body weight is momentarily supported on the hands but does not pass directly over the hands. Thus, if the arms give way or begin to collapse, the student falls safely to the feet.

- Design a basic warm-up routine that is required at the start of every gymnastics session.
- Do not allow a student to resume practice after an injury or serious illness without written permission from qualified medical personnel.
- Prepare an individualized program for anyone you have identified as having special needs.

Psychological Readiness

- Teach students that they are responsible for their own safety and well-being.
- Assess each student's general self-control.
- Assess each student's ability to focus and concentrate on the skill at hand. Provide close monitoring of students who fail to display such ability on a regular basis.
- Assess each student's fear level, especially prior to the learning of new skills involving the inverted position.
- Encourage, without unduly pressuring, each student to overcome fear.[6] Do not force students to attempt skills of which they are afraid.

Falling Techniques

Falling is a given in gymnastics. Not only is it inevitable, it is a skill that can be learned and improved. There are elementary falls, intermediate falls, and advanced falls. Learning to fall safely involves using progressions that start with a prepared, low fall involving little energy so that if mistakes are made, there is little risk of injury or pain. The general strategy of safe falling is to spread the force of the landing across the greatest possible distance, time, and area of the body. Short, quick, localized impacts are the most likely to cause injury.

To start, beginner gymnasts should master falling forward, falling backward, and falling sideways. All falls should start low to the ground to minimize the impact of falling, and further energy should not be added until the student has mastered the falling technique safely. Once the proper falling techniques have been mastered, the instructor should always reinforce them. Since falling is often sudden and unexpected, the skills of falling should be habits

---

[6] Do not put extra pressure on students to perform skills that they fear by making class grades dependent on such attempts. Provide alternatives for successful grades. For example, students should be able to earn satisfactory grades by moving through horizontal progressions as well as through vertical progressions. Experiencing skills with spotters or spotting belts should be viewed as one way of satisfactorily completing assignments.

that are as automatic as possible. If instructors see a student perform a fall incorrectly during the instruction of other skills, they should remind the student of correct falling technique immediately.

Forward Falling Progressions

1. Start on your knees in a push-up position on a soft mat (e.g., 4" or 8" landing mat). Lower your torso to a landing that maintains support on the palms of the hands and the chest. The face should be turned to the side to protect the nose and face.

2. From the push-up position, repel from the floor and, as you fall back to the floor, land with your elbows bent, turning your head to the side, landing on your chest while breaking the fall with your bent arms.

3. Repeat the previous drill from a vertical starting position on your knees. Fall forward and repeat step two.

4. Starting from a standing position, drop to the knees and repeat step three. Repeat several times, adding force and momentum as your control increases.

5. From a slightly raised platform such as folded panel mat, fall from a standing position onto the soft mat, absorbing the impact with bent arms and landing on the thighs and chest to distribute the energy safely.

6. After mastery has been demonstrated on the falls with less energy and less impact, repeat step five from a slight jump instead of a standing position to add more energy to the fall.

Backward Falling Progressions

1. Lying on your back on a soft mat (e.g., 4" or 8" landing mat), round your back and shoulders, bend your knees, bringing them upwards to your chin on your chest, and rock backwards and forward to experience maintaining a rounded back while moving. The neck and shoulder muscles should be tightened sufficiently to keep the chin on the chest while moving to create a protective round shape and avoid whiplash. Palms and forearms should be placed on the mat to absorb the impact of later, more powerful, falls (thumbs in toward the body, fingers pointed towards the toes).

2. From a squatting position, fall backward while holding the same rounded position as in step one. Be certain to hold the chin on the chest as repeated attempts are done with more and more force.

3. Start from a standing position, drop to a squatting position and fall back immediately to the rounded body position described in step one.

Sideways Falling Progressions

1. From a kneeling position, fall forward while turning sideways and perform a shoulder roll.

2. From a standing position, drop to your knees while turning sideways slightly

to fall further to your thigh, then to your hip, and ultimately to your shoulder, rolling sideways to your back and completing a shoulder roll.

Spotting

Providing physical assistance to a student performing a gymnastics skill is referred to as spotting.[7] The purpose of spotting varies considerably from student to student and from circumstance to circumstance. Often, spotting is used to protect the student who is performing a risky or new skill. At times it is used to help students overcome fatigue, particularly when they are training for endurance by using a sequence of skills. At times it is used to help novice students minimize fear and develop confidence in their ability to perform a skill. Sometimes it is used to guide the student through an unfamiliar movement so the student will understand how a specific skill "feels" and be able to identify proper body position and body position changes and transitions. Spotting may also involve simply standing by and being ready to assist should help be needed while the students attempt the skill on their own. There may be no contact if the student is successful, but the instructor anticipates protecting the student should an error occur.[8]

Spotting also has some potential drawbacks. Students may become overly dependent on spotting. Such an overdependency can result in slower learning, a false sense of security, and an inflated belief in one's competency. It may also result in placing the instructor at risk of injury if the spotting technique is done incorrectly, if the instructor attempts to spot a student who is heavier than what the instructor's strength can handle, or if the student is attempting a complex skill that is beyond the instructor's ability to spot safely.

Some literature has inappropriately cautioned instructors and students to "never perform a gymnastics skill without a spotter." Such a caution is not only unrealistic, it is contrary to a major purpose of gymnastics instruction, which is to teach students to safely and independently perform gymnastics skills within their skill levels. A much more appropriate guideline is to caution students not to perform a skill by themselves until it has been safely mastered as judged by a qualified instructor.[9]

---

[7] The term spotting is also commonly used to describe an entirely different phenomenon, that of visual cueing or visual sighting. Visual spotting is an excellent technique for maintaining body awareness. Teachers stress identifying visual focal points before, during, and upon completing gymnastics skills.

[8] The primary difficulty of this type of spot involves anticipating precisely where assistance may be needed and understanding the limitations of the spotter's reaction time.

[9] **Spotting vs. mastery for progressive learning:** The mastery approach is a strategy in which gymnasts dedicate significant periods of time to mastering skills without relying on spotting from instructors. The gymnast typically receives little or no spotting while learning but is required to master prerequisites at a very high level of stability before moving on in the vertical progressions. This method requires prolonged periods of time for complete mastery and is often used on events such as the balance beam, where the skills are first learned on the floor and then transferred to the beam. This method has the advantage of avoiding the transition from being spotted to a sudden withdrawal of the instructor's spot, a situation that is often quite frightening to novice performers. It has the disadvantage of requiring prolonged periods of time for mastery and the development of self-confidence before progressing to the next step in a series of vertical progressions.

Spotting is used in conjunction with safety mats—not as a replacement for mats or as a substitute for the lack of safety matting. Spotting should be considered just one of many techniques that instructors can use to aid in the athletes' skill development and well-being.

The following are guidelines for the safe use of spotting by the instructor:

- Do not substitute spotting for sound fundamentals. Avoid putting students through skills for which they are not prepared. Spot only as much as is required.

- Have a thorough understanding of the biomechanics of a skill before attempting to spot it.

- Be aware of possible performer errors and station yourself where the greatest risk and most probable safety errors are likely to occur.

- Be prepared to protect yourself as well as the performer.

- Make certain the performer is aware of how you are going to spot them.

- Practice spots you are just learning with performers who can already safely execute the skill and with an experienced spotter assisting you whenever possible.

- Avoid reaching across the bars of the apparatus to spot. Broken bones or serious sprains and bruises can result if the performer falls on your arm, crushing it into the bar below.

- Spot only students whose weight, size, and speed you can reasonably assist. If you cannot safely spot by yourself, four options are possible:

    - Use a second spotter to assist you.

    - Use a second spotter to assist you, using a handheld spotting belt.

    - Use an overhead-spotting rig.

    - Eliminate the skill.

- Generally, the most effective spot is executed by assisting performers near their center of gravity. Guiding and supporting the center of gravity minimizes stress on the spotter while providing effective safety spots for the performer.

- Make physical contact with the performers before they become airborne to enhance the coordination between their attempts at the skill and your physical assistance.

- Establish a means of effective communication between the performer and yourself to ensure that both of you know when an attempt is to be made.

- **NEVER** say you will spot and then withdraw that spot in an attempt to convince performers that they are ready to perform the skill on their own.

- Although your focus must be on the performer when you are spotting, between attempts take time to observe the status of the other students in the class (general supervision).

- Be careful not to "overspot," providing performers with more force and/or rotational energy than they need to perform the skill.

- Anticipate providing assistance on the landing after successful performance of the skill. Injuries may occur from over-rotation or from landing without the body awareness to absorb the impact of the landing.

- The instructor makes the final judgment concerning whether a performer is ready to attempt a new skill. Although performers may be willing to attempt the skill, they must still rely on the instructor's judgment regarding whether they are ready to initiate a new skill.

Student Spotters

Student spotters can be a valuable addition to quality instruction, assisting other students and gaining insight into safe procedures and proper execution of gymnastics skills. They cannot, however, substitute for the instructor or for the instructor's judgment. Properly taught and properly supervised, mature, responsible student spotters can add substantially to the amount of activity and the safety level of gymnastics instruction. The following are guidelines for safe, appropriate use of student spotters:

- Train student spotters in the recommended techniques.
- Test them for competency in performing the desired spots (i.e., make certain they can adequately do what you have taught).
- Provide them with ample practice with students who can already perform the skill safely before you ask them to spot someone who is just learning that skill.
- Match student spotters with students of comparable size, height, and skill.
- Screen the performer who is about to be spotted to ensure the performer has all necessary prerequisites to attempt the skill.
- Use student spotters for basic spotting skills.
- With intermediate skills, make certain the performer needs only slight assistance.
- Never use student spotters for spotting difficult skills unless you are spotting with them.
- Give spotters frequent rest breaks to reduce their level of fatigue.
- Monitor student spotters on a regular basis to ensure that they are not deviating from the recommended techniques you have taught them.
- Teach student spotters to request assistance from the instructor if they ever become uncertain concerning their ability to handle a specific skill or specific student performer.

Spotting Belts

Spotting belts are typically supported by two ropes, one on either side of the performer, connected to the belt with safety latches that allow the belt to rotate through a circular skill (e.g., back handspring or a backward or forward somersault) without entangling the rope and without danger of the ropes separating from the belt. With hand spotting belts, the ropes are each held by a separate spotter. With an overhead spotting belt the ropes pass through overhead pulleys attached to a ceiling beam so that both ropes can be held by a single spotter. With overhead traveling rigs, the ropes pass through pulleys and are both held by a single spotter just as with the overhead rig, but the pulleys can slide along two parallel cables suspended from the ceiling, permitting the performer to run short distances into the skill or perform several skills in sequence along a tumbling run.

These latter two rigs are less common in secondary school classes, both because they are more expensive and because they require substantial technical skill to be used safely. Spotting belts are typically used with advanced intermediate skills and advanced skills, and, although they clearly provide an enhanced measure of safety, they are time-consuming to use and often detract from general classroom instruction.

The following guidelines should be followed when using safety belts:

- If a safety belt is to be used, you must practice with it on a regular basis so that you can work the equipment safely and efficiently and do not present an additional hazard to the performer.

- For all types of spotting belts, the ropes should be kept taut, without lifting the performer, to prevent the belt from being jerked when support is provided for the performer. Keeping the ropes taut also minimizes the possibility of the performer's arms becoming entangled in the ropes while performing the skill.

- Safety equipment should be inspected before each use.

- Only qualified instructors should use overhead safety equipment.

- Performers should be taught to keep their stomach and back muscles taut to avoid whiplash when support is provided by the spotters as they pull on the ropes.

- The belt should have a snug fit with no slippage and a firmly secured safety buckle.

- Never fit the belt with towels or foam.

- The use of a sweatshirt with long sleeves is often more comfortable for the performer while wearing the spotting belt.

The "No Zones"[10]

Occasionally, an instructor may inadvertently touch a performer on a part of the body that normally would be socially unacceptable, e.g., the buttocks, the genital areas, and/or the female chest. Such contact, while infrequent, is almost impossible to totally eliminate. Likewise, occasionally, a performer will strike the instructor in a similar zone while being spotted. In either case, a quick phrase such as "oops," "excuse me," or "sorry about that!" should suffice to acknowledge that the touch was unintentional and that both the gymnast and the instructor are aware of its unintentional nature. Fear of inadvertently touching a "no zone" should never be allowed to impede effective spotting.

---

[10] This term was first introduced in the 1998 *USA Gymnastics Safety Handbook*.

Progressions

Progressions are the backbone of effective instruction in virtually every sport. In gymnastics, proper progressions are critical. Because of the vast number of different skills that can be taught on a variety of different apparatus, a list of progressions could literally be endless. Further, there is clearly more than one way that progressions can be used to safely teach any given specific skill or sequence of skills. Nonetheless, there are six areas that each set of progressions should include. The following "lesson plan" or skill analysis can be used for skills of virtually any difficulty, from the basic and intermediate skills for recreational gymnasts to high-level skills used by competitive gymnasts working with advanced coaches. This skills analysis allows for a variety of safe and effective progressions to teach virtually every gymnastics skill.

Knowledgeable gymnastics instructors should, at a minimum, be aware of the following gymnastics skills analysis involving six analytical steps for every skill:

- **Prerequisites** for successfully performing a skill (e.g., strength, flexibility, body awareness, and essential prior skill learning and/or practice).

- **Progressions for teaching** of a skill (i.e., the specific learning steps and/or skill breakdowns).

- **Teaching cues** (such as verbal commands, feedback signals, and what to look for and/or how it feels).

- **Common errors** typically made by students during the initial stages of learning.

- **Potential risks and/or hazards** (i.e., where the likelihood of falling is greatest; what part of the body must be protected).

- **Appropriate spotting techniques** (i.e., where to stand relative to the apparatus and the gymnast; where to place the hands; what student mistakes should be anticipated).

Illustrative Example: The Cartwheel

1. **Prerequisites:** Requires the ability to support the entire body on one's hands without collapsing. Assumes the student has the ability to perform a handstand. The ability to perform a Russian Split is helpful but not essential.

2. **Progressions:** Lunge to a side handstand and step down to a stand. Perform a mini-cartwheel where the body weight does not pass directly overhead. Perform the cartwheel on a straight line.

3. **Teaching Cues:** A left-leg lunge requires that the left hand be placed down on the floor first. Alternate hand, hand, foot, foot placement with a definite rhythm or cadence. Place the first hand down as far away from the lunge foot as possible. Place the second hand down as far from the first hand as possible. Look for the floor without raising the head excessively.

4. **Common Errors:** Opposite hand is placed down first. Head is raised excessively, causing the back to arch and resulting in a loss of strength, balance, and direction.

Elbows bend, causing the sensation of falling and the fear of collapsing. Lunge on a straight leg preventing the student from pushing the body weight over the hands into the cartwheel.

5. **Potential Risks:** Arms collapse, causing a fall to the head.

6. **Spotting Techniques:** Stand behind the gymnast so that, as the cartwheel is initiated, the gymnast's back is towards the spotter. The spotter's first hand supports the gymnast's hip during the lunge and push-off. Both hands guide and support the gymnast's body during the handstand phase. The spotter's second hand supports the hips during the step-down phase at the completion of the skill. The spotter should anticipate an arch in the student's back and a bending of the leg during the handstand phase of the cartwheel. Such an error increases the possibility that the spotter may be kicked in the face or the chest by the gymnast's feet.

Horizontal and Vertical Progressions

An important curriculum guide for instructors who work with classes of individuals with diverse skill levels is a set of horizontal and vertical skill progressions for each gymnastics event. Vertical skill progressions refer to related skills that become progressively more difficult, typically demanding higher and higher levels of technical skills and higher and higher physical demands such as strength, flexibility, and cardiovascular conditioning.

Horizontal progressions refer to related skills that typically require the same level of strength, flexibility, and cardiovascular conditioning for successful mastery. Horizontal progressions permit a safe variety of skill learning within the same class or series of classes for students with limited strength, flexibility, and cardiovascular conditioning. Such prerequisites typically take a significant period of time to develop, and simply repeating the same skills from class to class can be quite demotivating. Vertical progressions require increasing physical and technical demands on students. Table 2 presents a small sample of horizontal and vertical progressions for tumbling.

Table 2. Sample Horizontal and Vertical Progressions for Tumbling			
Vertical Progression: **Easier**	**Horizontal Progression—Difficulty Level Remains Relatively Constant**		
	Handstand	Lunge to a Sidewise Handstand	Cartwheel
| | |	Front Walkover	Front Walk Over, Stepout on One Leg	Front Walkover, Switch Leg
More Difficult	Front Handspring	Front Handspring, Stepout	Front Handspring Stepout to Cartwheel

Environmental Concerns

In addition to providing safe supervision, appropriate activities, and proper teaching techniques, instructors have the responsibility of providing a safe environment and well-maintained equipment. The following guidelines help create and sustain a safe environment for students.

General Considerations

- Spectators, including students with medical excuses, should not be permitted in the gymnastics instruction area. A place should be set aside for nonparticipants that keep them away from the path of performers.
- Be certain your equipment meets or exceeds all safety specifications established by a national association or manufacturer.
- Develop and carry out an inspection policy that stipulates the following:
  - The regularity (yearly, monthly, weekly, or daily) with which each piece of equipment and aspect of the facility should be inspected.
  - The specific personnel or outside organization that is responsible for the inspection.
  - The items to be inspected and the conditions that are considered acceptable.
  - The records to be kept and the location of the filed records.
  - The procedure used to determine whether an item is to be replaced or repaired.
- Be certain the floors are cleaned daily and-between classes, if need be—that chalk, dust, and other slippery material have been removed.
- When not in use, facilities should be locked and equipment should be stored and locked away.
- Be knowledgeable in first aid and be capable of administering it.
- Have an appropriately stocked first aid kit available.
- Have a pre-planned and practiced Emergency Action Plan for dealing with emergencies and securing the assistance of qualified medical personnel should they be needed.

Gymnastics Area

- The gymnastics area should be large enough to accommodate the number of students participating.
- The area should be free of any pillars or posts, or such obstacles should be padded.
- The walls should be free of any protruding parts. Protrusions that cannot be removed (such as drinking fountains) should be padded or protected via padded barriers.
- The area should be physically separated from all other activities, especially those that require the use of balls. Partitions should be ceiling to floor netting or a ceiling to floor moving door as opposed to cones or floor markings. These latter means are unacceptable unless the activity is compatible, such as dance or fitness activities.

- Windows in the area should be capable of being covered so that light is muted. Bright, direct light, such as sunlight through the window, may interfere with the vision of the performers or spotters.

Matting and Apparatus

- Students should not be permitted to move and/or adjust equipment unless they have been taught how to do it properly and have been given explicit permission to do so. Gymnastics involves multiple pieces of equipment, each with its unique requirements for continual adjustment to fit the performers (e.g., height and width of uneven bars and parallel bars); a serious risk is created if the equipment is improperly set or heavy equipment "falls."[11]

- Match the size and/or the settings of the equipment to the skill and size of the performer. Use matting and apparatus only for purposes for which they were designed. Information on recommended uses can be obtained from the manufacturer and the national governing body (USA Gymnastics).

- Remember that mats are not a substitute for proper progressions, good landing techniques, and competent spotting.

- The amount and kind of matting required will depend on the following:

  - The skill being performed—typically, but not always, the more difficult the skill, the more matting that is required

  - The ability level of the performer—the lower the ability and the less experienced the performer, the more matting that is required

  - The age of the performer

  - The resiliency of the matting due to aging and/or use

- Check mats/apparatus daily for rips, gashes, worn surfaces, cracks, cleanliness, deterioration of cushioning material; resiliency and absorption, and quality of connecting surfaces (e.g., Velcro fasteners).

- Be certain you use the correct matting for the intended purpose. There are three different types of mats: base mats, landing mats, and safety mats.

  - Base matting is 1"-2" and is used for tumbling and as a foundation mat (i.e., the first layer of matting) under all pieces of apparatus

  - Landing matting is 4"-8" and is used whenever performers will be executing dismounts from a piece of apparatus

  - Safety matting is 8"-36" and is used for learning new skills

---

[11] For example, performers should never stand under the parallel bars when lifting the safety collars and adjusting the height or width of the rails. A rail is quite heavy and can drop quickly, striking anyone standing directly under them and creating the possibility of serious injury.

- Place mats/apparatus in a pattern that allows activity on them to be viewed clearly by the instructor from any place within the gymnastics area. Many safe organizational patterns are possible.

- Be sure that ample space is left between each mat/apparatus to accommodate traffic flow.

- Place mats so you can specify the exact direction in which everyone should tumble.

- Place mats/apparatus a reasonable and safe distance from walls and obstacles.

- Avoid placing mats/apparatus, especially for landing areas, near doors, including equipment room doors, even if the room is not normally used during the class period.

- Be sure ample space is provided for safe dismounts from all apparatus. Place these landing areas away from heavy traffic patterns (e.g., entrances and exits).

- Never use the same space as the dismount area from two different apparatuses at the same time.

- Never overlap mats in a fashion that creates uneven surfaces on which the performer can trip or turn an ankle.

- Always place mats so that open folds face the floor. Open folds that face upward are a significant hazard.

- Be certain all t-handles, spin locks, safety collars, springs, cables, and floor plates are secure and in proper working condition.

- Avoid placing equipment so that runways (visible and invisible) are in the middle of the gymnasium where performers must cross over them as they move from area to area.[12]

Example #1: Student Safety Checklist

For Your Safety
Maintaining personal safety in gymnastics is your responsibility. To minimize accidents and to protect yourself from injury, conduct your own personal safety checks at the beginning of EVERY practice session using the guidelines below.

Before Performing - Check Yourself for:
Jewelry: Remove all jewelry, including rings and earrings.

---

[12] Perhaps the most common, and most blatant, error is to place the vault runway down the middle of the gym to maximize running distance. Vault runways are typically extended the length of the gymnasium, requiring students to cross over them to reach the other portions of the gymnasium. Thus, the possibility is increased that a collision can occur when a vaulter is running full speed down the runway. A much safer design is to place vault runways along a sidewall where a nonperformer has little or no need to cross the runway.

Hair:	Be sure your hair is tied back so it does not block your vision or the vision of your spotter. Do not wear long ponytails that might strike spotters.
Footwear:	Wear nonslip, lightweight footwear. Heavy sneakers or shoes can be dangerous to you and your spotter. Nylon tights can be slippery and dangerous also.
Food & Gum:	Never chew gum or have anything in your mouth while performing.
Clothing:	Wear comfortable, but not baggy, clothing; baggy clothing can interfere with your spotter and/or your vision, particularly when you are upside down. Be sure all clothing is free of protruding buckles, buttons, rivets, and zippers.
Eyeglasses:	If eyeglasses are necessary, be certain they are held securely in place with a safety strap and wear only glasses with safety lenses.

Before Performing - Check the Area for:

Sufficient Matting:	Always use enough mats. The less familiar you are with the skill and/or the more difficult the skill, the more matting you should have.
Bottoming Out:	Always check the landing surface to ensure it can absorb the weight of your landing or fall and is the appropriate mat for the intended use.
Clear Matting:	Check the matting/apparatus to ensure that they are not slippery, that they are free of faults such as rips or gashes, and that they are free of clutter.
No Gaps:	If using more than one mat, be certain all mats are securely fastened together, with no gaps or crevices.
Safe Buffer Zones:	Be sure mats and gymnastics equipment are located a safe distance from walls, beams, or other apparatus or teaching stations.
Traffic:	Be certain the pathway you have chosen for your tumbling, your vaulting run, and your apparatus mounts and dismounts does not interfere with someone else's pathway. When you are not performing, be sure to yield the right-of-way to those who are.
Settings:	Be sure all t-handles, spin locks, safety collars, springs, cables, and floor plates are secure and in proper working condition.

Before Performing - Check Your Spotter and Yourself for:

Permission: Do not attempt a skill with a student spotter unless your instructor has given you explicit permission to do so.

Understand: Be sure to have a thorough understanding of a skill before you make your first attempt at it.

In Shape: Make certain you are in the proper physical condition to safely execute the skill. You must be strong enough, flexible enough, and have sufficient cardiovascular endurance to safely perform the skill. Do not attempt skills that require a level of fitness beyond your present physical ability.

Know Your Ability: Do not attempt skills for which you have not mastered all prerequisites.

Progression: Use proper progressions.

Communicate: Be certain your spotter knows what skill you are about to try and that the spotter knows how to spot the skill safely.

Anticipate: Be certain you know the problems you may encounter when attempting each skill.

Fatigue: Stay within your fatigue level. Only attempt skills when you are sufficiently rested to permit success. It is a good idea to attempt most new skills early in the workout before you become excessively fatigued.

At the Time of the Performance - Check Yourself for:

Warm-up: Be certain to warm up sufficiently so that your muscles and joints are prepared for the demands you are about to make on them.

Rest: Stop and rest when you or your spotter are tired. Your body cannot perform as well when you are tired; if you attempt a skill when tired, you may cause yourself serious injury.

Progressions: Follow the progressions step by step, just as your instructor has outlined for you.

Know Your Limits: Perform at your level and not above. Do not try skills on a dare or because someone other than the instructor says it is easy. Know your limitations and abide by them. Only attempt skills for which you have received instruction. Instructions given to another individual may not apply to you.

Commit: Always follow a skill through to its conclusion; never change your mind in the middle of a movement. You can seriously injure yourself or your spotter if you do.

Communicate: Be certain your spotter knows exactly what you intend
                                to do and when you intend to begin.

Event-Specific Safety Issues

Although not every safety issue is discussed in detail, common issues for typical usage
at the beginner and the low-intermediate levels are outlined.

Tumbling

Tumbling is the basis for virtually all gymnastics. Tumbling skills not only provide the
foundation for all gymnastics events, they also set the groundwork for falling properly.
Although tumbling can be designed for students of all skill and experience levels, adequate
strength, flexibility, and body awareness are the general, but still essential, prerequisites for
both safety and adequate skill progressions in tumbling.

- The tumbling lanes and landing areas should be smooth, level, free of gaps, free of
  obstructions, and clear of chalk or moisture that might make the surface slippery.
- Mats should be appropriate for the activity but no less than that required
  for competition.
- Spotting should be available as needed but overzealous spotting should be avoided.

Balance Beam

The beam is essentially tumbling and dance movements performed on a straight line. As
a result, virtually all learning should take place on the floor prior to attempting skills on the
beam itself. Falls from the beam are quite common because of the narrow width (10 cm for
competitive beams). Thus, fear is a particularly prominent part of this event as the height of
the beam is increased. Beam safety requires a great emphasis on proper progressions, safe
matting, and proficiency in safe-falling techniques. Matting is particularly essential in those
areas where falls are most likely to occur. Padding should also be placed on all beam support
legs. Serious injuries have occurred from gymnasts falling while using the beam as a seat
while watching other gymnasts or receiving instruction.

- Skills should be learned first on straight lines on the floor.
- Whenever possible, skills should be learned on lower beams, wider beams, and softer,
  padded beams prior to attempting those skills at competitive heights and on competitive equipment.
- Beams should be placed sufficiently far apart to preclude collisions between gymnasts
  falling from adjacent beams at the same time.
- Beam footings should be stable; beam supports should not be placed on soft mats.
- Whenever possible, beams should be aligned with ceiling beams and other straight
  lines in the gymnasium to assist performers in maintaining safe spatial orientation
  while performing.

- Mats should be appropriate for the activity but no less than that required for competition.

Bars

Three different types of bars are used in gymnastics: uneven bars, parallel bars, and horizontal bars. Each will be analyzed in turn, but there are two prerequisite skills common to all three events: swing elements and support work.

Swing elements are skills in which the apparatus is grasped with an extended or semi-extended body position. These skills start from a basic vertical hanging position, progress through a basic swinging motion and finally advance to more advanced swings often referred to as "tap swings." Proper grips and sufficient grip strength must be demonstrated in order to move on to more advanced swinging skills on each of the three events. Students who use incorrect grip and/or lack sufficient grip strength can be clearly identified during early, safe vertical swings under the bars.

Support skills sustain the body's weight on extended arms and, thus, require a significant level of upper body strength. A variety of basic support positions should be mastered on low bars before attempting more advanced skills that move into, out of, or through these basic support positions.

Uneven Bars

Beginning performers should be taught basic handholds, support positions, and basic hangs and swings that are initiated on the low bar set at approximately chest height for most adolescents. The height of the bar can be regulated by building up mats under the bar to reduce the height from bar level to the landing mat.

- Stay within each student's strength and body control. Pushing too fast slows learning and increases the risk dramatically.

- Teach students to support their body weight on the bar on the heel of their hands, not the palm or fingers.

- Although the performer must hold onto the bar, safe progressions require that they push away from the bar rather than "clutch" the bar to hold on. Too tight a grip creates the possibility for chaffing the skin of the hands or even creating a "rip," where the skin blisters and breaks.

- Mats should be appropriate for the activity but no less than that required for competition.

Parallel Bars

Teaching proper swing technique is crucial for preventing injury and increasing self-confidence which, in turn, leads to faster learning and more fun. Spotting beginners is usually done from underneath the bars to avoid the performer pinning the spotter's arm between the parallel bar and the performer's body. A fall through the bars from a swinging move may cause the performers' momentum to carry them into the upright supports of the apparatus or to over-rotate onto the head, neck, or spine. Therefore, performers should be cautioned to minimize the height of the pendulum swings to reduce the forces that can tear the performer's grip from the bars.

- Encourage performers to wear long-sleeved sweatshirts and long pants to protect against painful scrapes and bruises. Padding portions of the bars where the performer's body will contact the bar is also a method to minimize discomfort during the initial learning stages.

- Emphasize straight-arm support and straight-arm swings. Bent or flexed arms and partially extended shoulders result in a jerking and/or ripping action at the bottom of the swing, dramatically increasing the likelihood of losing one's grip and falling in an uncontrolled manner.

- Constantly monitor the performer's strength as progressively more difficult skills are attempted to determine if the performer's strength is sufficient to safely perform each skill. If in doubt, slow the progressions and increase the emphasis on strength training before progressing to the next skill.

- Mats should be appropriate for the activity but no less than that required for competition.

Horizontal Bar

Virtually every skill requires supporting the gymnast's entire weight by the hands. Thus, upper body strength, power, flexibility, and coordination are absolutely essential for safe skill execution. The greatest risk of injury occurs from improper dismounts, falling back onto the bar itself, and "ripping off" the bar at the bottom of the swing (where the gymnast is hanging vertically but the angular momentum can cause the body to rotate to a landing on the head and neck. Performers must learn to maintain pressure against the bar instead of pulling on the bar. The mistaken tendency to pull is extremely strong in the beginner, and, thus, mastery of proper technique through proper progressions is critical for safety.

- Avoid dowel grips with beginners.

- Set the bar at chest height for learning beginning skills.

- Mats should be appropriate for the activity but no less than that required for competition.

Vaulting

All beginner vaulters, male and female, should be taught with the horse positioned sideways. The basic run, hurdle to board, vaulting from the board to a stand on soft mats, safe landing techniques, and basic falling techniques should be taught before actual vaults are attempted. Basic vaults should be taught first from short, controlled runs. Students should be taught to focus on the vaulting board during the run, shifting their vision to the horse after they have hurdled to the springboard.

It is often helpful to place a visual target such as nonslippery athletic tape or chalk marks on the "sweet part[13]" of the vaulting board to aid students in focusing on the appropriate part of the springboard. Although fast runs are essential for successful vaulting, students should be cautioned to run only as fast as they feel in control. Gymnasts should be taught to anticipate the impact of the horse on their hands and arms to allow a quick push or repulsion to aid the vault and avoid collapsing into the horse.

- Place the springboard on a nonslippery surface to prevent the board from moving as the gymnast's feet contact the board.

- Make certain the horse is set at a height appropriate for the gymnast and the skill and that all safety locks are in the correct position.

- Have gymnasts note their starting position and the number of steps they wish to take for consistency (12 to 14 steps are typical of advanced vaulters, although fewer steps are quite appropriate for beginner vaulters performing basic non-inverted vaults such as a basic squat or straddle vault).

- Spotters should anticipate performers who hesitate and who do not have sufficient momentum to vault completely over the horse. Such performers often fall backwards towards the springboard.

- Spotters and performers should anticipate a lack of repulsion (pushing with the arms), a deficiency that causes performers to fall forward, often catching their feet on the horse.

- Spotters and performers should anticipate over-rotation in the post-flight and landing stages with inverted vaults such as headsprings and handsprings.

- Use thicker landing mats for beginners, anticipating that, despite practice in safe landing techniques, a common error will be that of landing out of control, often with excessive arch in the lower back.

- As the performer's proficiency and confidence increases, the spotter should anticipate longer and longer post-flight phases (i.e., the gymnast travels further beyond the horse) and should be prepared to side step without crossing his or her legs to stay with the performer until the landing is safely completed.

- With intermediate level boys vaulting long horse, the straddle vault should be taught before the squat vault because of the length of the horse. Proficiency in a fast, controlled run and adequate repulsion from the horse with the arms should be regularly demonstrated by the performer before converting from side horse to long horse.

- Mats should be appropriate for the activity but no less than that required for competition.

---

[13] The "sweet part" is where the contact with the vaulting board provides the maximum spring.

Pommel Horse

Typically regarded as one of the safest gymnastics events, the pommel horse is nonetheless a difficult event for beginners to master. The mushroom is by far the most recommended preliminary station for learning circling for the pommel horse.

- Matting should completely surround the pommel horse or mushroom.

- Encourage performers to wear long pants to protect against scrapes and bruises.

- Mats should be appropriate for the activity but no less than that required for competition.

Still Rings

The rings should never be used while swinging. They should be lowered to chest height during initial skill learning, or the mats should be built up from the floor level to achieve the same effect.

- Emphasize mastering proper handgrip on the rings.

- If the beginner gymnasts cannot reach a full support position using their own strength, only the qualified coach should provide a spot or assistance in achieving that position.

- Check that the performer's hand can close securely around the rings and that the grasp on each ring is directly beneath the straps holding the ring.

- Dowel handgrips can help the beginner gymnast hold onto the rings more securely during basic skills such as inlocates and dislocates. Because "grip lock" is not a potential hazard on rings as it is on bars, such grips may be safely used under the direct supervision of a qualified instructor.

- Mats should be appropriate for the activity but no less than that required for competition.

References

Caine, D., Cochrane, B., Caine, C., & Zemper, E. (1989). An epidemiologic investigation of injuries affecting young, competitive female gymnasts. *American Journal of Sports Medicine, 17*(6), 811-820.

USA Gymnastics Safety Handbook. (1998). Indianapolis, IN: USA Gymnastics Publications.

CHAPTER 25

Ultimate

Ken Demas
Mamaroneck, New York

Introduction

Since its beginning in 1968, ultimate has grown from an informal meeting of interested participants to an internationally recognized sport. In the United States, ultimate can be played at many levels. In schools, it can be found in physical education classes, intramural programs, and as an interscholastic sport. Recreationally, players may choose to play in formal leagues, in sanctioned events, or in friendly pickup games. In any case, the "spirit of the game," specifically, sportsmanship, fair play, adherence to the rules, and the joy of play are valued over all.

The very nature of play in ultimate leads to some concerns regarding safety. Students need to be familiar with throwing and catching skills, the flight characteristics of the disc, and legal play and movement patterns. Ultimate is normally played without the use of referees. This requires that students have the skills, knowledge, and control to monitor their own actions.

The proper sequencing of skill instructions and providing adequate opportunities for practice will make for a safe and rewarding activity. The foundations established here should provide participants with the tools they will need to take their play to whichever level they choose.

Supervision

- Students need to be warned of the inherent dangers associated with playing ultimate and how to avoid them. Specifically, they need to be taught the importance of staying on their own playing field, avoiding physical contact, and playing within their abilities. Giving reasons for these concerns and examples of each is helpful. Occasional reminders during the course of the unit also aids in refocusing students on these potential causes of injury.

- Evaluate the situation with regard to the number and placement of supervisors. It is likely, in a physical education setting, that more than one playing field will be laid out or that, during practice activities, students will tend to disperse around the field area. If this is the case, supervisors should consider the following: Is my field of vision clear? Will I be able to get to a potentially dangerous situation in time to prevent injury? Am I visible and accessible to all the students in the class? Is my emergency first aid pack (i.e., latex gloves, Epi-pen, etc.) near at hand? Am I in a position to mediate disputes, enforce rules, and control discipline?

- Planning and organization are the backbone of good instruction and careful supervision. Know how you will be moving students from point A to point B. Establish clear, consistent signals that the students fully understand and are familiar with. The ability to establish control for transition or in the event of an emergency is an essential skill for a competent supervisor. Planning and organization also provide you with a structure from which to anticipate potential problems.

- In the event of an injury or incident, know the proper protocols and procedures used at your site. The appropriate forms and reports must be filed; be sure you know who is responsible for doing so. Collect all the necessary information that will be needed for a complete and accurate report. Your direct supervisor should be informed of the incident. It may be appropriate to evaluate the incident and investigate whether there is a pattern associated with this type of injury or during this particular activity.

Selection and Conduct of Activity

Develop a well-organized and appropriate unit plan. Using a block plan for the unit, even if just for an outline, is extremely helpful in establishing a sound format. It will make the establishment and visualization of clear progressions and a sense of continuity more clear and will allow you to anticipate and plan for a range of skill levels.

The plan should allow for students to begin by acquiring basic skills like catching and throwing. Using stationary targets at first and then graduating to moving targets will give students the opportunity to test their accuracy, distance throwing, and ability to lead the receiver. Catchers will be presented with tracking and judgment challenges. The plan should allow for opportunities to work on fundamental offensive and defensive techniques. Moving to find the open space on offense or judging whether to step in front of the receiver to intercept or to stay behind and limit forward progress on defense can be learned in games of keep away. Two-on-one and three-on-one games help students acquire these skills. Then, modified small-sided games on smaller fields should be initiated. These games engage students more fully and still reduce speed, distance, and confusion on the field. Safe play is more likely to be the norm if a developmentally appropriate progression is used.

Warm-up and cooldown activities need to be incorporated into your plan. Keep in mind that the warm-up should be preparing the students for the level of activity they will be engaged in. Ultimate is a highly active sport that includes both aerobic and anaerobic elements. In addition, attention needs to be spent on stretching the arms, shoulders, and backs, as all players are expected to throw as well as catch.

Ultimate is a noncontact sport, as required by the rules. Drills, practice, and modified games should all reinforce this concept. When on defense, learning to read the intended direction of a throw and to anticipate and track the throw based on the disc's rotation and tilt are important skills. The offensive players can work on cutting and patterns to allow themselves to get free. Students are more likely to play by the rules if they are not frustrated by their inability to compete on an equal footing. Knowledge, skill, body control, and the ability to anticipate will help maintain a safe playing environment.

Constantly reinforce the "spirit of the game." The precepts of sportsmanship, fair play, adherence to the rules, and the joy of play will enhance an atmosphere of safe and active participation.

Environmental Concerns

Equipment

Select discs that are appropriate for the age and ability level of your students. Discs weighing 100g or less are excellent for kindergarten through third grades. They are lighter and smaller and work well indoors; outdoors, however, the wind can make their use difficult. Discs weighing up to 120g fit nicely for grades three through five. The 141g disc is a good multipurpose disc and can be used at both the middle school and high school levels. The heavyweights, at 161g and 200g, are better suited for ultimate, tricks, and disc golf.

Soft foam discs and models with varying degrees of flexibility and padding along the edge are available. You may want to consider these as an option for those students who might be more tentative or unskilled. Do not use long distance throwing rings. They are constructed of metal rings covered with semisoft plastic and can be thrown for great distances and with great force. They also have a knack for finding any tree in the area.

Over time, exposure to the sun and hard play can cause a disc to crack across the copula or dome and even across the edge. Cracked discs should not be used. The cracks can cause erratic flight, resulting in someone misjudging a throw and being injured. The cracks can also cause cuts to the hands. Discs can be replaced quite inexpensively—check your local dollar or discount store.

Another type of wear may occur if students have been playing on or skipping the discs on rough surfaces. The bottom edge of the disc can become rough. This, too, can cause cuts to the hands or at least make catching uncomfortable. This rough surface can be corrected by lightly buffing it with steel wool or fine sandpaper.

Facilities

If you are using the gymnasium for any part of your unit, be alert to any of the usual potential hazards. Floors should be clean and dry. Extraneous equipment, wall fixtures, and closet doors all need to be secured or stowed away. Keep in mind that the disc in the hands of a novice does not always go where it is intended, and the catcher's attention will be on it—not on any potential obstruction.

Limit the number of discs and students on the gym floor to a manageable number. For the same reasons mentioned above, errant throws or poor catching can result in an injury. Try to keep the lines of flight as parallel as possible. Think through your practice activity to eliminate any potential safety issue.

Playing ultimate indoors is not encouraged. Most gymnasiums do not provide enough of a buffer zone around playing areas. Carefully evaluate your situation before playing indoors. Students could potentially run into walls or obstructions. In addition, students not engaged in the games and on the sidelines are not likely to have enough space to insure their safety.

If you are using the playing field for any part of your unit, be sure to inspect it for any potential hazards. This is particularly important after a weekend or after use by some outside group. Trash and trashcans, holes and depressions, and equipment and obstacles on or in the vicinity of the playing area all need to be removed or remedied. A written report should also be filed with the proper authority, outlining the specifics of the hazardous condition.

The playing surface itself should be in good condition. Ultimate is a game that inspires players to sometimes dive or fall in their efforts. A well-grassed playing field will greatly reduce the number of bruises and abrasions.

For your practice sessions, allow for adequate spacing. Be certain to inform your students as to the boundary limits of the practice facility. Use some type of marker to delineate the area. The marker should be easily seen and of such material that it does not become a safety hazard in its own right.

When laying out playing fields, be certain to clearly mark the fields with appropriate markers and lines. Allow for adequate buffer zones between the fields. Players can drift off their assigned fields and onto adjoining fields when chasing down a disc. For the same reason, it is important to remember to keep obstructions well clear of the field and outside surrounding buffer zones.

Students who may be waiting on the sidelines to substitute for or replace other players need to be kept outside the playing area. It is also recommended that they not be placed in the buffer zone between two games, as there will be action in front of and behind them.

Ultimate is an exciting sport that invites spontaneous and active play. It requires little more than a disc and an open playing field to invite that play. Because of this, it is likely to be played by children and adults alike in any number of venues. By providing a good, solid foundations in skills, knowledge, strategy, respect for the rules, and at the same time an appreciation for safe practices and procedures, we can feel more secure in our knowledge that it will be played in a hazard-free and safe environment.

CHAPTER 26

Volleyball

Barbara L. Viera
Retired
Newark, Delaware

Volleyball is an activity that is relatively safe when played at all levels of ability and by different age groups. For this reason, it is a popular activity for backyard barbeques, picnics, parties, and any occasion where people get together to socialize and have a good time. The main reason that this activity tends to be safe is that it is truly a noncontact sport. The two opposing teams are separated by the net; thus there is usually little to no body contact between opponents.

If, however, the game is played by two highly competitive teams, there can be contact above and below the net between spikers and blockers. During games played by less skilled players, the danger is greater because players lack effective body control and often fall into their opponent's side of the court. Because players are confined to a small area and the game demands constant jumping and movement on the court, it is not surprising that an occasional injury does occur when one player runs into or falls on top of another.

These injuries are usually minor. The two body parts that are most susceptible to such injuries are the ankles and the fingers. It is, nevertheless, extremely important to the safety and success of the game that the players maintain a high level of communication on the court. Every time players know that they are going to play the ball, it is essential that they call for it to notify their teammates of their intentions. Good communication can eliminate accidental collisions between teammates, reducing the potential for injury.

There are four major areas that need to be addressed when discussing volleyball safety: the teaching of the skill, the selection of proper teaching strategies, the proper setup and use of equipment, and the use of proper clothing and protective equipment by the players.

Because the repeated use of a body part in an inefficient position can cause muscle pulls, strains, or sprains, players using improper technique are often injured. Teachers must be able to select the correct teaching strategy for the level and strength of their students. A teacher who hits a ball at a student who is incapable of receiving it at the given intensity puts that student in a dangerous situation. The equipment must be up to standard and safely set up. Perfectly good equipment can become very dangerous if it is improperly installed. Finally, students need to prepare themselves for a game by wearing any necessary protective equipment and by making sure that they are not wearing anything that will be a hazard on the court.

Supervision

When teaching volleyball, instructors should consider several things in order to make the class as safe as possible. The ideal situation is to have at least one volleyball available for every student in the class and at least one court for every 12 to 15 students. Students will learn more quickly if they have the opportunity to handle the ball as often as possible. Unfortunately, however, the ideal situation is rarely found in the everyday teaching environment. When faced with a group of students working in a small, enclosed area, teachers must establish some control over how and where the students move. The following is a list of suggestions for making the class fun and safe.

1. In the initial class sessions when basic ball handing is being learned, do not set up the nets. They are not needed and could be an obstruction to free movement.

2. When running drills involving two or more players, make sure that all groups are moving parallel to each other and far enough from each other that there is no danger of collision.

3. The teacher must be in a position in the gymnasium where all students are within view and must be aware of any extraneous activity that could cause an accident.

4. When the teacher uses a piece of equipment as an instructional aid, it must be used so that it is not a hazard to the students. For example, if the teacher uses a chair or box to stand on when spiking or serving the ball to the students, it must be far enough away from the net so that there is no danger that the blockers will come down on the chair and suffer an injury.

5. In teacher-led drills, the goal is to extend the students toward their potential. At the same time, however, it is essential that the teacher know the capabilities of each student so that none are forced to participate beyond their capabilities.

6. When the activity of the day is volleyball, that is the only activity that should be allowed. If the balls are available at the beginning of class for students to use in warming up, they should not be allowed to shoot at the basketball hoop, kick the ball, or play variations of bombardment.

7. No students with injuries should be allowed to participate unless they have clearance from a doctor. This is particularly true of finger and ankle injuries.

8. Students should not be allowed to begin their warm up unless the teacher is in the gymnasium.

9. At the end of class, all the volleyballs should be collected and put away until the teacher is ready to begin the next class.

10. Students should practice their drills on the court so that they gain an appreciation of the size of the playing area. Developing an awareness of the players around them helps students build the ability to react appropriately in a game setting.

11. When running drills that involve both spikers and blockers, the teacher must make sure the students are aware of the danger of balls rolling under the feet of the jumping players. Players who are serving in the role of retrievers for the drill should be told where to return the balls and how to get them there. Players should also be taught to react to a given signal during drills in case the ball does accidentally roll under the feet or toward the feet of jumping players. A simple "NO" spoken with an authoritative voice should be warning enough for players not to jump until the area is safe.

12. When more than one adjoining court is being used at the same time, players must be prohibited from entering an adjoining court to play the ball. As soon as the ball enters an adjoining court, it should be whistled dead by the official or teacher.

13. A volleyball team consists of six players. A variation of the game is played with nine players. It is not advisable to put more than nine players on one side of the net. This is not teaching the sport as it should be taught and can be dangerous.

Selection and Conduct of the Activity

Many injuries occur in volleyball because the student attempts to perform a skill without the proper technique. Students must be taught the proper beginning position and method of execution of each of the basic skills in volleyball and when and how each is used in a game situation. It is also extremely important that the teacher uses the proper terminology in the teaching of the skills. Often, students use the incorrect technique because they have misunderstood or misinterpreted the teacher's explanation. A good example of this is the expression, "hit the ball with the fingertips," used when teaching the overhand pass in volleyball. In this skill, the ball should be contacted with the upper two joints of the fingers, not the fingertips. If players attempt to hit the ball with their fingertips, they are likely to jam their fingers. Following is a list of considerations for teaching the basic skills of volleyball. Understanding and implementing them will help to insure that the students learn proper technique and therefore play a safe game.

1. Make sure that the correct terminology is used so that students thoroughly understand what is expected of them.

2. Teach the students the skills they need to gain body control. This is particularly important in three areas:

a. Teaching spikers how to stop forward momentum into the net. Planting the heels before takeoff is essential.

b. Teaching blockers how to move to join a teammate for a double block without knocking that player over. It is the middle blocker's responsibility to move to the outside blocker, not to the ball.

c. In defensive techniques in which the player hits the floor to save a ball, the player must be skilled in the proper method of falling. It is important that, when falling, the player learns to land on the body parts that have sufficient padding and not on parts that are bony such as the knees, elbows, and hips. The body should always hit the floor from a position close to the floor and not from a high position.

3. When teaching the block and spike, make sure that students learn to land on both feet simultaneously. Landing on only one foot puts extra strain on that foot. If the player comes down on one foot and lands on a teammate's or opponent's foot, it is very likely that a serious sprain will result.

4. When teaching the spike in volleyball, make sure that the students hit the ball with a fully extended arm. Hitting the ball with a bent arm makes the player depend heavily on the rotator cuff muscles for attaining power. This added strain on the rotator cuff can cause tendonitis. Hitting with an extended arm uses the powerful muscles of the shoulder and back (Johns, 1977).

5. When teaching the dive or sprawl, make sure that players flex their knees and arch their backs. Failure to do these things causes players to jam their toes into the floor, resulting in bruised joints, especially of the big toe (Johns, 1977). It is also important to teach players to get as close to the floor as possible before executing these skills so that the fall is from a lower position and safer to perform.

6. Make sure that players condition their ankles.

7. If a student has weak ankles, they should be taped before each class and competition. Many players now use ankle braces for any volleyball competition as a precautionary measure to prevent injury.

Environmental Conditions

The equipment used in volleyball is relatively simple. It consists of standards for holding up the net, and volleyballs. If the competition is at a high level, the net also needs to be equipped with antennae. These should be attached to the net in line with the outside edge of the sideline. During competitive volleyball, it is also essential to have an official's stand. USA Volleyball, the National Association for Girls and Women in Sport (NAGWS), and the National Federation of State High School Associations (NFHS) all publish rules with specific regulations pertaining to the safety of participants. In 2002, the NCAA will begin writing rules, and the NAGWS will cease doing this. Following is a list of considerations for the teacher when setting up the gymnasium either for a class or for a competition.

1. The best standards are usually fairly heavy and must be handled with care when setting them up. Some standards include a base and will stand on their own as long as there is no tension placed on the net; however, the standards will fall over easily. When the teacher uses student assistants to set up, they must be aware of this danger. It is possible for a standard to fall over and hit a student, and the resultant injury could be serious. Teachers should make sure that the standards are held upright by someone until they are attached to the floor. This will greatly decrease the chance of an accident.

2. All metal fasteners and tensioning devices on the net must be covered with a soft, pliable material.

3. The standards must be placed at least three meters from the sidelines.

4. Round standards are less hazardous to the players than other types. Standards that fit into a sleeve in the floor are safer that those with a base that require guide wires. Support wires are very dangerous to a player who is moving to play a ball and is unaware of his or her location. Fixing the standards to the floor with guy wires should be avoided if at all possible. If guy wires must be used, the heavy chain type are better than the wire cable type, and any type must be covered with a soft, flexible material. The NFHS requires that this material be at least 1/2" thick and that it must be applied to a height of 5 1/2 feet (Doyle, 2000). Fortunately, most of the standards that require guy wires are no longer used.

5. The standards, referee's stand, and all the tensioning devices should also be covered by soft, flexible material. The NFHS recommends this material be at least 1/2" thick. The cranks that are used to place tension on the net should be removable if at all possible. If they are not removable, the next best option is the type that fold back so that they are not sticking out. If neither of these types is available, the tensioning mechanism must be completely covered with soft, flexible material (Doyle, 2000).

6. The antennae must be securely fastened to the net. Each antenna has a device to attach it to the net. Some antennae have a small rubber cup on the bottom that covers a metal fastener. This rubber cover must be in place or it creates a dangerous situation. The pieces fastening the antennae to the net must be smooth with no sharp edges.

7. The wire cable extending through the net should have a plastic covering on it. This prevents the wire from splintering and causing injury when anyone touches it as they try to set up the net. The cable at the bottom of the net should be rope, as rope is less likely to cause injury to a player who accidentally runs into it. Fortunately, most of the nets with wire cables have been replaced with the safer, rope variety.

8. Due to the high degree of tension placed on the nets to get the correct height, a great deal of stress is also placed on the floor plates used with standards that have a base. Often when these standards are improperly attached, or if no guy wires are

used when they are needed, the floor plates begin to rise up from the floor. These plates can become a hazard to unsuspecting athletes when the standards are not in place.

9. If wire supports are used for the standards, it is recommended that, in addition to covering them, strips of material be hung from the wire to alert players of their presence (Sanford, 1997).

10. A clear area should surround the court. USA Volleyball recommends that this clear space be at least three meters from the sidelines and four meters from the end lines (Sanford, 1997).

11. The surface of the court must be smooth and should not be abrasive in any way.

12. If an outdoor court becomes soft or slippery, the game should be stopped immediately (Sanford, 1997).

13. Any off-court areas where hazards exist should be declared nonplayable. Players should not be allowed to enter nonplayable areas for the purpose of playing the ball. Players should be made aware of this, and during play, the ball should be whistled dead as soon as it goes into such an area.

14. For beginners, the air pressure in the ball should be kept at the lower end of the acceptable range. Unfortunately, most teachers have a tendency to make the ball pressure too high, causing the ball to hurt the student's forearms and even causing some bruising.

15. During competition, the floor often gets wet after a player falls while making a good defensive effort. It is essential that the competition be halted until the floor can be toweled dry. The wet surface is extremely slippery and very dangerous.

16. Certain items worn by players can help protect them from injury. There are also several items that can be hazardous to the wearer or to other participants in the game. Following are suggestions for a player's personal equipment that help to prevent injury.

    a. Long-sleeved shirts help to protect the arms and elbows from floor burns, especially when the player is forced to hit the floor during a defensive maneuver (Johns, 1977). Long-sleeved shirts are not as popular as they were several years ago.

    b. Kneepads are highly recommended at all levels of play. They protect the knees from floor burns and bruises. Many players are not as inhibited about hitting the floor when they wear knee pads and thus have better defensive skills.

    c. Official rules prohibit the use of jewelry and certain other articles during play. Generally, rings, bracelets, earrings, and necklaces must be removed. Even post earrings can get caught in the net or another player's clothing and cause damage to the ear (Sanford, 1997).

d. The wearing of a hard cast is not allowed on any part of the body. Hard splints or other protective devices may be worn on any body part as long as they will not cause injury or give an artificial advantage to the player. Soft bandages of any type are allowed.

e. Protective-type braces for the lower extremities are allowed as long as there are no exposed metal parts that may be a hazard to other players. If a cast, brace, or headgear is used, padding or covering may be necessary (Sanford, 1997).

f. Prosthetic limbs may be worn under certain conditions. They may have to be approved by the governing body of the rules being used. It would be wise to check in advance and get approval in writing so that there will be no problem with the officials on the day of competition. These devises should be covered with padding and should not endanger the other participants in any way (Sanford, 1997).

g. Anything worn on the head should be soft and pliable. Hats are not allowed, but sweatbands, barrettes, and bandanas used as sweatbands are all allowed as long as they are being used to secure the hair and not just for adornment. Braided hair with beads must not be allowed to swing freely in a hazardous manner (Sanford 1997; Doyle, 2000).

h. All players should wear appropriate footwear.

i. Eyeglasses should have unbreakable lenses and should be firmly attached to the head.

j. It is strongly recommended that gum chewing not be allowed during participation.

References

Doyle, Cynthia. (2000). *Volleyball 2000-01 rules book*. Indianapolis, IN: National Federation of State High School Associations.

Johns, D. (1977). Care and prevention of common injuries in competitive volleyball. *Volleyball Technique Journal, 4* (1), 46-50.

National Association for Girls and Women in Sport. (1999). *Volleyball guide (1999-2000)*. Reston, VA: American Alliance for Health, Physical Education, Recreation and Dance.

Sanford, Becky (Ed.). (1997). *Official 1997-1998 United States Volleyball Rules*. Indianapolis, IN: Sport Graphics.

Tomasi, L. (1979). Injury prevention and treatment. In B. Bertucci (Ed.), *Championship volleyball by the experts* (pp. 245-259). West Point, NY: Leisure Press.

Viera, Barbara L. (1993). Volleyball. In N. J. Dougherty (Ed.), *Physical education and sport for the secondary school student* (pp. 346-365). Reston, VA: The American Alliance for Health, Physical Education, Recreation and Dance.

Viera, Barbara L., & Ferguson, B. J. (1996). *Volleyball steps to success*. Champaign, IL: Human Kinetics.

CHAPTER 27

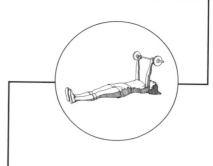

Weight Training

Barney R. Groves
Virginia Commonwealth University
Richmond, Virginia

Weight-training programs have been in existence for centuries. One question frequently asked by those contemplating the development of a weight-training program is, "How shall I begin?" Beginners frequently seek guidance form their friends and acquaintances, health club employees, parents, coaches and/or teachers. Although these persons are unquestionably well-meaning and may be active exercisers as well, they often lack an understanding of the many safety factors involved in the development of an effective weight-training program and, thus, may expose the lifter to an unwarranted risk of injury.

The purpose of this chapter is to suggest procedures for conducting weight-training programs that are safe for all. Environmental factors and training methods to aid in the development of safe and effective programs of weight training will be individually addressed.

The Lifting Environment

A good weight-training facility includes both machines and free weights. These areas should be separated so that they do not create a hazard due to overcrowding and traffic congestion in any given area. If Olympic and/or power lifting is practiced, a designated area on a specially built platform is preferred.

The weight-training room can be an intimidating place, especially for beginners, who are awed by the numerous pieces of complicated equipment. As the instructor in charge, you should be sure that you have created a safe, convenient, and interesting facility in which to participate. Guidelines to accomplish this include the following:

1. Clearly mark placement space for all equipment.

2. Post emergency procedures in a highly visible area.

3. Clearly mark traffic patterns.

4. In a highly visible area, post the maximum number of participants that can safely use the space.

5. Make sure equipment is used only for the exercise for which it was designed.

6. Ventilation and lighting should be adequate.

7. Clearly mark storage space for all equipment.

8. Inspect equipment and facilities daily. Careful inspection records must be maintained indicating the following:

   • The floor and wall anchor points are secure

   • There are proper weight pins on exercise machines

   • The floor area is free of slick spots, equipment, clothing, bags, etc.

   • The machines are properly lubricated and free of rust

   • Free-weight bars have locks available

   • Benches and platforms are stable and secure

   • Cables, pulleys, chains, fasteners, and other moving parts are safe to use

   • There is a procedure to assure cleanliness of mats, benches, seats, and pads

   • Deficiencies are immediately corrected or the faulty equipment is immediately taken is out of service

9. Make sure lifters are aware of what is going on around them.

10. Do not allow horseplay.

11. Require use of locks on free-weight bars.

12. Do not allow use of any equipment that is broken or damaged or that does not fit properly.

13. Require a spotter when students are using free weights that are to be lifted over the head, face, or chest or positioned on the back (squat).

14. Be sure the spotter is strong enough to help with the weight being lifted.

15. Have a system of signs and signals so that partners know when to help.

16. Have lifters check the bar before the lift for proper loading and that safety locks are in place.

17. Teach spotters not to touch the bar if the lifter can complete the lift without their help.

18. Lifter and spotter should communicate to assure safety during the lift.

Methods/Techniques

Introduction

Proper methods and techniques are the keys to a safe weight-training program. There are many people giving advice about techniques and training who know nothing about the physiological, psychological, and anatomical makeup of an individual. Many work on the principle of "no pain, no gain;" my addition to that statement is "no brain." If "pain" is the uncomfortable burn during an exercise, then it is good, but if the student complains of severe joint or muscular pain, it is the body's way of telling them that they are doing something wrong. Be sure the students listen to their bodies. Instruct the students to tell you what suggestions have been made to them and to clear all exercises and techniques with you. The other alternative is to have the students ask the person what credentials they have that qualifies them to do weight-training instruction. Instruct your students not to follow a stranger's advice until they ask someone whom they know is qualified.

There are conflicting thoughts regarding signs the students should recognize that tell them not to work out at any given time. Most of these signs are learned through trial and error because each individual is different. However, the most obvious signs of illness—cold, flu, severe joint pain, chest pain, etc.—must always be heeded. There are also conflicting theories concerning immediate muscular soreness after a workout and Delayed Onset Muscular Soreness (DOMS). Some believe that if soreness is noticed before a workout, the workout should be delayed or canceled. This type of well-meaning advice could cause the beginning lifter to wait a week or more to eliminate all soreness before doing another workout.

Muscle soreness varies depending on the intensity of the workout. If a person does a high-intensity workout, he or she can expect intense soreness in the middle or belly of the muscle. However, this type of workout also leads to rapid gains in muscular development. Soreness of this type is used, by experienced lifters, as a sign of a good workout. They also know from this soreness whether or not the intended muscles were involved. This soreness soon becomes a welcome feeling.

Proper Breathing

The importance of proper breathing while lifting weights cannot be overemphasized. Instructors usually mention the importance of breathing but do not continue to reinforce its importance after the first time. The "Valsalva maneuver" is the scientific name for a situation causing a person to pass out while lifting. The cause of this phenomenon is when a person holds his or her breath and strains against a weight while trying to perform a lift. This causes the blood supply to be cut off from the brain, thereby depriving it of oxygen and causing the person to pass out momentarily. Passing out does not cause any damage in and of itself, but if you have a weight over your face, chest, or head and drop it, the results could be tragic. Always remember to exhale (breath out) on exertion and inhale (breath in) during the relaxing phase.

Hyperventilation is the opposite of breath holding. Sometime lifters breathe rapidly, thinking that this helps their lifting ability. However, too much hyperventilation is dangerous because, as the lifter breathes rapidly, he or she blows off a large volume of carbon dioxide, which could cause dizziness and result in a loss of balance or dropping the bar, resulting in serious injury. Students should be told to breathe at least once during a lift but fewer than ten times.

Warm-Up

The value of warming up is usually not brought into question, but different methods of warming up merit some discussion. The idea behind warming up is to increase the blood flow to the muscle about to be exercised, which raises the temperature of that muscle or muscle group. Some sources recommend that a person do general exercise until light sweating begins. A general exercise is a total body exercise like walking, jogging, or riding a stationary bicycle, which warms up the entire body. Other sources recommend specific exercise as opposed to general exercise. Specific exercises warm up only the muscle or muscle groups to be used. An example of this would be to do a bench press with an empty bar before doing a bench press with weight. This causes the working muscles to be well-supplied with blood, producing an elevated temperature to relax the arteries and veins to promote a good supply of oxygen and glycogen and to carry away waste products. The specific warm-up seems to be the method of choice for most lifters.

Hand Care

Most bars used in lifting are deeply knurled or "grooved " to give a better grip. This knurling is necessary but can cause problems to the hands of beginners. As the students lift, they will begin to develop some protective calluses, which are desired by most lifters. However, if they don't want calluses, they should use gloves that are available in any sporting goods store. If they choose to have hands with protective calluses, they should care for them or the calluses will rip and cause problems. Students should be instructed to make sure, as calluses develop, that they are kept smooth by using a pumice stone or a very fine grade of sandpaper. Caution students to use common sense when using either stone or sandpaper and to do a little at a time until they know how much callus they want.

Also, after teaching students to use chalk to keep their hands dry for improved grip, make sure they know to wash their hands with soap and water to remove the remaining chalk. The chalk continues to dry the skin as long as it is left on. Instruct students to apply a lotion after washing to make the skin supple and flexible so it will not crack or tear. If a tear is noticed, it should be treated immediately before there is chance of an infection.

Foot Care

Students should always be required to wear shoes. This protects them from injury when stepping on an object left on the floor and reduces the severity of injury when a weight is dropped on a toe.

Lifting Techniques

Proper lifting techniques are the keys to injury-free and productive training. Experienced trainers teach that technique comes first and increases in the amount of weight lifted will follow. It is always best for students to have a training partner who will continue to watch for and immediately correct a break in technique. Remember, students often don't look like they think they do while lifting, so, if possible, match training partners who have an interest in each other's improvement.

Lifting from the Floor. This exercise is considered a "functional, total body lift" and is the exercise where learning proper techniques is the most important. People do this exercise daily when they lift a bag of groceries, small child, pet, bowling ball or golf bag from the ground. Lifters using this exercise should realize that no matter how perfect their technique is, they will experience some soreness in the lower back after an intense workout. This area is, for the average person, the "weakest link" and takes a long time to gain enough strength to match the strength of the legs.

When lifting from the floor, remind the students to do the following:

1. Bend their knees so that the major lifting is done by the legs.

2. Keep their shoulders high, hips low, chest out, and head up.

3. Keep their backs straight, and the weight close to their bodies. Keeping the back straight does not mean keeping it vertical; rather, it means keeping it straight "from the hips to the head," without letting it round out.

This exercise does not require a spotter.

Lifting Overhead/ Shoulder Press. When lifting overhead, a person should always have a spotter. The spotter stands behind the lifter, prepared to assist with the lift and keep the weight from injuring the lifter. This exercise is also important for daily life. When we place anything above our head, such as books in a shelf, dishes in the cupboard, or a bowling ball in the closet, we are using the overhead press.

Lifters should remember to do the following:

1. Not lean back—this could cause them to lose their balance and fall backwards with the weight, resulting in an injury.

2. Keep the eyes open—this helps avoid balance problems.

3. Keep the back straight—the entire back should be held rigid throughout the lift to eliminate injury.

4. Keep the abdominal muscles contracted to support the back—the abdominal muscles play a major role in supporting the lower back during a lift.

5. Wear a weight belt when lifting close to maximum—a belt aids the abdominal muscles in supporting the lower back during a near-maximum or maximum lift.

Spotters should remember to do the following:

1. Stay close to the lifters to assist if necessary.

2. Not allow the lifters to lean back.

3. Remind the lifters to keep their eyes open.

4. Remind the lifters to keep their backs straight.

5. Remind the lifters to contract their abdominal muscles.

Bench Press. When performing the bench press exercise, the lifter should always have a spotter. The bench press is one of the most favorite lifts of all. However it can be very dangerous if improperly performed. The weight is directly over the face, throat, and chest and, if dropped, could have tragic results.

Lifters should remember to do the following:

1. Not attempt to lift a weight that is too heavy.

2. Communicate with the spotter as to what they intend to do.

3. Use a closed grip (thumbs around the bar).

Spotters should remember to do the following:

1. Be sure they can lift the weight if necessary.

2. Communicate with the lifters as to what they intend to do.

3. Remind the lifters to breath with each repetition.

4. Focus on the lifters. Never look away.

Squat. When performing the squat, the lifter should always have a spotter. The squat is a favorite with power lifters, bodybuilders, Olympic lifters, and people needing great strength in the lower part of their body, e.g., football linemen, weight throwers, sprinters, high jumpers, and broad jumpers.

Lifters should remember to do the following:

1. Not attempt to lift a weight that is too heavy.

2. Use a safety squat rack if available.

3. Use two or three spotters if a safety rack is not available.

4. Communicate with their spotters what they intend to do.

5. Place the bar on their shoulders, not their neck.

6. Use a weight belt if near maximum weight.

7. Practice proper breathing by breathing out during exertion phase and breath in during lowering phase.

8. Lower their body until the top of their thighs are parallel to the floor.

9. Not train with knee wraps; they are to be used only when using very heavy weights.

10. Use wrist wraps if wrist pain is experienced during exercise.

Spotters should remember to do the following:

1. Be sure they are strong enough to assist the lifter and if not, get additional spotters.

2. Communicate with the lifter to determine their intentions.

3. Make sure the bar is on the lifter's shoulders, not the neck, and centered on the lifter's back.

4. Remind the lifter to breathe properly.

5. Stay close to the lifter and in position to help if necessary.

Olympic Lifting. Olympic weight lifting is probably one of the most recognized types of weight lifting by the general public, because of the exposure this sport receives during the Olympic Games. These two lifts (snatch and clean and jerk) are also the most dangerous and hardest lifts to learn. Because of the explosive movements and large amount of weight lifted, these two exercises should have an area set apart from the rest of the exercise areas. These lifts cannot be spotted, and no one should be close to the lifter because of the danger of the lifter missing the lift and dropping the bar. Anyone interested in becoming an Olympic lifter should get an expert to teach the proper techniques; it will be worth their efforts in the long run.

Latissimus Dorsi Pulldown, or Lat Pull. The Latissimus Dorsi (lats) muscles are the large muscles on the sides under the arm that contribute to the V shape of the back, which is desired by most weight lifters. These muscles are developed by pulling downward from overhead. The safety consideration for this exercise is to lower the weight slowly, under control, and to not allow the weight to "free fall," catching it just before it hits the weight stack. This practice could be injurious to the shoulder, elbow, and wrist joints if continued over a period of time.

Biceps Curl/Triceps Extension. The biceps muscle is the muscle on the front of the upper arm, and the triceps muscles are located on the back of the upper arm. These two muscle groups are the flexors and extensors of the elbow. The safety consideration is to not allow the elbow to hyperextend at the bottom of the lowering phase of the biceps curl, which could cause injury.

Conclusion

Safety in the weight room is the most important thing to teach a lifter, no matter what their reason for lifting. A lifter does not want to experience the pain of injury and the resultant loss of training caused by an avoidable injury. Also, the possibility of a lawsuit against the instructor is always present if negligence is proven. It takes only a small amount of time to make sure the weight room and equipment are safe, and constant attention to proper technique will pay off in large dividends for you and your lifters.